David Allen is Academic Director at The Queen's Foundation for Ecumenical Theological Education in Birmingham. He has a particular interest in the non-Gospel texts of the New Testament, and has published a number of works in this area, notably *Deuteronomy and Exhortation in Hebrews* (2008).

THE HISTORICAL CHARACTER OF JESUS

Canonical insights from outside the Gospels

DAVID M. ALLEN

First published in Great Britain in 2013

Society for Promoting Christian Knowledge
36 Causton Street
London SW1P 4ST
www.spckpublishing.co.uk

British Library Cataloguing-in-Publication Data
A catalogue record for this book is available from the British Library

ISBN 978–0–281–06470–0
eBook ISBN 978–0–281–07040–4

Typeset by Graphicraft Limited, Hong Kong
First printed in Great Britain by Ashford Colour Press
Subsequently digitally printed in Great Britain

Produced on paper from sustainable forests

Contents

Acknowledgements   vii
Abbreviations   viii

1 Introduction: locating Jesus outside the Gospels   1
   Sources for the study of Jesus   4
   Portraits of Jesus   12
   Framing the canonical Jesus   14
   Conclusion   18

2 'The witnessed one': Jesus in Acts   20
   The 'earthly Jesus' as character in Acts   25
   The life of Jesus in Acts   30
   The use of Jesus' teaching in Acts   32
   The story of Jesus in Acts   37
   Jesus the Baptist?   41
   Conclusion: the Jesus of Acts   43

3 'To know or not to know': Jesus in Paul   45
   Paul's 'knowledge' of Jesus of Nazareth   51
   Paul's 'use' of Jesus' teaching   57
   Indirect references   65
   Why not more?   67
   Paul's story of Jesus   70
   Conclusion: Jesus according to Paul   75

4 'The ascended Christ': Jesus in Deutero-Paul   77
   Jesus in Colossians   78
   Jesus in Ephesians   83
   Jesus in Second Thessalonians   86
   Jesus in the Pastoral Epistles   87
   Conclusion: the Jesus of the Deutero-Paulines   90

Contents

5 'The sacrificial high priest': Jesus in Hebrews   92
  Identity: Jesus – the heavenly high priest   97
  Identity: Jesus – the human 'high priest'   100
  Conclusion: the Jesus of Hebrews   110

6 'The remembered teacher': Jesus in James   112
  The epistle of James, the 'historical James' and
  the 'historical Jesus'   113
  James and the Jesus tradition   119
  The Jesus behind the Jacobean text   125
  James and the historical Jesus   127
  Conclusion: the Jacobean Jesus   130

7 'The model Christian': Jesus in 1 and 2 Peter and Jude   132
  Jesus in 1 Peter   133
  Jesus in Jude   141
  Jesus in 2 Peter   143
  Conclusion: the Jesus of the Petrine epistles/Jude   147

8 'The apocalyptic Son of Man': Jesus in the Johannine
  letters and Revelation   149
  Jesus in 1 John   149
  Jesus in 2 and 3 John   154
  Jesus in Revelation   155

9 Conclusion: the canonical Jesus   165
  The non-Gospel material and the earthly Jesus   165
  The plurality of the canonical Jesus   168
  The characteristics of the canonical Jesus   171
  But why not more?   175
  Conclusion – the canonical Jesus   179

Bibliography   180
Index of biblical references   195
Index of names and subjects   202

Acknowledgements

The bulk of this book was written while on study leave from my role at The Queen's Foundation, and I am grateful to the Principal and colleagues at Queen's both for enabling the period of leave and for ensuring that my responsibilities were covered during it. I am also grateful to students at Queen's who have been privy to the content of the work (consciously or otherwise!), and who have therefore contributed to its shape and format.

My thanks go to Chris Keith and to Robert Foster, who, in unconnected but significant ways, gave me the idea for this project. I also want to thank Philip Law at SPCK for his constructive editorial insight at various stages of the book's production, and the various staff at SPCK for their help in producing the finished version of the work.

And, of course, my thanks and love to my wife Beccy and sons Seth and Luke, all of whom gave Dad the time and space to get the book produced and completed. May they come to be passionate about the one whose character it seeks to discover.

Abbreviations

AB	Anchor Bible
AnBib	Analecta biblica
ANTC	Abingdon New Testament Commentaries
ASNU	Acta seminarii neotestamentici upsaliensis
AUSS	*Andrews University Seminary Studies*
BBR	*Bulletin for Biblical Research*
Bib	*Biblica*
BibInt	*Biblical Interpretation*
BZNW	Beihefte zur Zeitschrift für die neutestamentliche Wissenschaft
CBQ	*Catholic Biblical Quarterly*
Cor.	Corinthians
Dan.	Daniel
Deut.	Deuteronomy
Eph.	Ephesians
Exod.	Exodus
FF	Foundations and Facets
Gal.	Galatians
HBT	*Horizons in Biblical Theology*
Heb.	Hebrews
ICC	International Critical Commentary
Isa.	Isaiah
JBL	*Journal of Biblical Literature*
JSHJ	*Journal for the Study of the Historical Jesus*
JSNT	*Journal for the Study of the New Testament*
JSNTSup	Journal for the Study of the New Testament: Supplement Series
Lev.	Leviticus
Matt.	Matthew
NABPR	National Association of Baptist Professors of Religion

NIB	*The New Interpreter's Bible*, ed. Leander Keck (Nashville: Abingdon, 2002)
NICNT	New International Commentary on the New Testament
NIGTC	New International Greek Testament Commentary
NovT	*Novum Testamentum*
NovTSup	Supplements to Novum Testamentum
NT	New Testament
NTG	New Testament Guides
NTL	New Testament Library
NTS	*New Testament Studies*
par., pars	parallel(s)
Pet.	Peter
Phil.	Philippians
PRSt	*Perspectives in Religious Studies*
Ps.	Psalms
Rom.	Romans
SBT	Studies in Biblical Theology
SNTSMS	Society for New Testament Studies Monograph Series
SP	Sacra pagina
SJT	*Scottish Journal of Theology*
T. Naph.	*Testament of Naphtali*
Thess.	Thessalonians
TynBul	*Tyndale Bulletin*
WBC	Word Biblical Commentary
WUNT	Wissenschaftliche Untersuchungen zum Neuen Testament

1

Introduction: locating Jesus outside the Gospels

It does not take much exposure to Gospels studies, or to biblical scholarship more generally, before one encounters the term 'historical Jesus'. The expression itself is unattested within the biblical record, but is instead a scholarly phrase or construction, a term devised within the discipline to describe the Jesus of history, the Jesus 'who really was'. For a number of centuries now, scholars have sought to get to this 'true' Jesus, the Jesus behind the theological and doctrinal superstructure overlaid by the Gospel writers and the early Church, and thereby construct an objective 'life of Jesus' free of theological or ecclesial influence. The means by which this 'real' Jesus has been determined vary greatly from scholar to scholar, and the various criteria used to distinguish what ultimately goes back to Jesus are contested, manifold and diverse. The degree of suspicion with which the canonical material is viewed likewise varies, and a veritable industry of divergent methodological approaches has materialized, each reckoning to present the supposed 'real' Jesus.[1]

As such, the historical Jesus is the Jesus created by historians, a figure that is simultaneously delineated from the so-called 'Christ of faith' and focused solely around the supposed person of Jesus of Nazareth. It may be that other terms are more suitable – the 'historical figure' of Jesus,[2] the 'historic Jesus' or the 'earthly Jesus'

---

[1] For a helpful review of the historical Jesus project and its major protagonists, see James K. Beilby, Paul R. Eddy, Robert M. Price, John Dominic Crossan, Luke Timothy Johnson, James D. G. Dunn and Darrell L. Bock, *The Historical Jesus: Five Views* (Downers Grove: InterVarsity, 2009) 9–54.

[2] Cf. D. Moody Smith, 'The Historical Figure of Jesus in 1 John', in *The Word Leaps the Gap: Essays on Scripture and Theology in Honor of Richard B. Hays*, ed. J. Ross Wagner, Christopher Kavin Rowe and A. Katherine Grieb (Grand Rapids: Eerdmans 2008) 310–24.

perhaps – but the underlying principle remains the attempt to free Jesus from dogmatic overlay and present instead a life of Jesus that is historically rigorous and persuasive. Scot McKnight, albeit in an essay proclaiming the end of the historical Jesus project, construes its depiction in particularly dualistic terms as the 'Jesus whom scholars have reconstructed on the basis of historical methods over against the canonical portraits of Jesus in the Gospels of our New Testament, and over against the orthodox Jesus of the church.'[3]

In recent years, though, scholars have challenged some of the key premises of the historical Jesus project. Some have ventured that the distinction between the Jesus of history and the Christ of faith is a false dichotomy (and one not made by the biblical authors).[4] Some have challenged the very heart of an enterprise that seeks (subjectively) to distinguish the kernel of genuine, historical tradition.[5] Some have questioned the very purpose of the historical reconstruction, venturing that the only Jesus who matters is the living Jesus encountered and present today.[6] But even those who are sceptical about the aspirations of the historical Jesus project would still consider that Jesus of Nazareth is a figure of some interest; likewise, while historical Jesus is a contested term, with its depictions of Jesus essentially constructions, there remains the common focus that it is the earthly Jesus on whom attention is rightly focused.[7]

The key point for our purposes, however, is that by their very nature, historical Jesus studies inevitably focus on the Gospel accounts of Jesus' life, canonical and non-canonical alike. The scholarly

---

[3] <http://www.christianitytoday.com/ct/2010/april/15.22.html>.

[4] Paul Barnett, *Finding the Historical Christ*, After Jesus 3 (Grand Rapids: Eerdmans, 2009) vii–ix, 176.

[5] Dale C. Allison, Jr., *Constructing Jesus: Memory, Imagination, and History* (London: SPCK, 2010) 459–60.

[6] See, for example, Luke Timothy Johnson, *Living Jesus: Learning the Heart of the Gospel* (San Francisco: HarperSanFrancisco, 1999) 3–22.

[7] For our purposes, we will continue to use the term, recognizing that its referent is the earthly Jesus, and using the two phrases interchangeably. This is not to separate the historical Jesus and the Christ of faith – as we will see, the NT evidence seems to place them in continuity – but is merely to keep the scope of our exercise manageable.

portrayals so generated along the way certainly vary, sometimes in remarkably divergent fashion, as do the methodologies and techniques so deployed. The Markan Jesus, for example, differs significantly from the Jesus presented in the Johannine Gospel, often in quite radical terms. Likewise, the Jesus of N. T. Wright diverges from that espoused by Marcus Borg or Dominic Crossan[8] in ways that cause one to speculate as to how such divergent conclusions can be arrived at from what is effectively the same source material. However, laying such differences aside for the moment, the 'source material' used in Jesus studies tends to be restricted to Gospel texts, normally the canonical four, but with the occasional inclusion of other non-canonical, evangelical material (notably the *Gospel of Thomas*) as and when deemed appropriate.[9] The other New Testament testimony is commonly rendered secondary as a result, its 'value' supposedly limited by either genre, late dating or merely disavowal; these texts are deemed to be more interested in the Christ of faith than in any remembrance of the Jesus of history. There is something of a parallel here, perhaps, even with Gospel studies and historical Jesus discussions, with the Gospel of John commonly sidelined in such historical questions, as it too is invariably seen as more interested in the (theological) Christ of faith.[10]

This book seeks to address such neglect, by focusing specifically on the non-Gospel material in an attempt to discern how these other texts of the NT contribute to framing the picture and identity of the earthly Jesus. It will have constituent chapters on Jesus in the respective later NT texts, along with a concluding chapter that seeks to tease out any overarching themes or findings

---

[8] See the debates, for example, in Marcus J. Borg and N. T. Wright, *The Meaning of Jesus: Two Visions* (London: SPCK, 1999), or Robert B. Stewart (ed.), *The Resurrection of Jesus: John Dominic Crossan and N. T. Wright in Dialogue* (Minneapolis: Augsburg Fortress, 2005).

[9] The Jesus Seminar, for example, advocates a fivefold Gospel comparison – see Robert W. Funk and Roy W. Hoover, *The Five Gospels: The Search for the Authentic Words of Jesus* (New York: Macmillan, 1993).

[10] See, for example, the discussion in Marianne Meye Thompson, 'Jesus and the Victory of God Meets the Gospel of John', in *Jesus, Paul and the People of God*, ed. Nicholas Perrin and Richard B. Hays (London: SPCK, 2011) 21–40.

from the analysis. It will consider the implications of these non-Gospel texts for our understanding of Jesus and the emergence of traditions about him, while offering a bridge between the canonical Gospel portrayals of Jesus and the later apocryphal pictures that subsequently emerge. It is not a complete book-by-book analysis, and there is some element of generalization within our discussion. We will not, for example, be able to focus specifically on Jesus according to Romans; there are related books available that do embark on this book-by-book approach,[11] but for our purposes and strategy, space precludes that level of analysis. Instead, we will group together the respective letters of the Pauline and Deutero-Pauline corpuses, if only as a convenient way of marshalling the relevant data in a hopefully helpful fashion. But that should not limit our capacity for exploration; bearing in mind the diversity within the canonical testimony, there remains plenty of scope to explore the full contours of the canonical Jesus.

Sources for the study of Jesus

At the outset of our discussion, though, it is probably worth establishing the purpose or value of an exercise such as this. After all, books on Jesus abound, not perhaps to the scale alluded to in John 21.25, but to a significant extent nonetheless. This rather begs the question as to why another volume should be added to their number.[12] One might also venture that the Gospel genre, as a biography of Jesus, would seem appropriately fit for purpose, and more than capable of presenting Jesus as the one remembered by those who followed after him. This would be even more the case were the Gospels, as some have recently suggested, the product of eyewitness testimony to Jesus' ministry.[13] By comparison,

---

[11] For example, Keith Warrington, *Discovering Jesus in the New Testament* (Peabody: Hendrickson, 2009).

[12] See Beverly, Roberts Gaventa and Richard B. Hays, *Seeking the Identity of Jesus: A Pilgrimage* (Grand Rapids: Eerdmans, 2008) 1–3, for a similar (and persuasive) self-justification for adding to the plethora of Jesus-related tomes.

[13] Richard J. Bauckham, *Jesus and the Eyewitnesses: The Gospels as Eyewitness Testimony* (Grand Rapids: Eerdmans, 2006).

any recourse to the non-Gospel material would be only secondary, and of incidental value compared to these putative 'life of Jesus' accounts. Furthermore, and more significantly perhaps, scholars tend to view the non-evangelical accounts as uninterested in the earthly Jesus, and more concerned with the proclamation and worship of the exalted Lord. Beyond the Gospels, only Acts and Paul avowedly cite any dominical sayings – and, even then, only rarely so – and any appeal to Jesus' parables or mighty deeds is minimal in, or even absent from, the non-Gospel texts. Edgar McKnight's muted summation therefore articulates the challenge faced: 'the nongospel material in the New Testament, like non-canonical references to Jesus, adds little to the overall picture of Jesus, but it does confirm the historicity of Jesus and some of the events recorded in the Synoptic Gospels.'[14]

Viewed in such terms, investigation of the non-Gospel testimony might seem to have little purpose or add minimal value. The function of historical corroboration could just as well be attested by non-Christian sources such as Josephus, and to view the non-Gospel texts as merely endorsing Synoptic material effectively consigns them to a secondary status when compared with their Gospel counterparts. Even someone as reticent about the historical Jesus project as Carl Braaten ends up sidelining the non-Gospel material (inadvertently perhaps), opining that: 'My view is that the only Jesus is the One presented in the canonical Gospels *and that any other Jesus is irrelevant to Christian faith*.'[15] To be fair to Braaten, he does subsequently offer some reflection on the NT epistolary corpus's witness to Jesus, and ventures that the 'access we have to the real Jesus of history is solely through the picture of faith left behind by the apostles.'[16] By this, one suspects, he includes Paul, John, Peter and others. But the point still remains, that engagement with Jesus tradition – be that in historical terms or otherwise – tends to be focused primarily,

---

[14] Edgar V. McKnight, *Jesus Christ in History and Scripture: A Poetic and Sectarian Perspective* (Macon: Mercer University Press, 1999) 39.

[15] Carl E. Braaten, *Who Is Jesus? Disputed Questions and Answers* (Grand Rapids: Eerdmans, 2011) 3, my emphasis.

[16] Braaten, *Who Is Jesus?* 46.

sometimes exclusively, on the *Gospel* accounts of his life. There is the common tendency to remove the rest of the New Testament from the equation in terms of framing Jesus tradition, preferring (once the canonical four Gospels are taken as read) to look to other (non-canonical) sources for reference, be they the so-called apocryphal gospels or other *agrapha* found in Early Christian writings.[17] This may reflect the expectation or prejudice that such texts have little to contribute to Jesus studies – notably those focusing on historical matters – but any such assessment remains surely that: a prejudice.

Now of course, some caution in handling the non-Gospel texts is certainly appropriate, and one must concede that the respective genres of the NT material necessarily impact upon how one goes about the study of the earthly Jesus. The Gospels are 'about Jesus' in a way that the non-Gospel texts are simply not. Both in terms of genre and content, the canonical Gospels encapsulate the life of Jesus, whereas the NT epistles testify to the communal life of congregations gathered in his name. The letters of Paul or Peter are situational in nature, addressing particular concerns and contexts, and one commonly has to read between the lines as to the situation or issue that they address. The nature of the documents should also caution us from *over*-expectations as to the role

---

[17] This seems implicit in Robert L. Webb's otherwise excellent review of historical method in historical Jesus studies (Robert L. Webb, 'The Historical Enterprise and Historical Jesus Research', in *Key Events in the Life of the Historical Jesus: A Collaborative Exploration of Context and Coherence*, ed. Darrell L. Bock and Robert L. Webb (Grand Rapids: Eerdmans, 2010) 9–93). He carefully addresses the appropriateness and relevance of various sources, but omits to consider what value the rest of the NT might have for this exercise. Likewise, in his review of potential historical Jesus sources, Darrell L. Bock, *Studying the Historical Jesus: A Guide to Sources and Methods* (Grand Rapids: Baker Academic, 2002), covers a number of salient texts, including Talmud and midrashim, but does not include the NT. Bart D. Ehrman, *Did Jesus Exist? The Historical Argument for Jesus of Nazareth* (New York: HarperOne, 2012) 105–17, is therefore quite unusual for giving attention (albeit relatively briefly) to the way in which the non-Gospel material (and particularly the non-Pauline texts) attests to the existence of Jesus. Michael Labahn, 'The Non-Synoptic Jesus: An Introduction to John, Paul, Thomas, and Other Outsiders of the Jesus Quest', in *Handbook for the Study of the Historical Jesus*, ed. Tom Holmén and Stanley E. Porter (Leiden: Brill, 2011) 1933–96, also includes some discussion of how certain non-Gospel texts impact upon historical Jesus concerns. His titular designation of these texts as 'outsiders of the Jesus Quest' sums up our point well.

occupied by the earthly Jesus in the particular texts, and one cannot ignore the important datum that the non-Gospel texts do not yield substantial information in this regard. Indeed, the relative silence of the rest of the NT on Jesus' life and teaching is something of a given, even in relatively conservative scholarship, and we shall explore the important implications of that fact for Jesus studies particularly in the final chapter. However, rather than viewing the (relative) silence on Jesus in the NT texts as a matter of embarrassment that has to be assuaged, we will consider what such silence means for the remembrance of Jesus within the life of the early Church.

Moreover, the genre difference between the Gospels and the non-Gospel material does not preclude the latter having something significant to contribute to constructing a portrait(s) of Jesus. One might, for example, distinguish between the Gospels as *biographies* of Jesus, interested in recalling the events of his life, and the non-Gospel material as sources for, or windows onto, the *identity* of Jesus – a different lens, perhaps, but one that seeks to spread the vision wider than just 'historical' or biographical questions. To use James Dunn's titular phrase,[18] the non-Gospel material contributes to the portrayal of 'Jesus Remembered' in a different way or function from the Gospel presentation, but it contributes nonetheless.[19] The NT epistles possess (potentially genuine) testimony to Jesus tradition, and reflect it as such, offering different ways in which such tradition is utilized; they yield other ways by which Jesus is remembered – be that in liturgy, in proclamation, in teaching or in paraenesis. References to Jesus' life need not be limited solely to the biographies/lives of Jesus, and the celebration, worship and preservation of Jesus memory in the life and practice of those who followed after him is both a window onto the identity of Jesus and also something fundamentally rooted in the discussion of who he is. To put the matter another way, if the Gospels are still valid sources for recollecting Jesus' significance,

---

[18] James D. G. Dunn, *Jesus Remembered*, Christianity in the Making 1 (Cambridge: Eerdmans, 2003).

[19] This distinction is made in Gaventa and Hays, *Seeking*, and in Hays's chapter within the volume ('The Story of God's Son: The Identity of Jesus in the Letters of Paul' 180–99). Note, though, the criticism leveled at it from N. T. Wright concerning the book's lack of attention to historical questions, and the critique of Richard J. Bauckham, 'Seeking the Identity of Jesus', *JSNT* 32 (2010): 337–46, that eyewitness memory is similarly undervalued.

and if the dichotomy between the Christ of faith and the Jesus of history is a false one, as many now conclude, it would seem warranted to ensure that the non-Gospel texts (those that still appeal to Jesus as central to their self-understanding) are allowed a voice in the shaping of the identity of Jesus. It may, of course, be that the exercise proves to be a fruitless one; it may be that they have little to say, or contribute, to the question. But equally it may prove a rich and fruitful enterprise, and suggest that the canonical Jesus is more than just the evangelical Jesus.

One might add some further reasons to suggest that the non-Gospel material has something to contribute to Jesus studies. First, *to restrict the non-Gospel materials' contribution merely to echoing or confirming Jesus' historicity is simply to place false restrictions on them*. The non-Gospel material certainly has something to say about Jesus, about how he was remembered, how he was proclaimed and celebrated; such testimony is not lacking in historical value, quite the reverse. Indeed, it is hard to think otherwise from this – one would surely expect to encounter at least *some* reference to, or *some* invocation of, Jesus' life and ministry within the non-Gospel material. The testimony of the Pauline literature, for example, is that Jesus tradition formed part of Paul's preaching when founding churches; he can speak of publicly proclaiming Jesus' death before the Galatians (Gal. 3.1) or of passing on Jesus traditions to the Corinthians (1 Cor. 15.3), both, it seems, as part of his missionary preaching.[20] Likewise, Hebrews can speak of Jesus' salvific message being proclaimed by him and passed on to the Hebrews by his first followers (Heb. 2.2). As such, 'it remains very unlikely that there ever were Christian communities who lived only with the tradition about Jesus, or only with the confession of his death and resurrection without knowledge of his earthly activity.'[21] One would therefore expect such tradition to feature

---

[20] Cf. Martin Hengel, 'Eye-Witness Memory and the Writing of the Gospels', in *The Written Gospel*, ed. Markus N. A. Bockmuehl and Donald Alfred Hagner (Cambridge: Cambridge University Press, 2005) 70–96: 'The message they proclaimed was too uncommon, even offensive, for them not to have to report something definite about Jesus' (75).

[21] Eduard Schweizer, 'The Testimony to Jesus in the Early Christian Community', *HBT* 7 (1985) 77–98 (96).

in, or be alluded to, within the epistolary discourse, however incidentally. To push the matter further, there also seems to be little direct evidence of *Gospels* functioning as texts used in very early Christian worship.[22] By contrast, we have clear evidence of letters and epistles being read (cf. 2 Pet. 3.16), such that when it comes to remembering the story within a liturgical framework, or encouraging each other through written discourse, it is evident that the epistles bear that mantle more than the Gospels. Thus, even if the volume of data on Jesus is not huge, it is still historical data per se, and contributes in some fashion to the overall 'biblical' picture of Jesus, and to both the recognition of the diversity of the canonical witness and the multivalent portrayals of Jesus therein.

Second, *the person of Jesus and the Jesus movement that followed after him are surely intertwined* – a rigorous historical method seeks to account for why/how people became committed to his cause, particularly after his death. That which people followed has to make sense of what has come before, and it 'is not at all easy to detach Jesus from his followers'.[23] First-century historian Paula Fredriksen, for example, takes this approach, beginning with the movement that followed after Jesus and then working *backwards* to the Gospels in order to try and explain the historical data from that point.[24] In this sense, then, the NT material is historically valuable, both for (perhaps) reflecting on the life of Jesus and also for bringing out how Jesus was understood by those who followed after him. Furthermore, recent developments in historical Jesus studies make the inclusion of non-Gospel material all the more valid, especially in the appeal to *memory* as the way in which Jesus tradition is preserved. There are different takes on how memory may be seen to operate,[25] but core to all of them is the language

---

[22] So W. A. Strange, 'The Jesus-Tradition in Acts', *NTS* 46 (2000) 59–74 (73).

[23] Francis Watson, 'Veritas Christi: How to Get from the Jesus of History to the Christ of Faith without Losing One's Way', in *Seeking the Identity of Jesus: A Pilgrimage*, ed. Beverly Roberts Gaventa and Richard B. Hays (Grand Rapids: Eerdmans, 2008), 96–114 (114).

[24] Paula Fredriksen, *Jesus of Nazareth, King of the Jews: A Jewish Life and the Emergence of Christianity* (New York: Knopf, 1999) 74–8.

[25] See inter alia Bauckham, *Eyewitnesses*; Dunn, *Jesus Remembered*; Allison, *Constructing*; Anthony Le Donne, *The Historiographical Jesus: Memory, Typology, and the Son of David* (Waco: Baylor University Press, 2009).

of remembrance, and a move away from reliance on the written word as the means by which the tradition is preserved. If this is the case for the Gospels, if they are 'Jesus Remembered' – that is, remembered for the impact or relevance to their situation – then the same logic surely applies to the other NT material whereby the effect of Jesus on the various communities is recalled and articulated. Anthony Le Donne helpfully reminds us of the impact of memory, averring: 'Memory is the impression left by the past, not the preservation of it. In memory, we do not re-experience the past. What we experience is the impact left by the past . . . Memory is what is happening in our minds *now*.'[26] If the remembered Jesus impacts *now*, then the contextual aspect of that 'now-ness' is as valid for the non-Gospel texts as it is for the Gospels. They offer an alternative insight or milieu by which the remembrance happens – by reflection upon life and practice, rather than by biographical testimony.

Third, *it is probable that many of the NT texts* – the Pauline corpus certainly, but possibly James and/or Hebrews as well – *actually predate the canonical Gospels* (in their written form at least) and, on temporal grounds alone could stake a claim to record and present genuine Jesus tradition. As Dunn opines: 'the forty-or-so-year gap between Jesus and the written Gospels was not empty of Jesus tradition. The stream of tradition did not disappear underground for several decades only to re-emerge when Mark put pen to paper.'[27] Moreover, the purported authors of some of the non-Gospel texts (i.e. Peter and James) seem to be figures named elsewhere as knowing Jesus, and even if the attribution of the texts is pseudonymous, there still remain good grounds to investigate what particular picture the texts yield. After all, if Jesus studies have 'arrived' at any consensus in recent years, it is to provide 'a Jewish Jesus who is credible within first-century Judaism, who gave rise to the basic contours of the early Christian movement,

---

[26] Anthony Le Donne, *Historical Jesus: What Can We Know and How Can We Know It?* (Grand Rapids: Eerdmans, 2011) 24–5.

[27] James D. G. Dunn, *Beginning from Jerusalem*, Christianity in the Making 2 (Grand Rapids: Eerdmans, 2009) 111.

and who can truly be Lord to the church and human enough to be brother to the church as well as other humans on the face of the earth'.[28] If it is legitimate to consult other first-century sources to ascertain how they might speak to historical Jesus questions, be they early Christian texts such as the *Didache* or other material such as Josephus, then one must at least accord the non-Gospel texts the same invitation. Surely, as texts of those who follow after this figure – as brother and Lord – it is only good historical practice to consider what picture such sources might portray, and how different or distinctive their respective portrayals might be.

Fourth, *the non-Gospel material can actually cause the reader to re-evaluate or reassess the portraits of Jesus offered in the Gospel accounts.* While one can understand and, to an extent, justify the prioritization of the Gospels as those texts giving the clearest presentation of Jesus, this customarily leads to the tendency to make them the authoritative texts against which others are measured or judged. Inverting such relationships, however, can yield some different and interesting results. The depiction of James the Just (Jesus' brother) would be one such example. James is commonly seen as unsympathetic to his brother's ministry (John 7.3–5; Mark 6.3–4) and therefore not part of the Twelve; he is then only 'converted' post-resurrection (cf. 1 Cor. 15.7) and subsequently assumes the leadership of the Jerusalem church (Gal. 1.19; 2.9, 12; Acts 12.17; 15.13–21). When we read the epistle of James, which may (though not necessarily) go back to James the Just himself, however, we notice a number of similarities with Jesus' teaching in the Gospels, perhaps suggesting that James was more familiar with, or supportive of, his brother than is often thought; he may well have been both brother and 'believer' from the pre-Easter period, possibly even from the outset of Jesus' ministry.[29]

---

[28] Scot McKnight, 'Jesus of Nazareth', in *The Face of New Testament Studies: A Survey of Recent Research*, ed. Scot McKnight and Grant R. Osborne (Grand Rapids: Baker Academic, 2004) 149–76 (176).

[29] For this more positive view of James's attitude to Jesus, see John Painter, *Just James: The Brother of Jesus in History and Tradition*, Studies on Personalities of the New Testament (Minneapolis: Fortress, 1999) 11–41; Richard J. Bauckham, 'James and Jesus', in *The Brother of Jesus: James the Just and His Mission*, ed. Bruce Chilton and Jacob Neusner (Louisville: Westminster John Knox, 2001) 100–37 (106–9).

Portraits of Jesus

If, then, the non-Gospel material does have something useful to contribute to studies of Jesus, how might we go about using them? Our approach in this book will be to try and answer two distinct but related questions. First, we are seeking to find out what, if anything, we may discern about the historical Jesus from the non-Gospel texts under consideration. This may be partly about how they inform or confirm the Gospel testimony, the degree to which common or shared material may be found. But it may also elucidate aspects of the portrayal of Jesus that are extra or supplementary to the Gospel record, data or information that adds to the portrait of Jesus gleaned from the evangelical corpus. To put it another way, we will be looking to see how the non-Gospel material contributes to our understanding of Jesus' life, and of the remembrance of him by others beyond the Gospel writers and their communities. This may mean setting the Gospels theoretically to one side and letting the non-Gospel texts speak for themselves, answering the question: 'What would we know about the earthly Jesus from these texts if we didn't have the Gospel testimony?'

At the same time, though, texts do not exist in a vacuum – historical, canonical, intertextual or otherwise – and one cannot, of course, remove the Gospels completely from the discourse. Indeed, to do so would be counter-productive. A key feature of our discussion will be identifying the commonalities between the respective materials and discerning where there is shared data or testimony between the Gospels and the non-Gospel corpus. And where there *is* common ground between them, the principle of multiple attestation would suggest that such data has a stronger claim to being historically 'genuine'. Furthermore, sometimes knowledge of the Gospel tradition is a prerequisite for uncovering Jesus tradition elsewhere; it is only by *making* the comparison that one identifies usage of Jesus tradition. The epistle of James would be a case in point; as we shall see, the letter has many parallels with the so-called Q material, and seems to be making some Jesus connection accordingly, but one can only arrive at that conclusion by making the comparison with the Gospel witness.[30]

Second, and more expansively, we will consider the particular picture or portrayal of Jesus gleaned from each of the constituent authors. If we can speak of distinctive evangelistic portraits such as the Lucan or Markan Jesus,[31] each of which contribute to the diversity of our understanding about Jesus, what do the other canonical texts have to contribute in this regard? What is the Petrine Jesus, the Pauline Jesus, the Jacobean Jesus or the Jesus of Hebrews? How does the Jesus of Revelation compare with the Jesus of the Deutero-Pauline corpus? In short, what contours and shape are there to the 'canonical' Jesus?

A word on scope is probably in order at this point. The focus of our enquiry is not so much *Christological*, but rather '*Jesus-ological*'; Jesus – rather than Jesus *Christ* – is the subject of our attention. This is not to negate the idea that the NT testimony acknowledges Jesus as Lord and Christ, nor that the NT writers consider there to be a fundamental continuity between Jesus of Nazareth and the risen Christ. The Jesus remembered is a Jesus who is worshipped as Lord and in whom post-Easter faith is placed.[32] Rather, it is to focus – or, in effect, limit – our attention to discussion of Jesus' earthly existence, and to what the non-Gospel writers made of it, how they understood that life and its (historical) consequences for them and the communities they addressed. The appellation – and preservation – of the Jesus title is therefore significant; why did the non-Gospel writers preserve the name Jesus? More provocatively, if the life of the earthly 'Jesus'

---

[30] A similar case, though with fewer examples, can be made for 1 Peter and Revelation.

[31] For helpful reviews of the distinctive, individual Gospel portrayals, see Edward Adams, *Parallel Lives of Jesus: A Guide to the Four Gospels* (Louisville: Westminster John Knox, 2011); Richard A. Burridge, *Four Gospels, One Jesus? A Symbolic Reading* (London: SPCK, 1994).

[32] Cf. Braaten, *Who Is Jesus?* 33. He treats the term Jesusology with some suspicion, suggesting that it becomes merely an exercise in 'hero worship'. He therefore prefers to think in Christological terms, which 'account for the central place of Jesus as the Christ in the life and worship of the church'. Our approach seeks to uphold both aspects, proposing that good history seeks to take account of how the Church's life – as exemplified in the non-Gospel accounts – testifies to, and utilizes, Jesus' earthly existence.

was supposedly incidental to the non-Gospel materials, why do they not speak only of *Christ*?

Christology as a discipline, of course, has a wider focus than earthly Jesus concerns; it addresses the full gamut of Jesus Christ's identity, engaging with notions of pre-existence, exaltation, worship and divine identity among many other aspects. Such topics are important ones, but they are outside our immediate concerns. The landscape of 'New Testament Christology' is terrain relatively well traversed, with a number of volumes available that give a book-by-book analysis of the respective NT authors.[33] While we shall refer to such works as a matter of course, their contribution is generally speaking less concerned with the particular *historical* questions that Jesus studies normally invoke. Terminology, therefore, is not unimportant here, and some may wish to speak of the 'historical Christ',[34] particularly for the way that such phrasing prevents the (false) separation of Jesus of Nazareth and the Christ of faith. As we shall observe, the apostle Paul sees no discontinuity. However, in order to keep our focus Jesusological, we shall speak of the 'Jesus of faith' – or 'remembered Jesus' – as the better focus for our concerns.

Framing the canonical Jesus

What, then, is the overall aim of our project? At one level, its aspirations are somewhat modest. It recognizes the limitations of the historical Jesus enterprise, acknowledging that any attempt to get behind the Gospels, whatever one's motivation for so doing, will always be fraught with challenge. And if one is working with situational, contextual texts such as the NT epistles, their very

---

[33] See inter alia: C. M. Tuckett, *Christology and the New Testament: Jesus and His Earliest Followers* (Louisville: Westminster John Knox, 2001); Richard N. Longenecker, *Contours of Christology in the New Testament*, McMaster New Testament Studies (Grand Rapids: Eerdmans, 2005); Frank J. Matera, *New Testament Christology* (Louisville: Westminster John Knox, 1999); Mark Allan Powell and David R. Bauer (ed.), *Who Do You Say That I Am? Essays on Christology* (Louisville: Westminster John Knox, 1999). Other text-specific Christological studies will be mentioned in the relevant chapters.

[34] Barnett, *Finding* 176; cf. also Dale C. Allison, Jr.'s deliberately titled *The Historical Christ and the Theological Jesus* (Grand Rapids: Eerdmans, 2009).

nature and genre are even less geared to separating the layers of tradition and to piecing together the true Jesus. That is why our discussion is orientated towards the 'Jesus of faith', recognizing that that is how memory functions in the preservation of tradition and (hi)story. As to whether events categorically happened or not, one cannot really say, but the fact that they were *remembered* in the present for being so gives them some value as historical data.

And that surely is the nub of our task. We are seeking the Jesus articulated by the 'confessional', avowedly faith-geared position of the biblical authors, and specifically those responsible for the non-Gospel material – what we might term the 'canonical Jesus'. This is a phrase we have already used but not properly defined. Scot McKnight adopts the appellation to define the reflection that biblical writers used when describing Jesus in terms of redemptive categories or titles such as Messiah or Son of God, and he does so wanting to distinguish the discussion from any historical Jesus attempt to construct a 'pure' Jesus.[35] Now, such 'canonical Jesus' terminology reflects a faith consensus, and avowedly so, but that should not limit the value or import of the approach/title, and we will retain it as part of our historically orientated inquiry. For as many have recently proposed, such theologizing is not alien – and is indeed integral – to the historical task. It does not preclude reflection on the life and teaching of the earthly Jesus in whom many came to put their faith pre-Passion; indeed it is necessary to it. It is nonsense – or just perhaps merely 'bad history' – to think that people would follow after a crucified Galilean only after his death; there must have been some reason to attach oneself to him pre-Easter, and one is duty bound to explain how/why such things happened. Moreover, a key part of establishing the identity of any figure is to consider how they are afterwards interpreted and understood; we understand their significance through subsequent reflection upon a person, or by attention to their impact upon the world after their death. Karl Marx, for example, is a case in point of someone better understood after his death, and in the light of the subsequent impact and appropriation of his thinking and writing.

---

[35] See McKnight: <http://www.christianitytoday.com/ct/2010/april/15.22.html>.

But the 'canonical Jesus' appellation pertains to more than just the Jesus remembered through subsequent theological reflection and consideration. The canonical appellation is also a reference to the specific composition of texts that comprise that library we know as the 'New Testament' – it is the composite picture of Jesus' identity as outworked through the constituent canonical voices. Our task is to tease out the nature and diversity with which (if at all) a canonical portrait of Jesus is framed, and it is done in the explicit knowledge that some theological or qualitative claim is being made about the texts concerned. The Jesus remembered within such material is a Jesus to whom worship is offered and whose resurrection from the dead is celebrated and proclaimed.

At one level, particularly in terms of historical considerations, this decision to focus solely on the canonical testimony may seem somewhat specious or biased. If this were just a historical exercise, there would be good reason both to exclude some later texts (2 Peter would be, for many, the obvious contender) and introduce other, apparently earlier, texts into the discussion. We think of the *Didache* as a strong candidate in this regard, as it is normally dated to the latter part of the first century. 'Canon' is also a contested term; there are a variety of canons within the Christian tradition, and the term is commonly viewed as a (later) overlay onto the constituent biblical texts. We will work, though, with the generally agreed Protestant canon, neither wanting to exclude other significant contemporary texts of the time, nor to rule out the possibility that Jesus tradition isn't (similarly?) replicated in extra-canonical texts such as *1 Clement*. Rather, it is to accept that one has to start somewhere, and the received Protestant NT canon is as good a place as any, particularly if the canon somehow illustrates the rule of faith for a particular community of believers. One may say that this privileges the canonical texts at the expense of other non-canonical ones, but one must equally recognize that they have been privileged already; the very existence of the canon as a grouping of texts means that certain theological assumptions have been made. If the biblical canon is in some way linked to a greater story – or stories – then the other NT texts are at least fellow contributors to the framing and elucidation of that story.

One further point is worthy of mention. As well as being interested in historical questions, we are also concerned with narrative strategy, namely what portrait is painted of the particular Jesus in each of the respective sources. Stories have the capacity to yield a portrayal and perspective on a figure in a way that isolated quotations or statements do not. It is surely no accident that the four canonical Gospels – unlike *Thomas*, for example – are those that locate Jesus within a narrative framework, rather than just a list of sayings. Mark Allen Powell, for example, talks of the 'Jesus of story' rather than the 'Jesus of history' as a suitable label for summarizing the authoritative portrait of Jesus within the biblical record.[36] If anything therefore, we err on the side of narrative-canonical questions, and are advocating an approach to Jesus studies akin to that of Luke Timothy Johnson, in that the only Jesus that matters is the one encountered in the life of the Church (and specifically in the accounts of the life of the early Church as represented by the non-Gospel material).[37] But that is not at the expense of historical questions; we are still interested in the portrait of the figure of Jesus pre-resurrection (albeit mediated through post-resurrection glasses). 'History' does matter (more than Johnson tends to allow), and thus the celebrated memory of the figure, one suggests, must have some resonance or foundation in reality. Story and history are not in tension; story has the capacity to reveal or bring out history; Jesus' 'history' is part of Jesus' story.[38]

Let us put it another way. Borrowing from the approach taken by Gaventa and Hays in their edited volume,[39] our task is to tease out the 'identity' of Jesus as expressed within the non-Gospel

[36] Mark Allan Powell, *Jesus as a Figure in History: How Modern Historians View the Man from Galilee* (Louisville: Westminster John Knox, 1998) 8–9.

[37] See, for example, Johnson, *Living Jesus* 3–22.

[38] On such matters, see Samuel Byrskog, *Story as History – History as Story: The Gospel Tradition in the Context of Ancient Oral History*, WUNT 123 (Tübingen: Mohr Siebeck, 2000).

[39] Gaventa and Hays, *Seeking* 4–18. They speculate positively on the value of using the non-Gospel witness as sources for constructing the identity of Jesus, but the constituent chapters do not pursue every part of the NT canon.

material. Within the Gaventa/Hays book, Katherine Grieb outlines three ways by which identity may be articulated:[40]

1 *Sameness*: what do they have in common with others?
2 *Distinctiveness*: how do you spot them in a crowd?
3 *Singularity*: what really counts about a person?

Our discussion of the canonical Jesus will allude to all three characteristics. The criterion of sameness will not be absent from the account and, indeed, it will be easy to underestimate the extent to which the respective accounts 'share' common ground in their portrayal of Jesus. The fact that, for example, Jesus' death is a centrepiece for Paul, Hebrews and 1 Peter probably goes without saying, but it is worth underscoring nonetheless. At the same time, we will focus especially on what makes the respective accounts distinctive or singular in their portrayal of Jesus. We will attend particularly to the way in which the identity of 'Jesus remembered' is characteristic of that text and unique to it; one thinks, for example, of the lack of interest in Jesus' death in the epistle of James, or Revelation's particular association of the exalted Christ and the earthly Jesus. Each chapter finishes with a concluding paragraph that summarizes the distinctive or particular contribution to the depiction of Jesus given by the text(s) in question. Consequently, while this will undoubtedly require some comparative work with the Gospel depictions of Jesus, we will seek to give the texts themselves the space in which to unpack their own testimony. The aim is to let the respective texts or authors have their own voice, and to hear their particular 'take' or portrait of Jesus.

Conclusion

In sum, our object is not for 'pure' historical recovery or synthesis, but rather to tease out how the different depictions of Jesus function

---

[40] A. Katherine Grieb, '"Time Would Fail Me to Tell . . .": The Identity of Jesus Christ in Hebrews', in *Seeking the Identity of Jesus: A Pilgrimage*, ed. Beverly Roberts Gaventa and Richard B. Hays (Grand Rapids: Eerdmans, 2008) 200–14 (205–6).

within, and contribute to, the canonical identity of Jesus. Our approach is to see what these portraits of Jesus *outside* the Gospels might bring to the portrait of Jesus *in* the Gospels; that is, what happens, or what does 'canon' do, when different, or extra, portrayals are added. Throughout, our attention will be focused on the 'Jesus remembered'; what do the individual non-Gospel texts remember about him?

2

'The witnessed one': Jesus in Acts

Whatever one's reason for so doing, the task of engaging with the book of Acts is fraught with interpretative questions. The discourse has two distinct textual traditions – the so-called Western and Alexandrian versions, with not insignificant variants between them – and consideration of the integrity of Acts as a historical account is also not without its own problems. The difference, for example, between Paul's own recounting of his visits to Jerusalem potentially stands in tension with their depiction in Acts,[1] while Gamaliel's reference to Theudas and Judas the Galilean (Acts 5.36) is also chronologically problematic; according to the Jewish historian Josephus, Theudas operated around 45–6 CE, with Judas leading a revolt around 6 CE. Luke therefore differs from Josephus in terms of their respective chronological ordering (he places Theudas temporally first), and he also accords to Gamaliel a 'historical example' of which he could not have been aware (assuming that the events of Acts 5 date to the mid-30s CE).[2] When wanting to consider historical Jesus questions within the text, therefore, we can easily get distracted by these other matters and lose sight of what is actually the topic under discussion.

---

[1] Paul's visit to Jerusalem as outlined in Gal. 2.1–10 appears to be for the so-called Council of Jerusalem, as outlined in Acts 15. Paul describes it as his second visit to Jerusalem post-Damascus Road, but it is the third one as narrated by Acts. There are ways of resolving the discrepancy, and Gal. 2.1–10 need not equate to Acts 15, but the question still presents itself.

[2] Cf. therefore Luke Timothy Johnson, *The Acts of the Apostles*, SP 5 (Collegeville: Liturgical Press, 1992): 'Whatever historical basis there is to his account must be found at the level of substance and pattern rather than at the level of detail of specific incident' (4). For a defence of Luke's integrity as a historian, see Paul Barnett, *The Birth of Christianity: The First Twenty Years*, After Jesus 1 (Grand Rapids; Cambridge: Eerdmans, 2005) 187–205.

But even setting aside such matters, trying to tease out the 'Jesus of Acts' is a far from straightforward task, as several further complicating factors present themselves. Particularly in view of our interest in historical questions, the diversity of opinion as to the dating of Acts is an important question.[3] While specific matters of its date need not bother us too unduly, the insights of Acts into the earthly Jesus would probably be more nuanced or developed if it were a second- rather than a first-century text. Second, and more significantly perhaps, assuming that Luke–Acts share a common author (as Acts 1.1 seems to aver), one might well expect the second volume generally to mirror its predecessor's interest in the figure of Jesus. But as we shall see, that is not the case, and Acts does not yield an embarrassment of riches in terms of historical Jesus testimony.[4] Although following on canonically from the Gospel accounts, Acts takes a different track or focus; it presents itself primarily as a narrative of the *Church* rather than as a narrative of *Jesus* – its focus appears to be on the eponymous apostles, with information about Jesus gleaned on a more second-hand, indirect basis. Put simply, 'Acts is not about what *Jesus* did, but what his followers did',[5] and the portrait of Jesus in the text is therefore very much mediated through the portrait of other protagonists within the overall discourse.

We may, of course, surmise that Acts and Luke do not share the same author, therefore releasing Acts from any accusation that it ignores the Jesus tradition with which it is familiar, but that would seem to counteract the other, more persuasive evidence that they are in some sense connected narratives (cf. Acts 1.1–2). We will assume, with the consensus, that Luke and Acts (or Luke–Acts) are to be read in some way sequentially, and perhaps as two

---

[3] Richard I. Pervo, *Dating Acts: Between the Evangelists and the Apologists* (Santa Rosa: Polebridge, 2006), puts Acts well into the second century; Barnett, *Birth* 65–6, takes seriously Luke's testimony as Paul's travelling companion, thereby giving Acts a relatively early dating.

[4] Cf. W. A. Strange, 'The Jesus-Tradition in Acts', *NTS* 46 (2000) 59–74 (59): 'The author of Acts is as reluctant as Paul to make use of traditions about Jesus.' See Ch. 3 for further discussion of the apparent Pauline reluctance.

[5] I. Howard Marshall, *The Acts of the Apostles*, NTG (Sheffield: JSOT Press, 1992) 43.

parts of one overall discourse. But at the same time, one can actually overplay the (apparent) limitations of Acts in respect of Jesus testimony. Jesus (as a named figure, at least) is found in both the first and the last verses of the canonical text (1.1; 28.31),[6] and therefore 'bookends' the whole account. As the second volume of a narrative commenced in the Lucan Gospel, Acts may be seen as resolving, clarifying or expanding issues raised by the Gospel as to the nature of Jesus' identity. The promise to Mary, for example, that her offspring would exert an eternal kingship over the house of Israel (Luke 1.32–33), is left unresolved by the Gospel,[7] and it is only really in the first major speech of Acts, that of Peter at Pentecost, that the implications of the angelic prophecy are fully explained (Acts 2.22–36). Acts is notable for the volume of speeches found within its narrative, and as we shall see, much of the information about Jesus, or the portrayal of him in Acts, comes from these orations. As such, and as with the Pauline literature perhaps, one witnesses the emergence of a narrative of Jesus, a story by which the early Church was beginning to understand the particularity of Jesus as the resurrected, ascended and exalted Messiah.

In some, albeit limited ways, Acts also supplements our understanding of Jesus tradition, expanding on the Gospel's material and also providing information relating to Jesus that the Gospels themselves do not necessarily yield. This may include teaching of Jesus not found in the Gospel accounts (Acts 20.35, perhaps even 1.4–5), or it fleshes out incidents that are only minimally expressed within the Gospels (one thinks of the Ascension primarily in this regard). Acts may also utilize sources that are not specifically 'Jesus' tradition, but which can shed light on the impact of Jesus and how he was remembered (one thinks of the 'we' passages of the narratives – 16.10–16; 20.5—21.18; 27.1—28.16, or the tradition material that features in the kerygmatic speeches). Other background information also comes to the fore. We find out about

---

[6] Keith Warrington, *Discovering Jesus in the New Testament* (Peabody: Hendrickson, 2009) 58.

[7] Frank J. Matera, *New Testament Christology* (Louisville: Westminster John Knox, 1999) 64.

aspects of Jesus' family – the emergence, for instance, of James, the brother of Jesus, as a primary leader in the Jesus movement (though, admittedly, we only have the fraternal identification in Gal. 1.19). We have noted already that James may have been following Jesus earlier than the Gospels suggest, and will say more on that subject when considering the letter that bears his name; Acts does note, though, that Jesus' brothers were gathered with the Eleven post-Ascension (Acts 1.14), even if James is not specifically named therein. It is notable, then, that James is not taken in as the replacement for Judas (1.15–26); one would think him an obvious candidate if part of the broader pre-Easter Jesus movement. Acts also has other potential sources for Jesus tradition, with Manen/Menachem (13.1) possibly offering a window onto the Herodian court, and a source for Jesus of Nazareth testimony thereby.

More generally, Acts attends to how Jesus tradition is utilized within preaching (be that the simple fact that Jesus forms *part* of the content of such preaching – cf. 10.37–43) and the way in which the ongoing presence of Jesus in the community is acknowledged and enacted. Most importantly, perhaps, Acts ties key events within the life of the early Church to *Jesus*, and specifically to the work of Jesus *of Nazareth*, not Jesus Christ (2.22); within his Pentecost sermon, Peter recalls Jesus as one who had performed mighty deeds (2.22) and who had been crucified by the Romans (2.23), but who had been raised from the dead (2.32) and exalted as Lord at the right hand of God (2.33–36). It is this (now exalted) Jesus who has poured out the gift of the Spirit (2.32). From the outset, therefore, Acts serves to reduce the (potentially) false dichotomy drawn between 'Jesus of Nazareth' and the 'Christ of faith'; according to Peter, the one whom God has made Lord and Messiah is the same Jesus who has been crucified (2.36). As we have already noted in the Introduction, and as we will find with Paul and even Revelation, in the view of those who followed after him at least, the earthly Jesus and the risen Christ are portrayed as one.

In Acts, Jesus departs from his apostles, leaving them with the command to be his witnesses unto Jerusalem, all Judea and

Samaria, and eventually to the ends of the earth (1.8). The geographical demarcation is important here, and probably shapes how Luke recounts the spreading of the gospel from Jerusalem unto Rome, with the book being structured accordingly.[8] But the exhortation to be Jesus' *witnesses* is surely also significant for the text's overall *narratival* purpose, namely that one should expect witness or testimony to Jesus to form a core feature of the narrative to come. Now whether witness means proselytization (unlikely) or, more likely, the apostles acting as confirmatory 'eyewitnesses' to what Jesus had done, we would expect some reference to Jesus and his achievements to feature in the text, however indirectly. For being 'witnesses' to what Jesus had done seems to be an integral part of the apostolic standing – note the importance of Judas' replacement being someone who had accompanied the earthly Jesus (1.21–23) – and it would seem likely that the 'content' of what had been witnessed would feature at different points in the account (2.32; 3.15; 5.32; 10.40–41).

It is perhaps unsurprising, then, that those who follow after Jesus are found doing things similar to him, and thereby generating hints and associations to the Gospel tradition. When addressing the Jewish council as to the healing at the Beautiful Gate, Peter claims that they healed the man in the name of Jesus (4.10; cf. also 3.6 – 'in the name of Jesus Christ of Nazareth'). Not only does this label their activity as done in the name of Jesus, narrative-wise, they are also presented as acting *as* Jesus, healing as he healed. When recounting the Damascus Road episode, Saul/Paul is said to be persecuting Jesus of Nazareth – not Jesus Christ (22.8); the implication is that Saul's pursuit of the followers of the Way is vicariously a persecution of their (human) leader, that is, the earthly Jesus. Paul subsequently receives the accusation that he is a member or ringleader of a Nazarene sect or group (24.5); as the Nazarene/Nazareth label is applied to Jesus elsewhere in Acts (2.22;

---

[8] The expansion of the Church is reflected in the narrative flow of the book: Jerusalem (1.1—8.1); Judea/Samaria (8.1—13.1); the ends of the earth, ultimately Rome (13.1—28.31).

3.6; 22.8; 26.9), the suggestion once more is that Paul is part of a group associated with a figure from the Nazareth region, and with Jesus himself (there is little benefit, otherwise, in placing the appellation on the lips of Tertullus).[9]

The 'earthly Jesus' as character in Acts

On a cursory reading, Jesus can seem to depart from the narrative scene of Acts relatively quickly, as the Ascension brings a closure to his 'earthly' encounters until the promised Parousia (Acts 1.11). The text continues (at much greater length) to address the development of the group who seek to follow after him (the so-called followers of the Way), rather than focusing in on Jesus himself. We can therefore easily forget the role or character that Jesus assumes within the overall narrative, or overlook the significance of Jesus' ongoing presence in the retelling in Acts, but to do so is to miss Jesus' ongoing, continuing contribution. Peter claims that Jesus remains with them 'to this day' – that is, that of Pentecost (2.29), while Jesus meets with Saul on the Damascus Road or is seen by Stephen at the climax of his speech (7.55–56). Jesus even addresses Paul in the Temple, advising him to leave Jerusalem because some of his fellow Jews will not accept his witness/testimony about him (22.18). Thus, while he may be in some sense physically 'absent', Jesus remains very much 'present' in Luke's retelling, and the whole text (and not just 1.1–11) contributes to the book's articulation of Jesus' identity.

That said, the testimony of 1.1–11 is a good place to focus our analysis, as it is the only place where Acts presents Jesus in some form of extended earthly interaction. Jesus appears in Acts as a character and/or participant from the very outset of the book (1.1–9). The accounts of the resurrection appearances

---

[9] As an aside, we might observe that Tertullus' allegation suggests that the movement following after Jesus was conceived as an essentially Jewish movement, a 'sect' with Judaism, rather than a distinct group in its own right (cf. also Acts 18.12–16). See Carsten Claussen, 'Early Christianity and the Synagogue: A Parting of the Ways', in *Who Was Jesus? A Jewish-Christian Dialogue*, ed. Paul Copan and Craig A. Evans (Louisville: Westminster John Knox, 2001) 97–110 (102).

and Ascension found in Acts 1.3–9 parallel similar material in Luke 24.36–53, notably the exhortation to wait for the promise of the Father (Luke 24.49; Acts 1.4 – cf. Acts 2.33), though there are some points of tension or 'dissonance'[10] between the respective accounts. While both do (implicitly at least) restrict the appearances to Jerusalem (as opposed to the Galilean discourse of Matt. 28.16–20), Acts tells of forty days of resurrection appearances (1.3), whereas the Gospel suggests, implicitly at least, that the primary resurrection appearance and Ascension occur fairly quickly, possibly on the same day (Luke 24.50–51). In Acts, Jesus appears only to the apostles (the Twelve, one assumes); in Luke there are more general/widespread appearances (24.13–32). Such differences are not insignificant, and are difficult to harmonize historically, but they may reflect the particular narrative purposes of Acts at this point; the forty-day period is surely rhetorically significant and could be seen as paralleling the forty days of testing in the Gospel (4.2). If so, it is interesting that it is succeeded by a promise of baptism (in the Spirit – Acts 1.4–5), whereas in the Gospel account, the baptism (Luke 3.21–22) precedes the testing (4.1–13).

Narrative-wise, the post-Easter chronological discrepancies should not deflect from the picture Acts wishes to paint of Jesus.[11] From the outset of the Gospel account, Luke characterizes, or rather *continues* to characterize, Jesus as a teacher (Luke 4.15; 7.40; 19.39; 20.21); Acts summarizes the evangelistic discourse as comprising what Jesus did and taught (Acts 1.1), and then continues to depict Jesus doing such things for the forty days of post-resurrection appearances (1.3–5). Jesus is specified as instructing or commanding them (1.2), again akin to the teacher–pupil relationship established within the Gospel account. The content of Jesus' teaching is the kingdom of God (1.3), commensurate with the Gospel portrayal (Luke 4.43; 8.10; 9.2), and we therefore

---

[10] Richard I. Pervo, *Acts: A Commentary*, Hermeneia (Minneapolis: Fortress, 2009) 37.

[11] On the questions of the resurrection appearance chronology, see James D. G. Dunn, *Beginning from Jerusalem*, Christianity in the Making 2 (Grand Rapids: Eerdmans, 2009) 138–42.

encounter a strong sense of continuity across Luke–Acts in terms of this aspect of its portrayal of the earthly Jesus. As the Jesus of the Gospel preaches about the kingdom of God, it should be no surprise that questions as to the coming – or restoration – of that kingdom should re-emerge in the light of the resurrection event, even if the apostles still think that it is the kingdom of Israel, rather than of God, that is coming (Acts 1.6). There is continuity, then, between the pre-resurrection Jesus and the Jesus of the post-resurrection; the two men who exegete the account of Jesus ascending (1.10–11) may even be the same two men (however, figuratively) who are present on resurrection Sunday (Luke 24.4–6). The testimony of Acts concurs with the evangelical datum that the kingdom of Jesus comprised a core element of Jesus' proclamation and teaching. The fact, therefore, that Acts closes with Paul preaching on the kingdom of God (Acts 28.30–31) may equally be stressing the continuity of the ministry of the apostles with that commenced by Jesus.

There are further suggestions of continuity in Acts 1.1–11. The Greek word translated by the NRSV as 'staying' (1.4) commonly has overtones of table fellowship, and therefore Jesus' gathering with the apostles (1.4) probably has implications of sharing food together, reminiscent of the Upper Room discourse (Luke 22.13–20). Jesus is also shown to be instructing the apostles via the Holy Spirit (Acts 1.8); the very agent that empowered him at the beginning of his ministry (Luke 4.1, 14) is the same figure used to instruct those who follow after him and continue on with his ministry. Similarly, the fact that Jesus' directives to the apostles are Spirit-enabled (Acts 1.2) suggests a continuum, or association of sorts, between Jesus' mode of instruction to the apostles and the work they carried on by the enabling of the Spirit.

Jesus' declaration regarding the *origin* of the promise of the Spirit also warrants further enquiry. Acts recalls Jesus' prior baptism by John (1.22), and the text speaks frequently of John's baptismal practice (10.37; 13.24; 18.25; 19.3–4). In 1.4–5, Jesus declares that they will be baptized in (or by) the Spirit, but uses language akin to that accorded to John's promise of Luke 3.16 (John has the additional 'and fire' – one might have expected Acts to include that, bearing in mind the imagery of Acts 2.3). The same text is used in Acts 11.16 as the evidence of the coming of Spirit, but the Lucan Peter remembers this to be *Jesus'* words, rather than those of John the Baptist. Within the Greek text of 1.4, the shift from Jesus' indirect to direct speech is awkward, and it is not clear as to exactly what comprises 'what you have heard from me' – that is, whether it is the exhortation to await the promise of the Father (1.4) or whether it is the 'baptismal' quotation of 1.5. If it were the former, the previous (Jesus) utterance could be Luke 11.13 or possibly Luke 24.49,[12] but might equally be a more specific appeal to the promise of the Spirit unattested within the Gospel account. If it were the latter, then it may suggest that the John tradition is well attested, and that it was permissible to (re)place it in the mouth of Jesus, thereby giving it some kind of dominical ratification. Alternatively, it is perfectly possible that Jesus is quoting himself, and that Acts 1.4–5 actually reiterates a prior prediction that he would baptize with the Spirit – that is, both he *and* John foretold the event, and in broadly similar terms. Again, this would represent 'new' testimony about the earthly Jesus that is not found in the Gospel record.

The earthly Jesus disappears from the scene in Acts 1.9, in a mysterious experience whose 'historical' reference point is hard to determine.[13] Appeal to such experience can serve to make Luke seem less than historical. Did the disciples actually see Jesus ascend into the sky – a visual theophany[14] – or is the language of 'seeing' implying that something 'happened' (i.e. akin to other events of the incarnation), but which is in essence still supernatural?[15] Or is the event (essentially) theological in its nature – an experience

---

[12] Robert C. Tannehill, *The Narrative Unity of Luke–Acts: A Literary Interpretation* 2 vols, FF (Philadelphia: Fortress, 1986) 12.

[13] See the helpful discussion in Rick Strelan, *Strange Acts: Studies in the Cultural World of the Acts of the Apostles*, BZNW 126 (Berlin: Walter de Gruyter, 2004) 33–7.

[14] F. F. Bruce, *The Acts of the Apostles: The Greek Text with Introduction and Commentary*, 3rd rev. and enl. edn (Grand Rapids: Eerdmans, 1990) 38.

[15] Charles K. Barrett, *A Critical and Exegetical Commentary on the Acts of the Apostles*, 2 vols, ICC (Edinburgh: T&T Clark, 1994) 1.61–4, 81–2.

whose 'historicity' cannot be put into words?[16] Questions as to the historical actuality of such an event are impossible to resolve, of course, but we have already suggested the strategy of considering historical concerns in the context of narrative retelling. Taking this narrative approach seriously, and taking account of inter-textual allusions, it is possible that Acts here intends to reveal Jesus as Lord – or heavenly Lord.[17] Building perhaps on other 'Ascension' traditions, such as those involving Elijah or Moses, Jesus is shown to be God's (hu)man, the one vindicated by God. To put it another way, within the narrative of Luke–Acts as a whole, '(s)omething was disclosed to them [i.e. the disciples] about Jesus that previously had been hidden ... They see, in an ecstatic, visionary state, Jesus for who he really is.'[18] Jesus' identity has been further disclosed and he is now *in Heaven* (cf. Acts 3.20–21). The Ascension therefore culminates in the picture of Jesus in Luke–Acts, the full identity of the figure now revealed, and, as such, the apostles are to be witnesses to this – and not just to the event of the resurrection (cf. 1.21).

Indeed, it is only in Acts that we have a clear distinction between Jesus' resurrection and Ascension. This may raise practical historical questions, such as where the resurrected Jesus was when not with his disciples,[19] but it is beyond the scope of this book to assess such theological conundrums! What Acts does illustrate is the 'cessation' of sightings at some point – an important datum, often forgotten. There is an 'end' to Jesus' *earthly* existence in a very marked way. By comparison, the Gospels do hold back on this. Matthew and John leave Jesus on earth (for good reasons, no doubt), and Mark, assuming the ending at 16.8, leaves the situation in some ambiguity. Luke's Gospel does have Jesus mysteriously drawn heavenward (Luke 24.51), but on its own it is left somewhat underdeveloped or unexplained, lacking the finality to the sightings that the Ascension according to Acts conveys. That does not mean that Jesus is

---

[16] Dunn, *Beginning from Jerusalem* 145–9.
[17] Strelan, *Strange Acts* 48–9.
[18] Strelan, *Strange Acts* 35, 39.
[19] Dunn, *Beginning from Jerusalem* 147.

absent from the rest of the account, as we shall shortly discuss; it just demarks an end to a particular phase of the Jesus story, that his earthly work is in some sense completed.

The life of Jesus in Acts

Acts also knows of a number of details from Jesus' life. While these are obviously far less than the Gospels include, they are not insignificant, and can (occasionally) enhance the portrait given by the evangelists, and particularly by Luke's own Gospel account. But laying aside the Gospels for the moment, and setting aside the connections with Luke, if we only had Acts as our historical record, what would we know of the earthly Jesus?

Acts includes little information about Jesus' birth or upbringing, except that he had brothers (1.14), that his mother was named Mary (1.14) and that he was part of the Davidic line (13.22–23). Within Acts, the brothers are now part of the community with the apostles (1.13–14), suggesting that Jesus' family had overcome any initial apprehension or tension towards him. In effect, Acts becomes interested in Jesus' life from the point of John's baptism, with the latter acting as the inception point for Jesus' ministry (1.22); this ministry is portrayed as having a public dimension to it – Peter points out that his audience already know, or have seen, what Jesus has done (2.22), but not much more is made of it. Little is said explicitly as to what the ministry comprised, other than that it happened (1.17) and that it extended across Judea (10.39); Jesus is said to have done good things (10.38) and healed those oppressed by the devil (10.38), along with other signs and wonders (2.22), but Acts has little interest in the details of such miracles or in Jesus' parables and debates with the scribes and Pharisees. It does say that Jesus chose apostles to follow after him (1.2), and there is the suggestion that Jesus may have predicted the end of the temple (6.14), something that Luke omits from his Gospel,[20] but that is really all in terms of biographical detail.

---

[20] Acts 6.14 perhaps represents Mark 14.58 (so Helmut Koester, *Ancient Christian Gospels: Their History and Development* (London: SCM Press, 1990) 63n1).

Acts knows of Jesus' death in Jerusalem, and that he was buried there (13.29). It ascribes responsibility for Jesus' death to the Romans, with both Pilate and Herod involved in it (4.27; cf. 3.13); Pilate is portrayed both as the one who effectively signs Jesus' death warrant (13.28), and also as the one who wished to release him (3.13). But particularly notable is the way in which Acts attributes Jewish responsibility for it too (2.23; 5.30; 13.27); Jesus' death at the hands of his own people is a key feature of the Acts testimony and, in places, becomes the dominant strand, notably Acts 3.15, where the Jews are explicitly accused of murder, even if acting in ignorance (3.17). Jesus himself is portrayed as an innocent party (13.28). Acts also includes the tradition that a figure was released when Jesus was condemned; the figure is not named (he is called Barabbas in the Gospel – Luke 23.18), but is described by Acts as a murderer (3.14).

While not explicitly tied to Jesus, Acts does, of course, also pick up on tradition relating to him in the case of Judas (1.16–19). Judas is recognized as one of Jesus' core followers (1.17), and is cast as assisting those who would arrest him (1.16). He is supposed to have purchased a field with the fruits of his efforts, the Hakeldama or Field of Blood (1.19), but is then said to have been engulfed by the field, with all his bowels flowing out (1.18). Luke does not include Judas' death in his Gospel account, and of the evangelists, only Matthew does so (Matt. 27.3–10), with Acts therefore serving to supplement the evangelical testimony within the Lucan tradition. Historically speaking, the Matthean and Acts accounts do stand in tension – in Matthew, the chief priests buy the field and bury Judas there as he has already hanged himself (27.9–10); in Acts, Judas is said to buy the field himself (Acts 1.18). Who can say what is the 'correct' historical scenario, but the episode attests the way that narrative and history combine, when seeking to extract significance through narrative retelling.[21]

---

[21] On the value of Luke's Judas tradition, see Bart D. Ehrman, *Did Jesus Exist? The Historical Argument for Jesus of Nazareth* (New York: HarperOne, 2012) 107–8.

The use of Jesus' teaching in Acts

It is true to say that direct appeal to Jesus' teaching in Acts remains somewhat limited, especially when one considers the putative common authorship with the Lucan Gospel.[22] In short, direct appeals to Jesus' teaching in Acts are minimal to say the least. Where you would expect Acts to appeal to Jesus' teaching to endorse a particular position adopted by the apostolic community, we actually find a veritable reluctance so to do. When the early Church is shown to be formulating its socio-ethical practice, such as in the sharing of possessions (2.44–45; 4.32–35), Luke offers no appeal to Jesus' teaching on, say, the Beatitudes to justify the approach taken (or even to vindicate Jesus for 'proving' that the poor and hungry would be blessed – Luke 6.20–21).[23] We might think, likewise, of the so-called Council of Jerusalem (Acts 15.6–29), arguably the centrepiece of the whole book. Its decision not to impose restrictions on Gentile believers would surely have been bolstered by appeal to Jesus' teaching on such matters (cf. Mark 7.15, 19), and such an appeal is doubly absent, as Luke lacks any corresponding Mark 7 content in his Gospel account. Indeed, it is striking how little mention the Council makes of Jesus and instead, as is common throughout the account, it appeals to Scripture to vindicate the point being made, with Amos 9, rather than Jesus' prior teaching, being the corroborating testimony (cf. Joel 2 in Acts 2).[24] Positively, this does portray Luke (as with

---

[22] Cf. Strange, 'Jesus-Tradition' 71: 'For Luke, it seems to have been unnecessary to refer to the historic Jesus in order to establish the practice of the church or to confer authority on its beliefs or actions, and his gospel is certainly not a manual of instruction on mission for his own church.'

[23] Charles K. Barrett, 'Imitatio Christi in Acts', in Jesus of Nazareth: Lord and Christ: Essays on the Historical Jesus and New Testament Christology, ed. Joel B. Green and Max Turner (Grand Rapids: Eerdmans, 1994) 251–62. He notes: 'Luke never even points back to his former treatise as supplying a model, or represents the Christian character that he describes as recalling the story of Jesus, the story being an example of Christian behaviour' (252).

[24] On the use of Scripture in Acts to support/endorse its arguments, see Steve Moyise, The Later New Testament Writers and Scripture (London: SPCK, 2012) 6–41.

the other NT writers) trying to make sense of Jesus in the light of what was familiar to them, namely their Scriptures. But it also cautions against over-expectations from the non-Gospel material as to what light they may shed upon the Jesus of history, and, as I shall draw out more in the final chapter, it sheds further light on the way in which Jesus was remembered.

What evidence, though, is there of Acts engaging with Jesus' teaching? The text alludes to the activity of Jesus in Judea and Jerusalem (10.39), and the suggestion is that such activity comprised mighty deeds and wonders (2.22), but very little is actually said to flesh this out. There are the occasional references to Jesus' healing and doing good deeds (2.22; 10.38), but they remain fairly generalized and occasional, and there is no reference to the specific nature of the healing activity. Luke's portrayal of Apollos, one suggests, is commensurate with this. Apollos knows, and is a teacher of, Jesus tradition, and he has been instructed in the way of the Lord (18.24–25); while there is something deficient about his understanding of the Spirit, there is no implication that he is limited in his knowledge of Jesus – quite the reverse. Yet Luke still does not elucidate what Apollos' knowledge is comprised of – it merely suffices to say that he was familiar with it.

Luke's reticence therefore in using, or appealing to, Jesus' earthly deeds is striking; to put it another way, the disparity of interest in Jesus' activity between the Gospel and Acts would be one reason actually to disavow common authorship of the two texts. Strange's analysis is therefore fairly brief and to the point: 'there is virtually no evidence in Acts that Luke wrote his Gospel in order to enshrine the authoritative teaching of Jesus for the church'.[25] Strange suggests that one reason for the absence is that Luke's key interest – Gentile inclusion – isn't really 'taught' by Jesus, so there is no tradition to which to point; instead, it is the Holy Spirit who directs the Church in that direction (with the Gospel correspondingly omitting Markan testimony that might have justified the Gentile mission, such as Jesus' encounter with the

---

[25] Strange, 'Jesus-Tradition' 69.

33

Syro-Phoenecian woman – Mark 7.24–30). Within the Gospel account, Luke 13.22–30 could have functioned as supporting Jesus' teaching, but Acts does not make the connection with it. In sum, Strange concludes: 'the teaching of Jesus in the Gospel was not a simple reflection of the mission practice of the church';[26] in this regard, Acts just does not behave as we might expect it to. Of course, it may be that Acts expects its readers to be acquainted with Jesus' teaching already, and they therefore do not need to be reminded of it. Luke regularly underscores the public nature of Jesus' ministry (Acts 2.22; 10.38–39); he may wish instead to draw out the significance of Jesus' actions, rather than restate them, particularly through the use of Scripture (e.g. 2.25–36). At the same time, Luke consistently draws out the irony of the public response to Jesus; although there was divine attestation of him (2.22; 3.13), and although his action and teaching seem well known (10.39), Jesus was nonetheless put to death by his own people (2.36; 3.14–15; 13.27–29).[27]

There is, though, one specific appeal to Jesus' teaching, made by Paul at the climax of his Miletus address (20.35). In the context of defending his exemplary character, Paul recalls Jesus' words that 'it is better to give than to receive'. The expression is presented as an explicit Jesus quotation that demonstrably 'proves' Paul's case. The quotation has no direct parallel in the Gospels (Luke 6.38 may share a similar sentiment, but it remains a different saying), and so if Acts 20.35 were a genuine Jesus saying, it would supplement existing canonical Jesus tradition. Few scholars, however, consider it to derive from Jesus, instead conceiving of it as either a Lucan creation or a popular proverb placed in Paul's mouth by Luke.[28] It is similar to the *agraphon* found in *1 Clement* 2.1, and also stands in tension with Luke 10.7.

---

[26] Strange, 'Jesus-Tradition' 71.
[27] See Beverly Roberts Gaventa, 'Learning and Relearning the Identity of Jesus from Luke–Acts', in *Seeking the Identity of Jesus: A Pilgrimage*, ed. Beverly Roberts Gaventa and Richard B. Hays (Grand Rapids: Eerdmans, 2008) 148–65 (149–50).
[28] The closest form is Thucydides 3.97.4, but scholars differ as to whether the dependency or connection can be proved.

The appeal to Jesus at Acts 20.35 is an odd inclusion at this point, however, and needs to be treated as such, particularly as citations of Jesus' teaching, genuine or otherwise, are so rare within the Acts account. It may be that Paul – or perhaps the Lucan Paul – actually did cite the logion at this point, and that it is actually genuine Jesus material.[29] Craig Blomberg seems to concur, averring: 'Paul cites a saying of Jesus not found in any existing Gospel . . . This is a salutary reminder that not all Jesus taught was by any means included in the written Gospels (cf. John 21.25) and that even before their composition, people were preserving Jesus' teaching by word of mouth.'[30] Perhaps a middle option suffices, and 'what 1 Clement notes in this matter may well be an alternate rendition of what Jesus actually did say and was passed on, in its own way, by the tradition used by the author of the Miletus speech'.[31] Whatever the origin, it remains interesting that Luke chooses to ascribe it to Jesus, or to use 'Jesus testimony'[32] when there is no apparent need to do so, especially when other Jesus teaching is so notably absent from the Acts account, and when – as some point out – it is in tension with Paul's own sense of self-supporting mission. The 'citation' occurs at the climax of Paul's address, the high point one might say, and in a context in which Paul seeks to commend his own conduct. It is further notable that the climax of Peter's speech before the believers (Acts 11.16) also has a Jesus statement at its culminating moment, and it is almost as if, in both instances, Jesus' teaching is used as some form of corroborative statement that vindicates each character before their assembled listeners. This could be seen as Acts evincing a high regard for Jesus' words, even if they are only used sparingly in the overall discourse.

---

[29] Colin J. Hemer, 'The Speeches of Acts: pt 1: The Ephesian Elders at Miletus', *TynBul* 40 (1989) 76–85.

[30] Craig L. Blomberg, *From Pentecost to Patmos: An Introduction to Acts through Revelation* (Nashville: Broadman & Holman, 2006) 67.

[31] John J. Kilgallen, 'Acts 20:35 and Thucydides 2.97.4', *JBL* 112 (1993) 312–14 (314).

[32] Pervo, *Acts*, 528–9: 'the "agraphon" indicates that for Luke the door for sayings of Jesus remained open and was not limited to his written Gospel'.

While the explicit appeal to Jesus' teaching is not prevalent, there does, however, seem to be a strand within the Acts portrayal that seeks to hold up Jesus as a model figure. This may function, as we shall see, in terms of a larger story, rather than through direct citation, but it may also operate through the identification of key protagonists in Acts with the actions and narrative of Jesus. We think, for example, of the familiar patterning of Stephen and Paul as righteous sufferers just like Jesus, or the frequent appeals to the innocence of both Jesus and Paul (and the latter's frequent trials in this regard). Likewise, there are the prolonged journeys of Jesus and Paul respectively to Jerusalem and Rome, each heading, in some sense, to their death. While the apostles are primarily called to witness to Jesus rather than to imitate him,[33] some patterning or connection between them is suggested by the text. It is the apostles' actions rather than their words that mirror Jesus, and thereby express the way they continue his ministry and act as his witnesses. Paul breaks bread in the fashion that Jesus does (27.35); the apostles perform wonders and signs (2.43) just as Jesus had done before (2.22), and Stephen is particularly demarked for so doing (6.8). Philip is found preaching the kingdom of God (8.12), the concern of Jesus in his proclamation. Jesus therefore becomes something of an exemplar for the apostles to follow; there is not the explicit *imitatio* that we will encounter in 1 Peter, but Acts may still be said to offer an essay on discipleship, so to speak, one where the character and life of Jesus are held up in model fashion; the text 'illustrates how the early church imaged Jesus in their own lives and ministries'.[34] We may say that Luke and Paul are on similar ground here. As we shall see, Paul also seems to self-pattern his own ministry and mission upon that of Jesus, and Luke characterizes the apostle likewise. Beverly Gaventa summarizes the

---

[33] Charles K. Barrett, 'Sayings of Jesus in the Acts of the Apostles', in À *cause de l'Évangile: Études sur les Synoptiques et les Actes offertes au Père Jacques Dupont, o.s.b., à l'occasion de son soixante-dixième anniversaire*, Lectio Divina 123 (Paris: Éditions du Cerf, 1985) 681–708.

[34] Douglas Buckwalter, *The Character and Purpose of Luke's Christology*, SNTSMS 89 (Cambridge: Cambridge University Press, 1996) 75.

situation well: 'the apostles do not so much substitute for an absent Jesus as they exemplify his present ongoing activity'.[35]

The story of Jesus in Acts

But does Acts have anything more explicit about Jesus himself? If Acts disavows the need to root the Church's practice and self-understanding in explicit appeal to Jesus' teaching, are there other ways in which Jesus is remembered in its retelling of the life and practice of the early Church? We might venture that there are. Perhaps it is the *story* of Jesus, rather than the *sayings* of Jesus that are attractive for Acts.[36] For although Acts offers some insights into Jesus tradition, and to the remembrance of it, it also reflects the development of, and reflection on, such tradition within the life of the early Church. At various points in the Acts account, the Jesus story is retold, with extra detail supplied and added to it, the medium of kerygmatic speeches dotted throughout the text particularly prominent in this regard.

Such mention of story also takes us back to the question of how far Acts conceives of itself as doing history. On the one hand, Acts does seem in some sense 'historical', in that it is seeking to present, through however particular a lens, the expansion of the gospel from Jerusalem, and record the activity of certain key protagonists within that. But it is 'historical' in a particular way. It offers no dates or chronological reference points, it repeats narratives (Saul's conversion occurs three times) and there is a weighty emphasis on some material (e.g. Paul's trials) with comparatively little attention to the life of the churches founded along the way. Its 'history' is highly subjective. Acts also presents itself as some form of narrative, or maybe a composition of several narratives; it is seeking to do history through the medium of telling story/stories. And as I suggested in the introduction, 'story' need not be in

---

[35] Gaventa, 'Learning and Relearning' 162.
[36] Strange, 'Jesus-Tradition' 65: 'The story of Jesus is far more prominent in Acts than the sayings of Jesus.'

tension with historical concerns; narrative is used for historical effect, and any redaction or literary shaping need not reduce historical interest.

Now, certain aspects of Luke's retelling differ from the narrative presented within the Gospels, or at least the terminology varies, and this may reflect the expansion or development of the Jesus tradition. Jesus, for example, is depicted as hanging on a 'tree' (Acts 5.30; 10.39; 13.29; cf. 1 Pet. 2.24) rather than on a cross (though he is still said to be crucified – 2.23). This arboreal relocation probably alludes to Deuteronomy 21.22–23 and the curse that fell upon a figure hung from a tree, and would therefore represent Lucan reflection on the significance of Jesus' death, rather than a specific declaration regarding the actual historical event. In this fashion, Acts may be seen as a supplement to the Gospel tradition, a retelling of the Jesus story; it is not that the picture of Jesus is dramatically altered, but rather that we encounter material that enhances or reinforces the given story. The sermons in Acts also remind us that Jesus' history is a core ingredient to belief – Jesus' past is included within the call to faith, within the exhortation to respond to him. To put it more explicitly, Jesus *past* mattered as much as Jesus *present*,[37] and tradition about Jesus was included in the kerygmatic preaching of the Church; 'Jesus remembered' was a core aspect of that preaching. And while certain events, especially Jesus' death and resurrection, would clearly assume prominence in that regard, other aspects of his life are included which suggest that the earthly Jesus and his conduct did matter to the early Church.

Let us take a couple of examples. In the opening Pentecost speech, Jesus remains the integral character. He is identified as Jesus of Nazareth (Acts 2.22), not as Christ, and Peter portrays him as a divinely chosen figure (2.22), one through whom God

---

[37] Cf. Samuel Byrskog, *Story as History – History as Story: The Gospel Tradition in the Context of Ancient Oral History*, WUNT 123 (Tübingen: Mohr Siebeck, 2000) 6: 'the kerygma, the story of the present Lord, remains . . . intrinsically linked with the Jesus of the past'. His observation is made of Jesus studies more generally, but it would seem to be also particularly true for Acts' portrayal of the Jesus story.

had acted with mighty deeds (2.22). He recalls Jesus' cruciform death (2.23) ascribing responsibility for it to the Jewish people (2.23) in co-operation with the Roman authorities ('those outside the law' – 2.23; cf. also 4.27). He continues by referring to Jesus' resurrection (2.24), and finishes by announcing Jesus' exaltation as Messiah and Lord (2.33, 36). It is notable, therefore, that 'Peter reminds his audience about Jesus, even though he assumes that they either know about or have seen the evidence of God's action through Jesus.'[38] This seems an important point to underscore: within the narrative context, there is limited need to say anything about Jesus, as Peter acknowledges that his hearers already know these things (2.22). The inclusion of such Jesus material therefore seems deliberate and significant: the life of the earthly Jesus (the man – Jesus of Nazareth, 2.22) is linked to his resurrection and exaltation, and will also be tied to this event known as Pentecost. Or to put it another way, the Lucan Peter refuses to separate the activity of the earthly Jesus (however minimally expounded) from the exaltation of the risen Lord and the gift of the Spirit. It is *this* Jesus who gives the Spirit (2.33): from the very outset of the Acts account, the giving of the Spirit is associated not only with 'Jesus as Lord' but also with 'Jesus the crucified one' (2.36).

Peter's next address, at Solomon's Portico (Acts 3.12–26), is also a retelling of the Jesus story, and one that displays further reflection upon the significance of Jesus – it is no 'pure' historical retelling. The speech is given in Jerusalem, so just like at Pentecost, there is no need to sketch out a life of Jesus, but Peter still includes articulations of Jesus' character, or reference to the kind of figure Jesus personified. Jesus is described as God's servant and as glorious in character (3.13). He is also labelled as the Holy and Righteous One (3.15; cf. 22.14) and the Author of Life (3.14), both with some titular sense but in neither case is there any implication that Jesus used the titles of himself. The description of Jesus as suffering Messiah (3.18) may go back to Jesus (cf. Mark

---

[38] Graham Stanton, *Jesus of Nazareth in New Testament Preaching*, SNTSMS 27 (London: Cambridge University Press, 1974) 15.

8.27–32), but the application of his work, the atoning for sins (Acts 3.19) and subsequent times of refreshing (3.20), is instead supported by an appeal to the Scriptures. Likewise, significant authority is invested in the name of Jesus (3.16), such that it is capable of healing the man. Jesus is 'present' and active by his name.

One other personification of Jesus worthy of mention may come, albeit indirectly, through the speech of Gamaliel, in which he compares Jesus with other failed revolutionary leaders, specifically Theudas and Judas the Galilean (5.34–39). Momentarily setting the historical questions noted above to one side, narrative-wise, the essence of Gamaliel's declaration is that the Jesus movement would succeed/fail regardless of the intervention of the Council. But behind his observation seems to lie the assumption that Jesus had been leading a political or restorationist movement in his lifetime; Gamaliel treats Jesus in similar terms to Theudas and Judas, and forges some kind of like-for-like comparison.[39] This more 'revolutionary' Jesus is also hinted at by the apostles' question regarding the restoration of the kingdom (1.6), and Luke could well be responding to existing portrayals of the earthly Jesus, either to refute them or to rework them for his own interests. To put it another way, to depict Jesus in political or revolutionary terms is not anachronistic; at least, Luke utilizes the category, even if he does not just leave Jesus there.

Appeal to the character and person of Jesus therefore permeates the sermons/addresses of Acts[40] and, with Graham Stanton, one

---

[39] Jeffrey A. Trumbower, 'The Historical Jesus and the Speech of Gamaliel (Acts 5.35–9)', *NTS* 39 (1993) 500–17 (507): 'This may indicate that the idea was current in Luke's own day that Jesus had indeed mistakenly expected some form of Jewish restoration in his own lifetime or with his own career, as Judas the Galilean, Theudas, and the Egyptian had done. The speech of Gamaliel would then serve in Luke's scheme to show that Jesus was similar to the other prophets in outward appearance, but unlike them, his mission was to be the true agent of God and he was not mistaken about God's inscrutable timetable.'

[40] It is true that the Areopagus speech does not name Jesus (17.22–31) and there is merely the hint at one resurrected (17.31), but that is surely related to the context of the Athens address. And, even then, Paul still points to a *man* being the agent of judgement, not necessarily a divine figure (17.31).

concludes: 'Luke wished to show the readers of his day that an account of the life and character of Jesus was part of the preaching of the church.'[41] This preaching tends, though, to expand the Jesusology of Acts – its Jesus is no longer just the earthly Jesus. He is not only resident in heaven (3.20–21) but also present with the believers, 'no longer constrained by place and time'.[42] In other speeches, he is affirmed as Leader and Saviour (5.31), proclaimed as Messiah (5.42; 9.22) and as Saviour (13.23), and he eventually becomes King Jesus (17.8). Jesus is also conceived of in prophetic terms: both Peter and Stephen compare Jesus with the prophet promised by Moses (3.22–23; 7.37). Indeed, Acts draws out the way in which Jesus is attested to by the prophets (3.23–26; 10.43) and how they predicted his suffering (3.17); the discussion between Philip and the Ethiopian is focused around Isaiah, but Philip's explanation points him to Jesus (8.32–35). Furthermore, Paul's teaching about Jesus comes from both the law and the prophets (28.23), just as the Lucan Jesus himself explained to the Emmaus travellers how Moses and the prophets attested to him (Luke 24.27; cf. also 24.44). The apostles' appeal to Scripture as foundational for understanding who/what Jesus is mirrors how the Lucan Jesus himself is presented as doing so in the Gospel account.

Jesus the Baptist?

If Peter's healing is partly about the continuation of what Jesus of Nazareth had begun, then one might ask the same question regarding baptismal practice. The first thing that Peter requires in the aftermath of the gift of the Spirit is that his hearers repent and be baptized (Acts 2.38; cf. 8.36). The text, however, offers no reason or justification for such a response, and is instead presented as some kind of normal reaction for those wishing to become part of the new community. Likewise, Paul can speak of baptismal

---

[41] Stanton, *Jesus of Nazareth* 28.
[42] Gaventa, 'Learning and Relearning' 163.

practice as the norm in the local congregation in 1 Corinthians 1.14–18, but without offering any comment as to why it should be so.

This raises some interesting questions for the practice of Jesus, historical and remembered. On the one hand, the Gospels don't record Jesus exercising a baptismal ministry, at least not for an extended period of time. John records Jesus baptizing (John 3.22), but subsequently qualifies the statement to say that it was his disciples who were actually doing so (John 4.2), perhaps so as to avoid any confusion with John the Baptist.[43] To attribute any baptismal activity to the earthly Jesus is therefore an argument from silence, even if it seems likely that someone embarking on their own ministry might utilize a practice with which they had already become familiar. On the other hand, we also have to find some way of explaining the emergence of baptism as a response to the Pentecost moment. Why, if the new community have had the predicted baptism of the Spirit (1.5, 8), do they also require an accompanying water baptism?

The difficulty here is that arguments from silence work in both directions, and one can only pose hypotheses at this point. Perhaps, though, what Acts might offer in terms of historical Jesus testimony is to support the notion that Jesus *did* indeed conduct a ministry of which baptismal practice was in some form a part (cf. Mark 10.38–39). Of course, the Synoptic silence on any baptismal practice is an important datum, but it is not a datum that cannot be explained. The default privilege given to the Synoptics can tend to obscure insights drawn from the other NT texts, particularly when there might be very good reasons within the Synoptic accounts themselves for not wanting to refer to 'Jesus the Baptist'.

---

[43] Graham H. Twelftree, 'Jesus the Baptist', *JSHJ* 7 (2009) 103–25, opines that Jesus did embark upon a baptismal ministry, but abandoned it once the miracles occurred – i.e. evidence of the coming of the kingdom and a different age. Baptism is only the prelude to the eschaton. However, just because there is a change in the pace of the Jesus narrative, just because the demise of John earmarks a change in pace – does that necessitate that baptism no longer happens? It seems easier to speak of a continuity of practice, than for it to be stopped and restarted.

The Synoptic silence could easily arise from the concern to avoid unhelpful comparisons with John the Baptist – Jesus is after all the greater one who will baptize with fire (Matt. 3.11) – and such silence is explainable for that reason; the Gospels seek to remember what is distinctive about Jesus, and to portray him as another 'Baptizer' would not serve that purpose. The later addition to John (4.2) seems to evidence such a wariness, or the attempt to prevent any confusion between the two figures. By contrast, it is less easy to think why baptismal practice becomes a mark of community entry for the followers of Jesus in the aftermath of his departure.[44] It may be that their baptism was supposed to mimic or replicate that of Jesus, as Acts knows of the event (Acts 1.22), but there is nothing in Peter's sermon itself to require making that connection.

Conclusion: the Jesus of Acts

As we have observed, one cannot really talk about the Jesus of Acts without simultaneously talking about the Jesus of Luke's Gospel; Luke–Acts presents one broadly continuous narrative in which Jesus is one of the central characters. Across both volumes, one encounters the way in which Jesus is firmly identified not only as teacher and healer but also as Messiah and ascended, exalted Lord. Indeed, he is portrayed as *the* Christ, the one who properly fulfils that mantle where other potential figures did not (5.36–39), the one who God himself has vindicated (2.22–24).

Yet Acts can often still be a forgotten or sidelined voice in discussions about the earthly Jesus. Despite its substantial length, and despite its (apparent) interest in the continuation of the ministry of the earthly Jesus (1.1–8), Acts tends to be used more to inform discussions about the work of the Spirit as the one that

---

[44] For a strong articulation of Jesus baptizing, see R. T. France, 'Jesus the Baptist?', in *Jesus of Nazareth: Lord and Christ: Essays on the Historical Jesus and New Testament Christology*, ed. Joel B. Green and Max Turner (Grand Rapids: Eerdmans, 1994) 94–111. He concludes: '[I]t [baptism] remained for Jesus, as it had been for John, the normal means of enrolling those who had joined this eschatological restoration movement' (107).

'continues' the work of the supposedly departed Jesus rather than contributing to the identity of Jesus himself. This neglect, I would suggest, is unwarranted on two grounds. On the one hand, it overlooks Jesus' continued presence with the apostles in and by the Spirit; Jesus gives the Spirit (2.33: cf. 1.4–5) and the Spirit is identified as the Spirit *of Jesus* (16.7). The risen Lord is therefore with and active among the apostles in their ministry (18.9–10). On the other hand, Acts, as we have seen, has much to say about the story and character of Jesus, even if there is surprisingly limited appeal to his sayings and teachings. The apostles are to be witnesses to him, testifying to his life, death, resurrection and Ascension, and such testimonial appeal is made across a number of the kerygmatic speeches that permeate the Acts account. Acts therefore reminds the reader that Jesus' 'history' or 'past' – that is, the *earthly* Jesus' 'past' – mattered in the life of the early Church; it is surely no accident that he both begins and ends the Acts account (1.1; 28.31). For Luke, the expansion of the gospel from Jerusalem to Rome has its origins in one person, Jesus of Nazareth.

3

'To know or not to know': Jesus in Paul

Whether because of the volume of NT literature attributed to him,[1] or whether because his correspondence probably represents the earliest canonical witness to the impact of the Jesus movement, it is unsurprising that one looks to Paul as potentially the most valuable source for material or data relating to Jesus of Nazareth. Although not a follower of the earthly Jesus, Paul was associated with leading figures who had previously been so (Gal. 1.18–19), and, as a former persecutor of the Way, he may have vicariously gathered information about the very group/person he had devoted his energies to persecuting (Gal. 1.15; Phil. 3.6).[2] Because his corpus of epistles probably predate the written Gospel testimony, he is temporally closer to Jesus' life, and his letters would therefore lack any putative influence that other post-Easter events such as the fall of Jerusalem (70 CE) might have had upon the recollection of Jesus' life and significance. Indirectly, but no less valuable perhaps, Paul also offers us a personal picture of a devout Jew of

---

[1] There are inherent assumptions and challenges in trying to treat the Pauline corpus as one entity in terms of its depiction of Jesus. Given more time and space, we would normally want to treat each letter individually, and seek to discern if and how Jesus is depicted differently across the various constituent texts of the corpus. In order, though, to try and limit generalization, we are separating the so-called *Hauptbriefe* or genuine letters (Romans, 1/2 Corinthians, Galatians, 1 Thessalonians, Philippians and Philemon) from the Deutero-Pauline texts discussed in the next chapter. Such differentiation, however, is not to be read as making any declarations regarding authorship of such texts; the distinction is as much practical and heuristic as anything.

[2] Cf. Victor Paul Furnish, *Jesus according to Paul*, Understanding Jesus Today (Cambridge: Cambridge University Press, 1993) 14: 'There must have been talk about Jesus in the Pharisaic circles within which he [i.e. Paul] moved.'

the era and therefore a window onto such perspectives;[3] while, of course, his Diaspora background and interest in Gentile matters offer some points of difference from Palestinian thinking, and whereas the plurality of first-century 'Judaisms' is recognized, his testimony to understanding Jesus' *Jewish* context is not to be dismissed lightly, especially bearing in mind the so-called Third Quest's common consensus that Jesus is first and foremost a first-century Jew. After all, confidence in our knowledge of the historical Paul is often far greater than any such knowledge of the historical Jesus.

At the same time, there are the inevitable caveats to such high expectations. Paul only knows of Jesus *after* his death, and much of his experience comes by 'revelation', seminally so on the Damascus Road (Gal. 1.11–12). The post-Easter nature of his encounter with the risen Jesus, even though, to Paul's mind, of equivalent significance to that of the other apostles (cf. 1 Cor. 9.1, 15.3–8), may have led to a similar emphasis on post- rather than pre-Easter events. Although some have suggested that Paul's career and training in Jerusalem may have given him some exposure to the earthly Jesus,[4] that is at best only speculation, and it lacks any evidence or basis within the epistolary corpus. Paul himself gives no reason to believe he had encountered the pre-resurrection Jesus,[5] and, although it is an argument from silence, one might have expected him to say so had that actually been the case. Paul also differs from the Jerusalem apostles on some points (cf. Gal. 2.11–14), and this could raise questions as to his reliability on matters relating to

---

[3] James D. G. Dunn offers a list of ideas within Second Temple Judaism that reading Paul help inform: *Beginning from Jerusalem*, Christianity in the Making 2 (Grand Rapids: Eerdmans, 2009) 102–3.

[4] Paul Barnett, *Finding the Historical Christ*, After Jesus 3 (Grand Rapids: Eerdmans, 2009) 184. Barnett ventures that Paul would also have gleaned information about Jesus from Stephen (cf. Acts 7.58); this is not implausible but depends on how much credence one gives to the Lucan account.

[5] Any appeal to 2 Cor. 5.16 misses the point of that verse: Paul's 'flesh–spirit' knowledge is adverbial and eschatological. He now knows Jesus in the (new) era of the Spirit rather than in the (old) era of the flesh.

the Jesus tradition to which they were (at least in a way that he was not) 'eyewitnesses'.[6]

But probably the most significant caveat is the simple fact that, despite all the expectation, Paul can seem surprisingly reticent to speak of Jesus' earthly life much beyond the fact that he died and was resurrected. Paul quotes the Jewish Scriptures far more than he quotes Jesus' teaching, and because much of what Jesus tradition there is in Paul is found in 1 Corinthians, had that text not formed part of the accredited Pauline witness Paul's contribution to historical Jesus questions might be very minimal indeed. Paul offers no explicit reference to the parables or to the mighty deeds of Jesus, a seemingly surprising omission bearing in mind the comparative attention accorded to them by the evangelists, and there is no mention of Jesus' engagement with the Pharisees, an interesting absence in view of Paul's own Pharisaical allegiance (Phil. 3.5). Similarly absent is any reference to notable events such as the Temple cleansing or Jesus' baptism, events that are pivotal in the Synoptic retelling of Jesus' life. What reference to Jesus one does find in Paul often comes by accident, or because of some form of 'mis-use'; the eucharistic words, for example, are cited in 1 Corinthians 11.23–26 because the Corinthians have been abusing the Lord's Supper, not because Paul is necessarily seeking to inform them of that tradition.

Consequently some, most notably the famous NT scholar Rudolf Bultmann perhaps, have argued that Paul himself disavows any interest in the earthly Jesus. Bultmann contended, for example, that 'the teaching of the historical Jesus plays no role, or practically none, in Paul and John, while on the other hand modern, liberal Judaism can very well esteem Jesus as teacher'.[7] It may therefore be that Paul's (apparent) silence on such matters is no 'embarrassment', but rather the apostle's own intent.

---

[6] Paula Fredriksen, *Jesus of Nazareth, King of the Jews: A Jewish Life and the Emergence of Christianity* (New York: Knopf, 1999) 78.

[7] Rudolf Bultmann, *Theology of the New Testament* 2 vols (London: SCM Press, 1952) 1.35.

One thinks of the scene in Martin Scorsese's *Last Temptation of Christ*, in which Paul encounters the (unresurrected) Jesus but remains unperturbed about still proclaiming a gospel of the risen Christ. If the apocalyptic Christ event has changed the way the world functions, if a new age has dawned (cf. 2 Cor. 5.16), then it conceivably follows that it is the future, rather than the past, that now matters for Paul; the earthly Jesus could well be construed as something of an irrelevancy for him.[8] The converse also applies, as Paul's arguments would surely have been bolstered by appeal to Jesus' teaching; the absence of any reference to Mark 7.15 in the discourse of 1 Corinthians 8–10, or when addressing the complexities of table fellowship in his dispute with Peter at Antioch (Gal. 2.11–16), seems startling. Furthermore, the idea, for example, that Paul could be seen as supplementing (maybe overriding or contravening?) Jesus' teaching in 1 Corinthians 7.10–12 and 1 Corinthians 9.14–15, and that he putatively invokes a different eucharistic liturgy from that passed on in 1 Corinthians 11.23–26 (cf. 1 Cor. 10.16), leads some to conclude that Paul is somewhat ambivalent about Jesus tradition, and is unfazed as to whether or not it actually originated from *Jesus*.[9] Consider one scholar's summary of Paul's perspective on such matters:

> His intention is thus not to hand on, word for word, what was spoken by the earthly Jesus but to connect to a tradition grounded in the authority of the Lord as the basis for early Christian teaching. In instances involving words that originated with the earthly

---

[8] Stephen C. Barton, 'Memory and Remembrance in Paul', in *Memory in the Bible and Antiquity: The Fifth Durham-Tübingen Research Symposium (Durham, September 2004)*, ed. Stephen C. Barton, Loren T. Stuckenbruck and Benjamin G. Wold, Wissenschaftliche Untersuchungen zum Neuen Testament 212 (Tübingen: Mohr Siebeck, 2007) 321–39 (328).

[9] Cf. Gerd Lüdemann, 'Paul as a Witness to the Historical Jesus', in *Sources of the Jesus Tradition: Separating History from Myth*, ed. Joseph Hoffmann (New York: Prometheus, 2010) 196–212: 'Paul's theology, together with its theological, anthropological and soteriological ideas, in no way represents a recapitulation of Jesus' preaching nor even a further development of it' (196). He continues: 'Paul cannot be considered a reliable witness to either the teachings, the life, or the historical existence of Jesus' (212).

Jesus, Paul is interested in the fact that they are Jesus' words only insofar as the earthly Jesus is also the one raised and exalted by God.[10]

James Dunn is perhaps representative of the scholarly consensus with his muted comment that '(h)ad we possessed only Paul's letters, it would be impossible to say much about Jesus of Nazareth'.[11] Wherever one stands on this question, Paul's apparent silence with respect to the earthly Jesus can be frustrating, and leaves the reader wanting large gaps of knowledge to be filled.

At the same time, while we find Paul little interested in composing a biography of Jesus, or in specifically citing dominical teaching to justify his position, he actually remains far from uninterested in the *character* or figure of Jesus.[12] The (relative) epistolary silence on biographical matters doubtless derives in part from the nature of the evidence, as the epistles address specific local scenarios rather than retelling or reciting Jesus tradition. It is quite possible that Paul referred more to Jesus' life and teaching as part of his evangelistic and church-planting ministry,[13] and the letters may therefore assume pre-existing knowledge on the part of the readers, with Paul

---

[10] Jens Schröter, 'Jesus and the Canon: The Early Jesus Traditions in the Context of the Origins of the New Testament Canon', in *Performing the Gospel: Orality, Memory, and Mark*, ed. Richard A. Horsley, Jonathan A. Draper and John Miles Foley (Minneapolis: Fortress, 2006) 104–22 (109).

[11] James D. G. Dunn, *The Theology of Paul the Apostle* (Grand Rapids: Eerdmans, 1998) 184. Cf. also Francis Watson, 'Veritas Christi: How to Get from the Jesus of History to the Christ of Faith without Losing One's Way', in *Seeking the Identity of Jesus: A Pilgrimage*, ed. Beverly Roberts Gaventa and Richard B. Hays (Grand Rapids: Eerdmans, 2008) 96–114: 'traces of the Jesus tradition in the Pauline letters are relatively scarce' (110).

[12] Richard B. Hays, 'The Story of God's Son: The Identity of Jesus in the Letters of Paul', in *Seeking the Identity of Jesus: A Pilgrimage*, ed. Beverly Roberts Gaventa and Richard B. Hays (Grand Rapids: Eerdmans, 2008) 180–99, avers that 'on virtually every page of his letters, Paul talks about Jesus' (182).

[13] Cf. Martin Hengel, *The Four Gospels and the One Gospel of Jesus Christ: An Investigation of the Collection and Origin of the Canonical Gospels* (London: SCM Press, 2000) 149: 'the narration of Jesus' activity and death, his crucifixion and resurrection, was fundamental in the foundation of a community, which as a rule took place over a period of time'.

not needing to cover familiar ground afresh.[14] The 'givenness' of Jesus tradition in Paul may parallel such 'givenness' in Acts: just as Luke perhaps intended Acts' readers to take into account what had already been laid out in the Gospel (and therefore only refer to it very occasionally), so Paul assumes that his audience know the narratives and they therefore do not require or warrant further repetition.[15] But it remains the case that 'Paul never speaks of the death of Jesus without speaking of this man in space and time',[16] and while the Christological nature extends far beyond earth and time, there is an inherent continuity across and through Paul's Jesus (Christ) narrative.

At this point, it is probably worth restating the scope of our enquiry. Pauline Christology is a wide and profound topic of study,[17] and Paul's portrait of (the earthly) Jesus is part of a much more extensive depiction of Jesus Christ, one that transcends historical time and space. 'The Jesus who is the focus of Paul's fierce commitment is the divine and pre-existent Son of God, the agent of creation . . . who came to earth, died by crucifixion, was raised and exalted and is about to return.'[18] But our interest has been, and continues to be, in the earthly dimension of this narrative of Jesus, and that will form the focus of the rest of our discussion.

---

[14] Cf. Calvin J. Roetzel, *Paul: The Man and the Myth*, Studies on Personalities of the New Testament (Edinburgh: T&T Clark, 1999) 95: 'we must assume that when Paul preached he told the story of Jesus, and when he wrote occasional letters to the churches, there was no need to tell the story'.

[15] Cf. James D. G. Dunn, 'Jesus Tradition in Paul', in *Studying the Historical Jesus: Evaluations of the State of Current Research*, ed. Bruce Chilton and Craig A. Evans, New Testament Tools and Studies 19 (Leiden: E. J. Brill, 1994) 155–78: 'It would be utterly astonishing then if the congregations to which Paul writes did not possess their own stock of Jesus tradition, much of which he would himself probably have supplied' (159).

[16] Hengel, *Four Gospels* 152.

[17] See, for example, the magisterial study of Gordon D. Fee, *Pauline Christology: An Exegetical-Theological Study* (Peabody: Hendrickson, 2007).

[18] Paula Fredriksen, *From Jesus to Christ: The Origins of the New Testament Images of Christ*, 2nd edn (New Haven: Yale Nota Bene, 2000) 56.

Paul's 'knowledge' of Jesus of Nazareth

The extent of Paul's knowledge/interest (or otherwise) in Jesus tradition is a longstanding question within the scholarship.[19] We can find ourselves swimming in a tide between maximalists and minimalists, between those who see barely any citation of Jesus within Paul and those who believe there to be a significant number of references – a combination of quotation, allusion and echo. Working with the same 'evidence', we encounter conclusions at both ends of the spectrum, varying from statements like '(w)e can detect no hint that Paul knew of the narrative tradition about Jesus'[20] through to there being 'a huge amount of evidence that Paul's gospel included, at its core, stories and sayings of Jesus'.[21]

In the midst of such inconclusiveness, one can easily forget that Paul does yield some very explicit information about the earthly Jesus.[22] Such testimony is delivered indirectly and one has to piece it together jigsaw-style from the various Pauline texts (with a number of the proverbial jigsaw pieces still missing), but it remains 'knowledge' all the same. Paul knows that Jesus is born of woman (Gal. 4.4 – a radical statement for one whom

---

[19] See the review of Victor Paul Furnish, 'The Jesus–Paul Debate: From Baur to Bultmann', in *Paul and Jesus*, ed. A. J. M. Wedderburn, JSNTSup 37 (Sheffield: Sheffield Academic Press, 1989) 17–50, or the more recent summary of David E. Aune, 'Jesus Tradition and the Pauline Letters', in *Jesus in Memory: Traditions in Oral and Scribal Perspectives*, ed. Werner H. Kelber and Samuel Byrskog (Waco: Baylor University Press, 2009) 63–86. Todd D. Still (ed.), *Jesus and Paul Reconnected: Fresh Pathways into an Old Debate* (Grand Rapids: Eerdmans, 2007), offers a set of essays that take a more positive view on the Paul–Jesus relationship. For an accessible and helpful analysis of many of the key issues, see Furnish, *Jesus*.

[20] Nikolaus Walter, 'Paul and the Early Christian Jesus-Tradition', in *Paul and Jesus*, ed. A. J. M. Wedderburn, JSNTSup 37 (Sheffield: Sheffield Academic Press, 1989) 51–80 (69).

[21] David Wenham, *Paul and Jesus: The True Story* (Grand Rapids: Eerdmans, 2002) 181.

[22] Luke Timothy Johnson, *Living Jesus: Learning the Heart of the Gospel* (San Francisco: HarperSanFrancisco, 1999), surveys the relevant data within the Pauline corpus and summarizes it as 'no small fund of information about the life and death of Jesus. Paul's letters, in fact, are the most comprehensive and reliable sources of factual information – apart from the Gospels themselves – about the human Jesus' (106).

Paul regards as worthy of worship), under the Law (Gal. 4.4) and of the Davidic line (Rom. 1.3). Some have ventured that Paul reflects knowledge of the virgin birth tradition here,[23] but any such reference would seem faint at best and difficult to justify. More securely, Paul knows that Jesus' brothers had married (cf. 1 Cor. 9.5), and that one of them was James (Gal. 1.19).[24] These brothers are known as 'brothers of the Lord', and at the risk of stating the obvious, Paul therefore explicitly recognizes the earthly existence of Jesus (as one who had physical siblings), but who could at the same time be known summarily as exalted 'Lord' (Rom. 10.9).

Paul characterizes Jesus' life in Jewish terms as one who rendered messianic service on the part of Israel (cf. Rom. 15.8). He can also speak of Jesus leading a life of humility (2 Cor. 10.1; Phil. 2.5–7), one to which Paul exhorts others to be conformed (Phil. 3.8–10) and modelled (1 Cor. 11.1); he can also say that Jesus was handed over (1 Cor. 11.23) and crucified by Jews in Judea (1 Thess. 2.14–15).[25] The attribution of Jesus' death to the rulers of this age (1 Cor. 2.8) doesn't specify their identity (and maybe the ambiguity is deliberate), but it could well recall Jesus' death under the Roman authorities,[26] particularly as the context of the passage is the shameful death on the cross, a central aspect of Roman practice. While Paul is more interested in the theological outworking of Jesus' cruciform death (Rom. 5.10), it remains historically

---

[23] See David Wenham, 'The Story of Jesus Known to Paul', in *Jesus of Nazareth: Lord and Christ: Essays on the Historical Jesus and New Testament Christology*, ed. Joel B. Green and Max Turner (Grand Rapids: Eerdmans, 1994) 297–311 (298–301).

[24] Gary R. Habermas, *The Historical Jesus: Ancient Evidence for the Life of Christ* (Joplin: College Press, 1996) 146, views Rom. 10.9 as an implied reference to Jesus' baptism, but his suggestion is not persuasive. Paul refers to Apollos' ministry in Corinth, and Acts identifies Apollos as knowing the baptism of John; while this could be implied as Paul knowing of John the Baptist, it cannot be proved from the Pauline material alone.

[25] Though Rom. 8.32 (and perhaps 4.25) appears to ascribe divine agency to Jesus' death – see Beverly Roberts Gaventa, 'Interpreting the Death of Jesus Apocalyptically: Reconsidering Romans 8:32', in *Jesus and Paul Reconnected: Fresh Pathways into an Old Debate*, ed. Todd D. Still (Grand Rapids: Eerdmans, 2007) 125–45.

[26] Dale C. Allison, Jr., *Constructing Jesus: Memory, Imagination, and History* (London: SPCK, 2010) 395–8.

notable still that he records it as death *on a cross* (1 Cor. 2.2).[27] Paul offers therefore wide – and early – attestation for Jesus' death, and likewise the shame that it comprised (cf. Heb. 12.2 which does likewise). He also records that Jesus was buried (1 Cor. 15.4; cf. Rom. 6.4), a datum not to be ignored bearing in mind that crucified corpses would often just be left to rot. Paul also describes Jesus as a paschal lamb (1 Cor. 5.7), and this might suggest that he followed the Johannine chronology of the Passion Week (i.e. that Jesus and the disciples did not celebrate the Passover meal),[28] but the reference is probably too indirect to make such a case.

Moreover, it is not just the event of Jesus' death, but the *manner* or flavour of it that Paul recalls and acknowledges. Indeed, Dale Allison observes that, if one were dependent *only* on Paul for the portrayal of Jesus' Passion, one would know a reasonably significant amount about it, namely that Jesus was crucified (1 Cor. 2.8), nailed to a cross such that blood was yielded (Rom. 3.25), under Roman authorities (1 Cor. 2.6–8), because of his messianic pretensions or 'kingly' claims (Rom. 1.3–4; 15.12). The death involved some Jewish responsibility (1 Thess. 2.14–16), took place in Judea (1 Thess. 2.14–16), involved some act of handing over (1 Cor. 11.23) and ended with Jesus being buried (1 Cor. 15.4).[29] It may even be that the expression 'crucified with Christ' (Rom. 6.6; Gal. 2.19), rendered by a very rare, specific word in the Greek text, actually meant that Paul was aware of the tradition of Jesus being crucified alongside others (cf. Mark 15.27, 32).[30] It is also notable that Paul cannot conceive of the earthly Jesus *without* the cross; cross and Jesus are inextricably intertwined, and this would seem commensurate with the Synoptic portrayal,

[27] See Robert L. Webb, 'The Roman Examination and Crucifixion of Jesus', in *Key Events in the Life of the Historical Jesus: A Collaborative Exploration of Context and Coherence*, ed. Darrell L. Bock and Robert L. Webb (Grand Rapids: Eerdmans, 2010) 669–773 (671–4).

[28] Gerd Theissen, *The New Testament: A Literary History* (Minneapolis: Fortress, 2012) 65.

[29] Allison, *Constructing* 392–403.

[30] Allison, *Constructing* 410.

but less so with the depiction of Jesus in, for example, *Thomas* or Q.[31] Peter Davids's observation teases out the way in which Paul complements the Gospel testimony: 'his letters are particularly concerned with topics such as the reason for the cross, on which the gospel traditions provide little helpful information (the sayings mainly indicating that it was necessary and that Jesus' death was necessary for others, not reflecting on why it was necessary and why it was for others, these being Paul's burden).'[32]

We might also point to other salient 'historical' information beyond Jesus' death. For example, Paul confirms the existence of a group identified as the 'Twelve', even if he doesn't articulate its precise composition. On this point Paula Fredriksen notes, 'Were it not for Paul's witness, we might be tempted to question the group's actual existence' and, as such, Paul's testimony gives us good grounds to think that, despite all the odds, the concept of such a group actually went back to Jesus.[33] Paul names those who followed after Jesus (notably James, Cephas and John – (Gal. 2.9)), and gives particular attention to the role of Cephas – Petros, the rock – and the Twelve (1 Cor. 15.5); the resurrection appearances, while probably a received or established tradition, accord Cephas a primary role within the Twelve, in a way that is consistent with the Synoptic portrayal. Within the canonical testimony at least, 1 Corinthians 15.7 gives a further pointer particularly to James's story of inclusion within the early Jesus community, information that is not readily available from the Gospel material (similarly the appearance to around five hundred people – 1 Cor. 15.6). Indeed, the historical significance of the 1 Corinthians 15.3–9 tradition should not be underestimated, and may reflect a core datum reflecting the Gospel tradition.[34] The appearance to Peter, for example, is notable for expanding on an event only alluded to

---

[31] Hays, 'God's Son' 189.

[32] Peter H. Davids, 'James and Jesus', in *The Jesus Tradition outside the Gospels*, ed. David Wenham, Gospel Perspectives 5 (Sheffield: JSOT Press, 1985) 63–84 (64).

[33] Fredriksen, *Jesus of Nazareth* 96.

[34] Cf. Birger Gerhardsson, *The Origins of the Gospel Traditions* (Philadelphia: Fortress, 1979) 41.

within the Synoptic tradition (Luke 24.34). It is possible even, though difficult to prove, that Paul's self-understanding as an apostle to the Gentiles derives in some fashion from Jesus tradition. Paul Barnett pursues this option, suggesting that Jesus himself established a two-stage approach to the gospel proclamation – to Jews first (Matt. 10.5–6; 15.24) and then outwards to the Gentiles/ nations (Matt. 8.1–12; 28.19). Paul, Barnett argues, embraces Jesus' dualistic approach, and the Pauline ministry functioned as 'a genuine extension of the mission of the historical Jesus'.[35]

In sum, even those at the minimalist end of the Jesus–Paul debate would have to concur: 'at the foundation of what he [i.e. Paul] preached was a body of knowledge about the ministry and character of the Lord he served'.[36] Likewise, as a minimum, Paul's testimony derails any contention that Jesus is merely a historical construct, that Jesus of Nazareth is a fiction composed to endorse a kerygmatic Christ myth proclaiming salvation for sin. Paul sees a fundamental continuity between the crucified/historical Jesus and the resurrected Christ (cf. Rom. 4.24–25; 8.34); he (Paul) still calls him *Jesus*, as well as the Christ, an obvious but often-overlooked datum that would suggest that Paul values the historical existence of this Jesus. After all, even a relative minimalist like Gerd Lüdemann concurs: 'the man Jesus and the preexistent and risen Lord are one and the same'.[37] The fact that the Jerusalem visit (Gal. 1.18) is mentioned within such a robust defence of his apostleship also points to Paul's being able to distinguish between the *gospel* to which he is called, and the Jesus tradition with which he seeks to inform himself.

---

[35] Paul Barnett, *Paul: Missionary of Jesus*, After Jesus 2 (Grand Rapids: Eerdmans, 2008) 111.

[36] Paul Rhodes Eddy and Gregory A. Boyd, *The Jesus Legend: A Case for the Historical Reliability of the Synoptic Tradition* (Grand Rapids: Baker Academic, 2007).

[37] Lüdemann, 'Paul' 199. Likewise, but reflecting a different theological constituency, cf. Barnett, *Finding* 178: 'Accordingly, the "Jesus of history"/"Christ of faith" dichotomy is historically unhelpful and should be abandoned.' See also Stanley E. Porter, 'Images of Christ in Paul's Letters', in *Images of Christ: Ancient and Modern*, ed. Stanley E. Porter, David Tombs and M. A. Hayes, Roehampton Institute London Papers 2 (Sheffield: Sheffield Academic Press, 1997) 95–112.

Two further points thus follow. First, ironically perhaps, the very *limited* testimony to Jesus' life makes the testimony offered all the more reliable. Why would Paul mention the detail he does if there were no reality to such a life, however minimally depicted? One cannot accuse Paul of 'protesting too much'! That is, Paul says enough to underscore Jesus' human experience – and thereby remove any 'docetist' allegation[38] – but does not say enough for it to be part of a bigger myth-making Pauline enterprise. Second, if, as seems probable, Paul never met or encountered the earthly Jesus, and if Damascus Road was the seminal (qualifying) event for him, then the fact that he *does* appeal to the earthly Jesus' teaching, and the tradition associated with him, becomes all the more significant. What Paul does offer – if perhaps not with the abundance we might desire – is awareness of data about Jesus from the 50 CE decade, well before the written Gospel texts come to birth (in their written form at least). Historically speaking, Paul's letters are important sources for the earthly Jesus, if only because of their date, and while their testimony may not be as expansive as some may wish, they remain valid testimony nonetheless.[39]

We might make final mention of 2 Corinthians 11.3–4. Paul here speculates on the possibility of another 'Jesus' being proclaimed or taught to the Corinthians, and the consequences of so doing. Within this 'fool's speech' (as 2 Cor. 11.1—12.10 is often termed), the necessity of preserving the 'same' Jesus is upheld. Why would Paul have made this plea if the character or identity of Jesus (and perhaps even his teaching and ministry) were not important to him? It is notable that Paul specifies the message as 'Jesus', rather than 'Christ' (11.4), therefore suggesting that

---

[38] See Watson, 'Veritas Christi' 108–9; also Edward Adams, 'Paul, Jesus and Christ', in *The Blackwell Companion to Jesus*, ed. Delbert Royce Burkett, Blackwell Companions to Religion (Malden, MA: Wiley-Blackwell, 2011) 94–110 (95).

[39] See C. M. Tuckett, *Christology and the New Testament: Jesus and His Earliest Followers* (Louisville: Westminster John Knox, 2001) 127–35 (125): 'These letters do give us some information about Jesus, even if it emerges in an apparently less direct form than in the gospel. Nevertheless, the very early date of the evidence suggests that it should not be ignored.'

the message in hand is inextricably focused on the person of Jesus. Paul does, after all, claim to have seen Jesus, not Jesus *Christ* (1 Cor. 9.1).

Paul's 'use' of Jesus' teaching

As well as the incidental references to Jesus' life, Paul also cites Jesus *logia*, or at least claims to do so, at several points within his letters (and most notably within the Corinthian correspondence). The comparatively high volume of material in 1 Corinthians may reflect pre-Pauline knowledge of Jesus tradition in Corinth, or it may relate to the presence of Peter as a recent visitor to the city and to the church(es) there (note that Paul is critical of the party spirit around Peter, but not of Peter himself). Whatever the reason for them, and while Paul does not explicitly refer to Jesus as a 'teacher', the citations do suggest Paul *characterizes* him as such, as one who bestowed teaching or bequeathed wisdom that was worth preserving or remembering. For example, appealing to the command of the 'Lord' (note, 'Jesus' is actually not named by Paul – cf. 1 Cor. 14.37), Paul recites his teaching on the matter of divorce (1 Cor. 7.10; cf. Matt. 5.32; 19.1–9; Mark 10.9–11; Luke 16.18). Similarly, 1 Corinthians 9.14, and its declaration that those who live by the gospel may earn their keep from so doing, appears to cite Jesus' maxim that workers deserve to be paid for their labours (cf. Matt. 10.10/Luke 10.7 – though it may be a conflation of other texts as well). Neither citation is verbatim to the Gospel accounts, and this cautions against thinking that Jesus tradition was absolutely fixed in terms of content.[40] In modern parlance, Paul could be said to be

---

[40] Gerhardsson, *Origins* 34–5, nuances this well, contending that there is a clear distinction between Paul's words and those of Jesus; and, where there is appeal to Jesus, it is to his 'intent', rather than to verbatim preservation, what Gerhardsson terms 'halakah' teaching. Holtz, in trying to differentiate two specific sources (Q and non-fixed), maybe pushes the distinction too far – Traugott Holtz, 'Paul and the Oral Gospel Tradition', in *Jesus and the Oral Gospel Tradition*, ed. Henry Wansbrough, JSNTSup 64 (Sheffield: Sheffield Academic Press, 1991) 380–93.

paraphrasing Jesus, rather than quoting him, conveying the essence of the teaching for the Corinthian context. There seems no compelling reason, therefore, not to view them as reliable appeals to Jesus' teaching,[41] particularly as, in the first example, Paul subsequently adds his own gloss when addressing the concerns of those married to unbelievers (1 Cor. 7.12), thereby differentiating his own teaching from that of the dominical logion. The declaration of 7.12 is not, as some have ventured, Paul disagreeing with Jesus, but is no more than Paul merely acknowledging his lack of knowledge as to Jesus' teaching on the matter in hand. Indeed, it is quite possible that Paul, while differentiating his command from dominical tradition (7.12), is still seeking to act in the 'spirit' of Jesus' teaching, providing some kind of extension of it into the Corinthian situation; he just does not have the literal tradition/ teaching to which to point, and is careful not to appeal to what could not be 'evidenced'.

One might make several further observations on 1 Corinthians 7.10. First, Paul's use of the divorce quotation parallels that of Jesus; that is, divorce is to be strongly avoided (cf. Mark 10.9), but in the event that it happens, those involved should not remarry (1 Cor. 7.11; cf. Mark 10.11–12). Paul and Jesus seem on common ground here. The suggestion that Paul is quoting Jesus ('don't divorce') only then to immediately refute his teaching ('but if/ when it happens, she should not remarry') misreads Paul's argument; the latter statement is best understood as a parenthesis between the other two, mutual declarations of 7.10–11,[42] a Pauline

---

[41] Lüdemann, 'Paul' 201, avers that the historical Jesus could not have said the logion ascribed to him in 1 Cor. 7.10, partly because of the way Paul focuses on the wife's role (something Matt. 5.32 and Luke 16.18 do not do), partly because a Palestinian woman would just not have been able to divorce her husband. Lüdemann also ventures that Jesus could not have spoken 1 Cor. 9.14 as mission practice was not sufficiently framed in Jesus' time. However, while the words may not have been Jesus' *ipsissima verba* (and how could it be proved either way?), it remains notable that (1) they have been attributed to Jesus and (2) they remain broadly consistent with the Jesus teaching found elsewhere. For a helpful, accessible discussion of the passage, see Bart D. Ehrman, *Did Jesus Exist? The Historical Argument for Jesus of Nazareth* (New York: HarperOne, 2012) 125–7.

[42] Anthony C. Thiselton, *The First Epistle to the Corinthians: A Commentary on the Greek Text*, NIGTC (Grand Rapids: Eerdmans, 2000) 519.

supplement to Jesus' teaching. It is true that Paul reorders the Synoptic record, prioritizing the woman separating from her husband (both Matt. 5.32 and Luke 16.18 restrict the discussion just to the husband's actions), but such adjustment may reflect Paul applying Jesus' teaching to the particular situation in Corinth. The distinction seems relatively minimal though: the 'spirit' of the citation is surely upheld and remains consistent with Jesus' teaching. Second, and not in opposition to this, Paul's subsequent elucidation may conceivably be more 'original' than the Synoptic material, seemingly more accommodating than the Markan parallel (Mark 10.9–12): Paul is more permissive of the possibility of separation/divorce if the unbelieving partner has initiated it (1 Cor. 7.15), a concession that one might think the earthly Jesus would have endorsed. Third, Paul does not believe he can just construct Jesus teaching out of nothing (1 Cor. 7.25) – there is some self-confessed restriction operative on him and his teaching.

Paul's citation of Jesus in 1 Corinthians 9.14 also requires further comment. He invokes the mission support logion, but then proceeds to exclude himself from its purview by refusing to accept financial support from the Corinthians (9.15). In that sense, therefore, he *does* contradict Jesus' teaching, or at least distance himself from it in fairly clear terms. Paul's response may reflect the particular relationship he has with the Corinthians, and his desire not to be dependent upon them and be tied to their expectations of what his apostleship should comprise (cf. 1 Cor. 4.14–16). Or it may illustrate a more general Pauline perspective, namely that part of the call to imitate Jesus Christ can entail setting aside Jesus' teaching; that is, Paul can override Scripture and/or Christ if necessary to be a genuine follower of Christ.[43] If the latter were the case, then it would suggest that Paul views the *actions* or story of Jesus Christ as more significant than the *words* of Jesus Christ.

---

[43] David G. Horrell, '"The Lord Commanded . . . But I Have Not Used . . .": Exegetical and Hermeneutical Reflections on 1 Cor 9:14–15', *NTS* 43 (1997) 587–603. He suggests there is a significant compulsion on Paul's part to override Jesus' teaching.

This would accord with the limited reference to Jesus' teaching elsewhere in the Pauline corpus. However, Paul's willingness to take money from other churches (even latterly from Corinth – Rom. 15.26) – and, by implication, to be supported by them, be that personally (Phoebe – Rom. 16.1–2) or corporately (Phil. 4.15–17), suggests that the reluctance of 1 Corinthians 9.15 should be viewed against the specific Corinthian context rather than displaying any more general relativizing of the dominical command. Besides, the very fact that Paul differentiates himself from Jesus' teaching actually gives further grounds for thinking 9.14 to be reliable dominical tradition. Paul actually gains nothing by creating the logion, quite the reverse. It is notable therefore that in the two places where Paul appeals to Jesus tradition he actually proceeds next to qualify or differentiate himself from it. Far from Jesus tradition being a trump card or final authority to which Paul appeals, the dominical sayings (in 1 Corinthians at least) serve only as bridges for the exercise of the practicalities of apostolic exhortation.

The third appeal in 1 Corinthians to dominical testimony is 11.23–26, in which Paul recalls the so-called eucharistic words of inauguration. He claims to have received these words from the Lord (11.23), and some have understood the source to be direct divine revelation to Paul,[44] perhaps on the Damascus Road. However, the language of 'handing on' suggests otherwise; the terminology differs from the more apocalyptic, revelatory language he uses of his encounter with the risen Christ on the Damascus Road (Gal. 1.12). Instead, it invokes the idea of a tradition Paul has inherited (probably from the Jerusalem apostles, though perhaps from the Antioch church) and that he is faithfully seeking to preserve and bequeath to the Corinthian congregations. It quite possibly formed part of a Passion narrative with which Paul was familiar, and would represent one part of a broader Jesus tradition he upholds within the Corinthian context. The same may be said

---

[44] Francis Watson, '"I Received from the Lord . . .": Paul, Jesus and the Last Supper', in *Jesus and Paul Reconnected: Fresh Pathways into an Old Debate*, ed. Todd D. Still (Grand Rapids: Eerdmans, 2007) 103–24.

of 1 Corinthians 15.3–8, the content of which Paul likewise speaks of having received and passed on to the Corinthians (15.1, 3); both represent core early Church tradition, focused around the person of Jesus Christ, and for whose preservation Paul exercises apostolic responsibility.

Paul's wording is closer to the Lucan eucharistic tradition (Luke 22.19–20), particularly in the separation of the cup and bread: in both Paul and Luke, the cup is taken 'after supper' (separately from the meal), whereas Matthew and Mark combine them into one act (Matt. 26.26–28; Mark 14.22–25). Paul also parallels Luke's designation of the cup as the 'new covenant' in Jesus' blood, thereby using different terms from that applied to the bread; Matthew and Mark retain the same terminology for both – 'this is my body/ blood'. Because the latter version seems more geared to liturgical interests, the case might be made that the Paul/Luke tradition actually reflects the more 'genuine' or 'historical' example, but ultimately we can only speculate as to Jesus' precise 'inaugurating' words. The 'historical' detail of Jesus' eucharistic wording is a complex subject, and full attention to the various possible reconstructions is beyond our scope here.[45] However, it should be mentioned that Paul does add his own interpretative gloss to the tradition (11.26), which is distinguished from the citation of Jesus' teaching. He also probably adds an additional 'in remembrance of me' to the words spoken over the cup (1 Cor. 11.25), phrasing that is absent from the Lucan version and that may reflect Paul's own interests in citing the tradition – that is, to remind the Corinthians that it is a meal in the memory of the Lord that they are not keeping appropriately.[46] If so, this once more suggests that Paul can exercise a certain amount of fluidity when using Jesus tradition; he can faithfully pass on tradition without being beholden to absolute fixity in terms of Jesus' words. But that does not mean,

---

[45] For an in-depth discussion of the matter, see I. Howard Marshall, 'The Last Supper', in *Key Events in the Life of the Historical Jesus: A Collaborative Exploration of Context and Coherence*, ed. Darrell L. Bock and Robert L. Webb (Grand Rapids: Eerdmans, 2010) 481–588.

[46] Gordon D. Fee, *The First Epistle to the Corinthians*, NICNT (Grand Rapids: Eerdmans, 1987) 555–6.

as some have suggested, that Paul is also able to offer a different take on the Lord's Supper (cf. 1 Cor. 10.16).[47] While it is true that, in 10.16, Paul speaks of the cup before the bread, the reordering may be for purely rhetorical reasons (probably the emphatic statement of 10.17 that they are all one bread), and there is nothing in 10.16 that requires it to be the specific wording for a eucharistic meal (cf. the more familiar food–drink ordering in 1 Cor. 10.3–4).

In sum, what the tradition of 1 Corinthians 11.23–26 does do, with the embedding of some form of words derived from early on in the tradition, is to make the 'event' of the Upper Room historically likely, with Jesus remembered for performing some act of eucharistic remembrance.[48] On the particular aspect of being 'betrayed' (11.23), it is tempting to think that Paul knows of the Judas narrative, and the casting of the latter as the one responsible for Jesus' betrayal. However, the translation of the Greek word here (*paradidomai*) is notoriously loaded, and commonly means just 'handed over', without any further negative overtones. Therefore, 11.23 may merely imply that Jesus was 'handed over' – to those who would take him unto his death – without any necessary association with a 'betrayer' figure, and it need not infer that Paul knew of the Judas tradition (though, equally, it is not incompatible with that). However, what it does do is explicitly link the eucharistic narrative with the Passion – they both happen 'on the night'; that is, the same one.[49]

The other possible Pauline appeal to Jesus' teaching is the declaration of 1 Thessalonians 4.15–17 regarding the timing of the coming of the Lord. Paul justifies his claim as originating by the

---

[47] So Werner H. Kelber, 'Conclusion: The Work of Birger Gerhardsson in Perspective', in *Jesus in Memory: Traditions in Oral and Scribal Perspectives*, ed. Werner H. Kelber and Samuel Byrskog (Waco: Baylor University Press, 2009) 173–206 (188).

[48] Though the Jesus Seminar remain sceptical about the Upper Room event/discourse: 'the accounts of the last meal Jesus ate with his disciples in Jerusalem is so overlaid with Christianizing elements that it is difficult – if not impossible – to recover the actual event' (Robert W. Funk and Roy W. Hoover, *The Five Gospels: The Search for the Authentic Words of Jesus* (New York: Macmillan, 1993) 388).

[49] Allison, *Constructing* 402.

'word of the Lord', but the phrase is ambiguous and could be understood in several contrasting ways, connected or otherwise to Jesus. E. P. Sanders, for example, argues that the Thessalonian allusion 'passes with flying colours' in terms of authenticity; he attributes it to Jesus and to Paul's claim as such.[50] If it were classed as Jesus tradition, then we would have here an additional saying of Jesus, one akin to the subject matter of Matthew 24.30–31/ Mark 13.26–27, but still a discrete form in its own right. Others, though, are more muted in their assessment, pointing out that the 'word of the Lord' need not imply a dominical saying, and may rather be Paul appealing to some form of prophetic oracle or utterance he had received, one entirely unconnected to Jesus.[51] The absence of an explicit Synoptic parallel also weighs against its being understood as Paul appealing to Jesus. The ambiguity of the phrase certainly cautions against jumping to the conclusion that it is a Jesus citation; in terms of introductory phrasing at least, it is different from the explicit dominical appeals of 1 Corinthians 7.10–12 and 9.14. However, just a few verses later (1 Thess. 5.2), Paul seemingly alludes to Jesus tradition and to the Day of the Lord coming like a thief in the night (Matt. 24.42–44). The next verse (1 Thess. 5.3) also shares some parallels with Jesus tradition found in Luke 21.34–36,[52] and the combination of 1 Thessalonians 5.2–3 might make the case for 4.15 likewise being an allusion to Jesus' teaching more plausible.

At some point, debates about parallelism and allusions break down, however, and the jury is probably still out as to whether Paul is ascribing 1 Thessalonians 4.15–17 to Jesus or not. But whether or not 4.15–17 was genuine Jesus tradition, and whatever Paul understood by the 'word of the Lord', it remains the case that Paul has associated some form of eschatological agency to the returning Lord Jesus, and that he will come unexpectedly

---

[50] E. P. Sanders, *The Historical Figure of Jesus* (London: Penguin, 1993) 182; see also Seyoon Kim, 'The Jesus Tradition in 1 Thess 4.13—5.11', *NTS* 48 (2002) 225–42.

[51] Hays, 'God's Son' 181n4.

[52] Holtz, 'Paul', avers: 'There can be no reasonable doubt that the two texts are related to each other' (388). He suggests that the tradition goes back directly to Jesus.

(5.2). This seems broadly in accord with the portrayal of Jesus in the Gospels (cf. Matt. 24.36), especially the Q material, or at least would be casting Jesus in particularly eschatological terms. It may be that Paul is reacting to eschatological misunderstanding among the Thessalonians, and offering a corrective to their anxiety at the picture of Jesus they have had portrayed to them.[53] It may well be, therefore, that Paul previously preached to them a Jesus who was more the apocalyptic prophet than the social reformer/teacher, a shift perhaps from the Jesus-as-teacher slant he postulates within the Corinthian paraenesis (though cf. 1 Cor. 16.22, for example). One does not want to overdo the distinction, and 1 Thessalonians, as probably the first Pauline epistle, is well known for its high eschatological expectation, but the portrait of Jesus rendered within the epistle does take this more eschatological slant or bent.[54]

What can we learn from this discussion? On the one hand, Paul seems able to adapt Jesus teaching/tradition in the light of particular circumstances, needs or context. This suggests some flexibility within the tradition, and we will see further evidence of this in James's adoption of Synoptic material. On the other hand, it remains notable both that appeal is made to Jesus to endorse particular aspects of Pauline teaching and that a core of Jesus-related tradition (1 Cor. 11.23–26; 15.3–9) existed that Paul sought to uphold and protect. Hence, one finds good reason to concur with Bird's pithy summary: 'On the whole, Paul's employment of the Jesus tradition is best described as a "re-presentation" rather than as a quotation.'[55] This is particularly the case if one defines 're-presentation' as framing the evidence or picture in a new light, one that takes account of the new circumstance and application within a fresh context.

---

[53] Kim, 'Jesus Tradition', 225–42.

[54] See N. T. Wright's *Schweitzerstrasse /Wredebahn* distinction (N. T. Wright, *Jesus and the Victory of God*, Christian Origins and the Question of God 2 (London: SPCK, 1996) 3–82). I shall comment further on this is in the discussion on James's Jesus.

[55] Michael F. Bird, 'The Purpose and Preservation of the Jesus Tradition: Moderate Evidence for a Conserving Force in its Transmission', *BBR* 15 (2005) 161–85 (165).

Indirect references

Beyond the direct citation of Jesus material, which does still remain somewhat limited, there are a number of other places in which Paul may be drawing on and reflecting Jesus tradition. These allusions to, or echoes of, Jesus' teaching are more subjective, and scholars regularly differ as to whether they find the particular allusion persuasive or not. After all, Paul does not accord the teaching to Jesus, but merely integrates it into his own discourse.[56] There is the possibility, even, that Paul reflects Jesus tradition not found in the canonical Gospels. We note the similarity, for instance, between 1 Corinthians 2.9 and logion 17 in the *Gospel of Thomas*: 1 Corinthians 2.9 appears to cite a scriptural text ('it is written'), but we find no direct parallel to it within the Old Testament (the closest is Isa. 64.4) and it may be that Paul is citing Jesus/*Thomas* tradition instead, but without formally citing the source.

What allusions can one identify?[57] They may be high-level, thematic ones that shape Pauline teaching. For example, within the broad, ethically orientated discourse of Romans 12—15, two particular topics emerge within Paul's discussion. A discourse focused around the significance of love and the great love commandment itself (Rom. 13.8–10) dominates chapters 12—13, while the exhortation not to judge one another encapsulates the weaker sister/brother discourse of Romans 14.1—15.13. The similarity between 13.8–10 and Mark 12.28–34 (especially vv. 29–31) is acute, and although Jesus is not named, Romans 13.8–10 'can scarcely be understood except against the background of the Jesus tradition'.[58] Similar appeal to the central love command is also found in Galatians 5.14, and perhaps even Galatians 6.2. Likewise, Romans 14.1—15.13 parallels the strong evangelical affirmation to humility

---

[56] We will see more of this in our discussion of the epistle of James.

[57] See Dale C. Allison, Jr., 'The Pauline Epistles and the Synoptic Gospels: The Pattern of the Parallels', *NTS* 28 (1982) 1–32; Seyoon Kim, *Paul and the New Perspective: Second Thoughts on the Origin of Paul's Gospel* (Grand Rapids: Eerdmans, 2002) 259–92; Wenham, *Paul and Jesus*, all of which are fairly positive about the extent of such allusions. For a more hesitant discussion, see Walter, 'Paul'.

[58] Holtz, 'Paul' 390.

and graciousness, and to avoid judging others (Matt. 7.1–5; Luke 6.36–38); that is, it is not only the verbal similarity that we encounter but also the particular focus that is common to both discourses and that makes the case for Paul building on the Jesus tradition more persuasive. In combining the dual exhortation to love (Luke 6.27–35) and to refrain from judgement (Luke 6.36–38), Paul has coupled together two key, successive injunctions from the Sermon on the Plain.[59]

We might add further specific correspondences here, such as Romans 12.14 (cf. Luke 6.27–28; Matt. 5.43–44; so also 1 Cor. 4.12–13), Romans 12.17/12.21 (Luke 6.29–30) and Romans 14.10 (Matt. 7.1–2), all of which seem to parallel Jesus tradition found within the Sermon on the Plain/Mount. The abundance and concentration of such material is highly significant. It would suggest that Paul is familiar with blocks of Jesus' teaching, substantial parts of the Sermon on the Plain/Mount, rather than just isolated sayings.[60] It might also suggest that Paul is somehow characterizing himself in Jesus' role, carrying on Jesus' mantle as an ethical teacher and figure, a significant point bearing in mind the centrality of Romans 12—15 within Pauline theology.

The echoes might equally be more specific, or more tied to particular turns of phrase. Paul's exhortation to the Roman Christians to pay taxes/revenue to whom they are due (Rom. 13.7) potentially recalls Jesus' famous maxim to render to the Emperor what belongs to the Emperor (Mark 12.17). More specifically, Paul's conjecture that he is persuaded *in the Lord Jesus* that nothing is of itself unclean (Rom. 14.14) has resonance with the discourse of Mark 7.1–23, and especially the editorial gloss of Mark 7.19 (so also Mark 7.15, 18). Paul can also speak of believers praying 'Abba! Father!' when they are adopted as children (or literally 'sons') of God (Rom. 8.15), and this may reflect reminiscence of Jesus' own use of such a prayer (Mark 14.36), particularly as he is from the outset of Mark described as the Son of God (Mark 1.1).[61]

---

[59] Theissen, *New Testament* 65.
[60] Allison, *Constructing* 346–8.
[61] The text of Mark 1.1 is, though, contested at this point.

Why not more?

Sometimes, Paul doesn't act quite how we might expect him to do. The Paul, for example, who appears as a quasi-liberator of women in Romans 16 is the same Paul, it seems, who issues some quite problematic commands to female believers in Corinth (1 Cor. 11.2–11). Similarly, Paul's epistles to Romans and Galatians are replete with Old Testament citation, but Philippians is almost bereft of it. Such is the case with Paul's use of Jesus tradition – we expect more from him in terms of appeal to Jesus than he actually delivers, and the (relatively) limited reference warrants some explanation.

It is, of course, possible that Paul actually knew barely anything of Jesus' life, and thus his (apparent) silence merely confirms such ignorance. But it seems improbable, bearing in mind Paul's concerns with the interpretation of Jewish practice in the Diaspora, that he would know of other, more secondary Jesus teaching (such as that on divorce or mission) but not that which would have been absolutely germane for his particular ministry interests (for example, Mark 7.15, 18). Likewise, it would be highly implausible that someone so passionate about the gospel message focused around the figure of Jesus, someone so qualified in terms of scriptural interpretation, would not have exercised some curiosity regarding the life and context of that figure. Paul recounts a visit to Jerusalem post-Damascus Road (Gal. 1.18–19), but the content of the discussions with Peter and (latterly) James are sadly not expounded, and it therefore remains unclear as to the exact purpose of the visit. Some have speculated, for example, that the visit was merely to gain Peter's support for Paul's own mission,[62] but if this were the case we might expect Paul to have mentioned it, particularly bearing in mind their subsequent altercation in Antioch (Gal. 2.11–14). It is more likely that Paul used this Jerusalem visit to inform his own understanding of the

---

[62] Harm W. Hollander, 'The Words of Jesus: From Oral Traditions to Written Record in Paul and Q', *NovT* 42 (2000) 340–57 (342).

Jesus tradition[63] – the visit lasted a full fifteen days, and one is reminded of Dodd's famous observation that Paul and the other apostles would not just have talked about the weather! The question still remains, though, as to why, assuming that he was sufficiently aware of Jesus tradition, Paul does not appeal to it more often. If, as seems possible, there is a reasonably strong tradition of allusion to Jesus' teaching, why does Paul not explicitly identify it as such?

A number of answers have been proffered, but none are especially persuasive. It may simply be that the Church as a whole simply did not link the tradition to Jesus; Paul would therefore not connect the material to Jesus because there would be no connection to make, and is merely drawing from a stock of early Christian paraenesis.[64] It may be that Paul referred more to Jesus' life in the other non-surviving letters, such as the 'real' 1 Corinthians (cf. 1 Cor. 5.9) or the so-called 'painful letter' referred to in 2 Corinthians 2.3–4, but that is both impossible to prove and contrary to the other surviving evidence. One has to admit that if there were substantial Jesus tradition in the 'lost' letters, then it would be in stark contrast not only to the received Pauline corpus but also (as we shall see) to the general non-Gospel NT portrayal. It may, of course, be Paul's embarrassment about not knowing the earthly Jesus and not having been part of his ministry. This seems especially the case in Galatians, where issues of comparative status and primacy come to the fore,[65] but would this have been so much of an issue in Philippi or Thessalonica? Paul's relative silence on Jesus therefore remains a pertinent question for Jesus studies.

How, then, can we explain the silence in one way, but equally note Hays's observation that 'on virtually every page of his letters, Paul talks about Jesus'?[66] It may be, of course, that much of Paul's

---

[63] Richard J. Bauckham, *Jesus and the Eyewitnesses: The Gospels as Eyewitness Testimony* (Grand Rapids: Eerdmans, 2006) 266: 'We should . . . presume that Paul was becoming thoroughly informed of the Jesus tradition as formulated by the Twelve, learning from the leader of the Twelve, Peter.'

[64] Walter, 'Paul' 74–8.

[65] But even here, the reference to the kingdom of God (e.g. Gal. 5.21) suggests that Paul may be aware of that Jesus tradition.

[66] Hays, 'God's Son' 182.

knowledge of the Jesus tradition is conveyed during his missional preaching, in the first encounter(s) he had with those to whom he would latterly send the epistles. While, in one sense, this would appear to be an argument from silence, there is some textual evidence to that effect, and a case might be made that the epistles assume prior knowledge of Jesus in order for the epistolary appeal to have effect. The missionary proclamation to the Galatians, at the very least, had reference to the Passion narrative (Gal. 3.1),[67] and it is hard to think how such an appeal would have made any sense had it not contained some biographical reference points beyond Jesus' death. Likewise, Paul claims to be handing on trad-itions of some form (1 Cor. 11.2),[68] and we assume that these were in some fashion Jesus-orientated. In his survey of early Christianity, Martin Hengel arrives at such a conclusion:

> We must assume that in his mission preaching – which fades right into the background in his letters – Paul of course told stories about Jesus . . . they too will have wanted more information about the man Jesus. In other words, it was only possible to describe the exalted Jesus by telling of the earthly Jesus, his work and his death.[69]

It could be that the Jesus tradition was deemed to be in the hands of Paul's Judaizing enemies,[70] but the (albeit limited) evidence still suggests that there was a broad unanimity over what is preached. Both Jerusalem and Paul hand on shared tradition (1 Cor. 15.11), each drawing on generic, common material (1 Cor. 15.1–8).

Of course, this all assumes what Paul *should* have done but does not, and is imposing our own (modern) expectations onto

---

[67] That the death of Jesus was portrayed before the Galatians' eyes (Gal. 3.1) is also suggestive of an extended narrative rather than just a sole reference to the event of the crucifixion.

[68] Furnish, *Jesus* 27–8.

[69] Martin Hengel, *Acts and the History of Earliest Christianity* (London: SCM Press, 1979) 43–4; cf. also Hays, 'God's Son' 180: 'Paul's own preaching must have included his own very specific account of the identity of Jesus, his own particular way of telling the Jesus story.'

[70] So Alexander J. M. Wedderburn, 'Paul and Jesus: The Problem of Continuity', in *Paul and Jesus*, ed. A. J. M. Wedderburn, JSNTSup 37 (Sheffield: Sheffield Academic Press, 1989) 99–115 (100).

Paul. Justifying the absence of Jesus-accreditation may then be the wrong way of going about things. Rather than seeking to resolve the embarrassment about *not* mentioning Jesus more often, perhaps the 'historical' datum to be acknowledged is that Paul utilizes Jesus teaching without reference, without making any direct attribution. For both Paul and for several of the other NT writers, the appeal to Jesus tradition goes against our expectation. Dunn surmises accordingly: Jesus' teaching and tradition is 'absorbed into the ethical teaching of Paul and James, so that it has become an integral part of their own paraenesis without any sense that particular exhortations would only be authoritative if explicitly addressed to Jesus'.[71] This, then, informs our picture of how Paul has remembered Jesus – Jesus is not a quasi-trump card for Paul to wheel out as necessary, but is one whose character, as we shall see, goes to the very heart of Paul's identity and practice. Indeed, this characterization of the Pauline Jesus goes some way to explaining the qualification Paul places upon the two logia discourses of 1 Corinthians 7.10–12 and 9.14; it is as if Paul is only attributing teaching to Jesus when he really has to. The appeal is exceptional.

Paul's story of Jesus

We are faced, then, with two points of apparent tension. On the one hand, Jesus seems to be a highly significant figure for Paul, or at least significant enough for him to assume portions of Jesus' teaching and tradition within his own epistolary discourse. On the other, there remains, as we have seen, something of a reticence on Paul's part either to associate Jesus with such teaching or to appeal explicitly to Jesus' life and ministry as a model for Pauline paraenesis. Is there, then, a way of resolving such an apparent tension?

Perhaps our starting point should be to hear Paul on his own terms, or rather to let him shape the agenda as to how we go about assessing his characteristic portrayal of Jesus. After all, our interest

---

[71] James D. G. Dunn, *Jesus, Paul, and the Gospels* (Grand Rapids: Eerdmans, 2011) 40.

is in how the particular NT writers address the *identity* of Jesus, and the characteristic means they choose to do so. For Paul, it seems that 'story' is intrinsic to his particular portrayal. His articulation of Jesus' identity is made through narrative exploration rather than biographical rehearsal, through the embrace of a broader story of Jesus rather than (slavish?) appeal to historical remembrance.[72] That is, Paul becomes an interpreter of the Jesus story, not just a storyteller per se; he is someone living out the Jesus story, rather than seeking to retell it just for its own sake. The Jesus story for Paul is not about making biographical appeal or citing dominical logia to reinforce his position and authority, but rather concerns a narrative or story of Jesus that informs not only his preaching and letters but also his behaviour and self-understanding.

Now, of course, Paul's 'story' of the earthly Jesus is part of a greater 'story' of Jesus Christ that may be said to transcend time and space.[73] This metanarrative certainly includes Jesus' pre-incarnational existence (Phil. 2.6), his heavenly Ascension as risen Lord (Phil. 2.9–11) and his future return to judge and rule (1 Cor. 16.22). It also finds its roots in, and involves the interpretation of, the Jewish Scriptures.[74] But one might also suggest that Paul still retains a story of *Jesus of Nazareth*, and that Paul's characterization of Jesus is more nuanced or creative than merely the limited reference to teaching or events might imply. We thus find Jesus included in creedal tradition (1 Cor. 8.6; Rom. 1.3–4), and perhaps in liturgical material as well (1 Cor. 11.23–25, or perhaps Gal.

---

[72] Hays, 'God's Son'. Cf. also Douglas A. Campbell, 'The Story of Jesus in Romans and Galatians', in *Narrative Dynamics in Paul: A Critical Assessment*, ed. Bruce W. Longenecker (Louisville: Westminster John Knox, 2002) 97–124; Johnson, *Living Jesus* 110–15.

[73] Cf. Alexander J. M. Wedderburn, 'Paul and the Story of Jesus', in *Paul and Jesus*, ed. A. J. M. Wedderburn, JSNTSup 37 (Sheffield: Sheffield Academic Press, 1989) 161–89: 'Paul clearly knows of a "story" of Jesus which is not simply the story of the earthly Jesus, and one which indeed passes very rapidly over the ingredients of such a story as we know it from the gospel tradition' (162). The narrative parallels with the Gospels may, though, be stronger than Wedderburn implies.

[74] See Hays, 'God's Son'. He argues instead for a 'plotline' akin to Phil. 2.5–11 – without any particular appeal to, or correspondence with, the Synoptic tradition.

3.28). But Paul's story of Jesus is deeper than this, in that Paul also seemingly patterns himself on Jesus – one might say he seeks to embrace Jesus' human identity for himself. He can therefore speak of sending Timothy to the Corinthians to remind them of his 'ways in Christ Jesus' (1 Cor. 4.17). Likewise, he advises the Roman Christians to 'put on Jesus Christ' (Rom. 13.14), and seems to act upon his own instruction; one sees a number of parallels between Paul's self-portrayal and his depiction of Jesus. Both suffered deprivation (1 Cor. 4.11–12, cf. Luke 9.58); as servants of God, both experienced extreme hardship and affliction (2 Cor. 6.4–5). Paul speaks of partaking in the sufferings of Christ (2 Cor. 12.3–7) and of knowing him in his suffering and death (Phil. 3.10); he declares that he carries the death of Jesus in his body (2 Cor. 4.7–12) and has the rhetorical stigmata, or marks, of Jesus branded on his body (Gal. 6.17). His enigmatic mention of the thorn in the flesh that continues to plague him (2 Cor. 12.7) may be a further, oblique reference to his sharing in Jesus' suffering. Most explicitly perhaps, Paul urges the Corinthians to imitate him, *as he imitates Christ* (1 Cor. 11.1; cf. also 1 Thess. 1.6; 1 Cor. 4.16–17); although it is technically *imitatio Christi* rather than *imitatio Jesu*, there seems no reason to exclude the earthly Jesus from the pattern Paul seeks to embrace. After all, the Corinthians' imitation can only be as human beings, so it must surely include a pattern of human behaviour, presumably that of the earthly Jesus. Likewise, Paul's exhortation that the Roman Christians bear with the failings of the weak is premised upon the example of Jesus (Rom. 15.1–3); the relational nature of the appeal suggests that the pattern of Jesus' life – and not just the manner of his death – are in view here, and therefore that Jesus' human character matters. Wright suggests that the portrayal of Christ 'not pleasing himself' (Rom. 15.3), such that insults that fell upon him (Paul here cites Ps. 69.9), captures the 'basic story of Jesus', and particularly the Gethsemane narrative where Jesus apprehensively awaits his fate.[75] Finally, the exemplary meekness and gentleness of Christ (2 Cor.

---

[75] N. T. Wright, 'The Letter to the Romans', in *NIB* 393–770 (745).

10.1) can only really pertain to Jesus' life ('gentleness' can hardly be said to characterize Christ's death or exaltation), perhaps to the exhortation of Matthew 11.29. As such, Paul does seem to have in mind a pattern/story of the living Jesus that he calls his readers to embrace. Jesus does have an exemplary function as a human being;[76] his obedience contrasts with Adam's disobedience (Rom. 5.19); and a key aspect of the Christ hymn of Philippians 2.5–11 is that Jesus is obedient *on earth* (Phil. 2.8; cf. also Rom. 15.2–3; 2 Cor. 8.9).

Of particular importance, then, for Paul is Jesus' obedience, particularly his obedience unto death (Phil. 2.8), and this central aspect of his character is one that Paul himself seeks to replicate. It is Jesus' manner or disposition – rather than Jesus' biography – that really interests the apostle, and that he seeks to mimic or imitate. In recent times, therefore, scholars have proposed a different translation for the Greek phrase *pistis Christou*, a common and significant one within the Pauline corpus (Rom. 3.22; 3.26; Gal. 2.16; 2.20; 3.22; Phil. 3.9). The phrase has been frequently rendered as what grammarians term an objective genitive, namely 'faith in Christ', thereby placing emphasis on how one's expression of faith in Christ is related to the process of justification. A contrasting position, however, is now relatively commonplace within scholarship,[77] whereby the phrase is rendered as a *subjective* genitive – the 'faith/faithfulness of Christ' – whereby the focus is placed rather upon Jesus Christ's action, his own, obedient self-giving on the cross.[78] It is perhaps, then, unsurprising that Philippians 2.5–8, the 'story' of Jesus' obedient, self-emptying unto death on a cross, is followed very shortly by Paul's own recounting of *his* story of

---

[76] So Adams, 'Paul, Jesus and Christ' 98: 'How Jesus lived, at least in general terms, was important to the apostle, certainly for ethics and arguably for salvation.' Specifically on the ethical dimension, see David G. Horrell, *Solidarity and Difference: A Contemporary Reading of Paul's Ethics* (London: T&T Clark, 2005).

[77] On this topic, see Michael F. Bird and Preston M. Sprinkle (eds), *The Faith of Jesus Christ: Exegetical, Biblical, and Theological Studies* (Peabody: Hendrickson, 2009).

[78] Cf. Hays, 'God's Son' 189: '[I]t marks him as the singular, irreplaceable individual in whom God's will for the salvation of a faithless world is made effectual.' See also Campbell, 'Story of Jesus in Romans and Galatians'.

self-emptying (Phil. 3.4–6); Paul then declares that he knows (Jesus) Christ most intimately in his suffering and seeks to become like him in his death (Phil. 3.10).[79] Seyoon Kim encapsulates the situation well: 'the "remarkable correspondences" between Jesus and Paul in a life of suffering and humble service suggest that it is more realistic to think that having learned the life and character of the historical Jesus, Paul as his apostle tried to imitate him.'[80]

While the Synoptic Jesus' pithy sayings and parables differ from Paul's long, worked-out argument, one might also identify parallels between the respective 'ministries' of the two protagonists. Paul's affirmation of celibacy (notable for an ex-Pharisee) chimes with the depiction of Jesus as one who remained unmarried. It is commonly observed that Paul makes little use of Jesus' Kingdom of God/Heaven imagery (though the motif is still found in several places within the Pauline corpus – Rom. 14.17; 1 Cor. 4.20; 6.9–10; 15.50; Gal. 5.21), yet there may actually be some continuity between this theme and Paul's focus on justification and righteousness.[81] Dunn also ventures a number of points of comparison between the two ministries. He finds Jesus' Kingdom of God motif to be a close parallel to Paul's message of grace, and contends that Jesus' embrace of sinners parallels Paul's distinctive apostleship to Gentiles. For example, Paul's robust defence of eating with Gentiles, and his sharp reproof of Peter on such matters (Gal. 2.11), has very much the flavour of Jesus' similar critique in the Gospel testimony. Dunn also notes how both figures have good news for the poor,[82] how both espouse a now/not yet theology,

---

[79] Horrell, *Solidarity*. The fact that Philippians is composed from prison, Paul having lost all of his former privilege, adds further resonance to this.

[80] Kim, *Paul and the New Perspective* 283. On Paul's imitation of Jesus more generally, see Richard A. Burridge, *Imitating Jesus: An Inclusive Approach to New Testament Ethics* (Grand Rapids: Eerdmans, 2007) 138–54.

[81] So Wedderburn, 'Paul and Jesus'.

[82] See here also Bruce W. Longenecker, 'Good News to the Poor: Jesus, Paul and Jerusalem', in *Jesus and Paul Reconnected: Fresh Pathways into an Old Debate*, ed. Todd D. Still (Grand Rapids: Eerdmans, 2007) 37–65.

and how both have a pivotal place and role for the work of the Spirit.[83]

Conclusion: Jesus according to Paul

What sort of figure is the Pauline Jesus? Paul's portrait or remembrance of Jesus is complex and multi-faceted, and manifests itself in a variety of ways. It may not be the type of picture we expect, nor exhibit the depth of Jesus tradition we would necessarily wish for, and it functions within a broader, complex Christological framework. Indeed, because of the continuity between the earthly Jesus and the Christ of faith, we recognize that there is something artificial – anachronistic even – about separating off a Pauline Jesus from the wider Christ narrative of which it is part. But one can justify it on the grounds that the earthly aspect of this story remains foundational. In Paul, we encounter a portrait of Jesus whose cruciform death and resurrection are central and whose humanity, as a new Adam (1 Cor. 15.45), matters much.

We have seen that much of the scholarly debate still concerns the continuity, or otherwise, between Paul and Jesus, and how much of the Jesus tradition the apostle to the Gentiles knew. Our presenting question, however, is ultimately somewhat different, and concerns the portrait of Jesus offered within the Pauline corpus. In some sense, the extent of the parallels between Paul and the Synoptics is irrelevant to it, except to the point where Paul actually associates Jesus with the material presented, or describes Jesus in a particular fashion. The relationship between Mark 7 and Romans 14 is possible (and to this author's mind, quite probable), but it does not move the argument forward very much in

---

[83] See Dunn, *Jesus, Paul, and the Gospels* 95–115. Wedderburn, 'Paul and the Story of Jesus' 180, arrives at a broadly similar conclusion, identifying parallels between Paul and Jesus by their respective 'deprivation (poverty, homelessness, hunger, and the like), by celibacy, by humble service, and by enduring persecution'. He concludes: 'Paul acts and preaches as he does because a tradition has come down to him either that Jesus acted and preached in a similar way or that such acting and preaching is the Christian way to act and preach' (180).

terms of the Pauline *portrait* of Jesus. Likewise, it seems feasible that Paul would have wanted to know more about the life of the one whose death and resurrection he proclaimed, and he had the opportunity to do so, but the epistles themselves (whether by accident or intent) remain fairly silent on biographical details, and it is difficult to know where the burden of proof falls in terms of proving Paul's interest or not in Jesus.

But the very fact that Paul does not allude to such biographical details suggests not that they are insignificant for him, but rather that there is a wider tapestry to which one should attend, a more substantial Pauline Jesusology to recount. Perhaps more than the work of any other NT author, the Pauline corpus illustrates the way in which the non-Gospel material reveals the identity of Jesus rather than his biography. And if 'Jesus remembered' is, not to put too fine a point on it, the 'Jesus who is remembered', then it may be that Paul's testimony causes us to reassess some of the expectations of the historical Jesus project: rather than trying to construct a 'life of Jesus' premised upon the 'historicity' of biographical details, we might instead take Paul at his word and attend to his depiction of Jesus. He presents Jesus as the obedient, faithful one, someone to be modelled, followed and embraced. In Paul, we see Jesus tradition taken over. Paul 'puts on' Christ so to speak (cf. Rom. 13.14),[84] and inhabits the persona or character of Jesus. In short, 'Paul . . . can be characterized as *one of the truest disciples of Jesus* – not simply called Lord Jesus Christ, but also of Jesus of Nazareth.'[85]

---

[84] Michael B. Thompson, *Clothed with Christ: The Example and Teaching of Jesus in Romans 12.1—15.13*, JSNTSup 59 (Sheffield: JSOT Press, 1991), works with this titular motif in his very helpful/balanced discussion of Jesus tradition in Rom. 12—15.

[85] Dunn, *Jesus, Paul, and the Gospels* 115.

4

'The ascended Christ': Jesus in Deutero-Paul

Any attempt to ponder the portrayal of Jesus in the Deutero-Pauline corpus necessarily invites some hesitation or caution. By separating the texts off from the so-called *Hauptbriefe* or primary letters of Paul, as is common practice within biblical scholarship,[1] the implication is that Paul is not the author responsible for these particular epistles. This, of course, heightens the expectation of diversity when considering their respective portrayals of Jesus; as soon as one discounts Paul as author, or if one attributes the texts to a particular 'school' following after him, one cannot necessarily expect to find a harmony or unity to their depiction of Jesus.[2] For this reason, I shall treat the letters individually, rather than, as I did with the Pauline letters in the last chapter, grouping them together under one banner (though I shall address the Pastoral Epistles as a collective unit).

A further caveat or cautionary note might be added. Analysis of the Deutero-Paulines commonly focuses on their presentation of Paul compared to that found in the *Hauptbriefe*; that, after all, is what causes them to be classified as Deutero-Pauline in the first place. Discussion on them therefore gravitates towards questions of the 'historical Paul' and/or the practice of the early churches

---

[1] Personally, I am more inclined to group Colossians with the *Hauptbriefe*, but partly to go with the consensus, and partly because of the different pictures offered of Jesus therein, I distinguish the texts accordingly. For convenience, I shall continue to call the author 'Paul', as per the textual attestation, but without drawing any consequence for association with the historical Paul.

[2] As Victor Paul Furnish, *Jesus according to Paul*, Understanding Jesus Today (Cambridge: Cambridge University Press, 1993) 96, surmises, we need not expect 'anything like a uniform "deutero-Pauline" theology'.

with which he was associated, rather than dealing with historical Jesus concerns. Chronological factors also come to bear. If the texts postdate the historical Paul – to whatever extent – then they lack any temporal priority that those genuinely of Paul might possess. As a result, we find the distinction between Jesusology and Christology harder to draw; the letters contain no dominical sayings, and, within the texts' more realized eschatology, Jesus is (already) the ascended Christ. The blurring between the earthly and heavenly figure becomes all the more enhanced. What, then, can we say of 'Jesus' in such letters?

Jesus in Colossians

Colossians knows of at least one earthly Jesus, but this is surely a different figure, one known as Justus (Col. 4.11). The shared name is surely no more than coincidence, and we know little else of this figure beyond the reference found here. The fact, though, that Paul includes the Justus cognomen probably reflects the need to deflect any potential confusion with the 'other' Jesus – that is, the one whose name is 'Christ' (1.1, 3–4; 2.6; 4.12). For Colossians is Christological to its very core; indeed, it is 'Christ' language rather than that of 'Jesus' that predominates within the letter, and its Jesusology is minimal by comparison. The Christ in Colossians is the ascended one, seated at the right hand of God (3.1), the head of every power and dominion (2.10) and the one who is portrayed as the mystery of God (2.2). At first glance, this can seem to subsume any reference to, or remembrance of, the earthly Jesus.

Colossians contains one of the most significant Christological passages in the NT, the so-called 'Christ hymn' of 1.15–20, in which Christ is portrayed as supreme in and over creation. The hymn divides into two sections. In the first unit (1.15–18a),[3] Christ's pre-eminence and pre-existence are vigorously asserted. Christ is the image of the invisible God (1.15), the firstborn of

---

[3] Some scholars make the break at v. 17 rather than 18a.

creation (1.15), one who is both the agent and the purpose of creation – all things are created through him and for him (1.16). Christ is therefore pre-eminent in time as well as in status.[4] This first section thus exudes a high, cosmic Christology, with little, if any, recourse, to historic Jesus concerns, or indeed any interest in incarnational or earthly matters whatsoever.

The second section of the hymn, however, is potentially more Jesus orientated, at least in terms of what is recorded about the (earthly) redemptive activity of Christ (even if Jesus is not explicitly named in the unit). Several aspects of Christ's earthly work and character are elucidated. First, Christ is described as the first-born of the dead (1.18; cf. 1 Cor. 15.20), presumably a reference to the event of the resurrection. No mention is made of Jesus' life, nor is Jesus even named here, but one ventures that he is somehow 'understood', for the subsequent verse probably also offers a second, further reference to the earthly Jesus as the one in whom the fullness of God dwells (1.19). That said, as Jesus is not named, 1.19 could be alluding back to the first part of the hymn, thereby formulating some kind of claim of divinity for the pre-existent Christ figure of 1.15–18a; 1.19 is, after all, fundamentally a theological statement, and offers no information or detail as to Jesus' life. However, the Greek verb used here (*katoikeo* – 1.19), particularly the *oikeo* root, is suggestive of incarnation, and therefore of the fact that 'god-ness' was somehow associated with the (human) figure of Jesus.[5] This seems to parallel the notion of 2.9, namely that, in Christ, the fullness of deity was found in bodily form (2.9) – one assumes Jesus, the enfleshed one, is implied.[6]

---

[4] Furnish, *Jesus* 98.

[5] Colossians is not exact as to when the fullness dwells within Christ but the incarnation as a whole is 'perhaps most likely' – cf. Douglas J. Moo, *The Letters to the Colossians and to Philemon*, The Pillar New Testament Commentary (Grand Rapids: Eerdmans, 2008) 133.

[6] Marianne Meye Thompson seems to arrive at this conclusion: 'God has become manifest in the particular person of Jesus of Nazareth and is therefore known in the particular narrative of this man's life, death and resurrection' (Marianne Meye Thompson, *Colossians and Philemon*, The Two Horizons New Testament Commentary (Grand Rapids: Eerdmans, 2005) 54.

The specific reference to *bodily* form (2.9; cf. 1.22) is an interesting one: although the hymn prioritizes the cosmic Christ, 2.9 suggests that Colossians is not uninterested in earthly matters, or in what one might term the historical aspect of the extended (Jesus) Christ story.[7] After all, Colossians can ascribe saving effect to the death of this Christ (a cruciform one – 2.13–14), can emphasize the very physicality of the death (1.22) and can associate the audience's baptismal experience with Christ's resurrection (2.11–12). Furthermore, Paul refers to the Colossians' receiving Jesus Christ as Lord (2.6), and this must surely have included the receipt of traditions about his earthly life, however undefined.[8] As Stephen Fowl surmises: 'When Paul tells the Colossians to be rooted and built up in Christ in 2.7, he is urging them to live in the light of what they know about Christ'[9] – that is, they possess some knowledge about Jesus' earthly conduct. It is therefore quite possible that Jesus tradition is echoed elsewhere within the letter's paraenesis; for example, the issue of food laws (2.21–22) could be linked to Mark 7.1–8/15–23, even though the letter makes no formal claim in that regard.

In terms of the letter's overall portrait of the earthly Jesus, it is Christ's death that is the most significant point of interest. The achievement of the death is articulated in a number of ways – redemption (1.14), forgiveness of sins (1.14), victory (2.15), rescue (1.13), atoning sacrifice (1.20), reconciliation (1.22) – and it is notable that a text that stresses Christ's cosmic

---

[7] Wedderburn suggests this is inspirational rather than incarnational, and that the hymn has very little to say about the incarnation (Andrew T. Lincoln and A. J. M. Wedderburn, *The Theology of the Later Pauline Letters*, New Testament Theology (Cambridge: Cambridge University Press, 1993) 33). This may be the case for Col. 1.19 alone, but it feels harder to sustain in the light of 2.9.

[8] Birger Gerhardsson, *Memory and Manuscript: Oral Tradition and Written Transmission in Rabbinic Judaism and Early Christianity*, ASNU 22 (Uppsala: Gleerup, 1961) 300–1, ventures that Col. 2.6 comprises a collection of traditions about Christ, 'some oral or written equivalent of one of our gospels' (301). So also Stephen E. Fowl, *The Story of Christ in the Ethics of Paul: An Analysis of the Function of the Hymnic Material in the Pauline Corpus*, JSNTSup 36 (Sheffield: JSOT Press, 1990) 131.

[9] Fowl, *Story of Christ* 131.

supremacy simultaneously renders the centrality of the cross for its efficacious achievements. Christ's supremacy (1.18) and his suffering (1.20) are inextricably intertwined. While it is true that the spiritual achievements of Christ are given particular emphasis within the letter (2.11–12, 20; 3.3; 1.22), Paul maintains that all things are affected by his death, both earthly and heavenly (1.20). Colossians may therefore have in mind the physical reference point or backdrop to Christ's work. For example, the 'rulers and authorities' over which Christ has triumphed (2.15) are normally understood as spiritual forces and dominions, and, in the letter's overall milieu, that would seem a reasonable conclusion to maintain. However, one wonders if 2.15 might also show further knowledge about the death of Jesus, namely that it reflects Paul's awareness of the public dimension to the cross and that it was the Roman authorities that had placed Jesus there in the first place.

Similarly intriguing is the reference of Colossians 2.14, and its pointer to a legal record (of trespasses) being nailed to the cross. The reference is allusive and one hesitates to read too much into it,[10] particularly bearing in mind the figurative context of 2.13–15.[11] But the mere fact of its mention does warrant some consideration. It may, for instance, derive 'from the actual nature of Christ's crucifixion',[12] in the sense that Jesus' hands were physically nailed through (cf. John 20.25). If this were the case, it would make for a notable datum on the actual modus operandi of crucifixion. However, the phrasing of the verse seems to indicate otherwise: it does not say that *Christ's hands* were pinned to a cross, but rather that the 'debt' was nailed to it. It is literally a 'cheirograph'

---

[10] Note, for example, that Allan R. Bevere, 'The Cheirograph in Colossians 2:4 and the Ephesian Connection', in *Jesus and Paul: Global Perspectives in Honor of James D.G. Dunn for his 70th Birthday*, ed. B. J. Oropeza, C. K. Robertson and Douglas C. Mohrmann, Library of New Testament Studies 414 (London: T&T Clark, 2009) 199–206, does not consider any of the putative 'historical' allusions, considering it to be an essentially figurative or rhetorical motif.

[11] Cf. the more sceptical assessment of Lincoln and Wedderburn, *Later Pauline* 44.

[12] Moo, *Colossians* 211.

that is nailed to the cross, and, particularly bearing in mind the gospel testimony, one might conceivably view this as some kind of legal document attached to Christ's cross, one offering a public record of the charge for which he was being crucified. The inscription, 'This is the king of the Jews' (cf. Mark 15.26; Matt. 27.37 pars) would be the obvious connection.[13]

In sum, Colossians is aware of a Jesus story in which his death was cruciform and in which the death was understood as in some sense efficacious or victorious (Col. 2.14). Some might speculate that the material on the cross is a later addition to the Colossians text, or to the Christ hymn at least,[14] as the letter's attention elsewhere is generally upon the exalted and pre-existent Christ. This is not impossible of course, but equally there is no compelling evidence to support it. Instead, the cruciform focus seems to open up a window onto Jesusology in Colossians, by setting out the core relationship between the physical death of Jesus and the cosmic character of Christ; the earthly Jesus becomes key to its overall Christ story, or to what Colossians calls the 'mystery of Christ' (4.3). Paul's own testimony is illustrative in this regard. He can speak of rejoicing in his present sufferings (1.24 – presumably his imprisonment (4.3, 10)), and compares these sufferings to completing what was lacking in those of Christ (1.24). In particular, Paul underscores that the sufferings are experienced in the flesh (1.24), commensurate with those of Christ in his fleshly body (1.22). This juxtaposition of flesh imagery seems significant, and it may be that Paul is portraying himself as carrying on the ministry (i.e. the suffering) of the earthly Christ, in similar fashion to that found in the primary Pauline epistles. Christ becomes a paradigm of living for Paul, a paradigm particularly marked by earthly suffering.

---

[13] Dale C. Allison, Jr., *Constructing Jesus: Memory, Imagination, and History* (London: SPCK, 2010) 413–14. He finds this to be a historically plausible account, if only because such practice in a crucifixion context is only attested in the depiction of Jesus' death (i.e. in the Gospels and Paul).

[14] Furnish, *Jesus* 99. He believes it to be an addition by the author of the epistle.

Jesus in Ephesians

The close similarity between Ephesians and Colossians is a well-established datum of NT scholarship. Ephesians shares, exceeds even, the emphasis on the exaltedness of Christ in Colossians and his supremacy over rulers, powers and authorities (Eph. 1.20–23).[15] It also echoes Colossians' focus on Christ's death, but attends more to its theological significance and efficacy (cf. Eph. 2.13–22), rather than addressing the historical 'actuality' of the event. The author of Ephesians seems more geared towards theologizing than to historical reminiscence, and the 'events' of first-century Palestine barely feature on the horizon, probably because of the high-level, supratemporal nature of the discourse. Partly this means a particular epistolary focus on the heavenly situation of Christ and the Church (1.20–23; 2.5–6), rather than on earthly matters (at least in terms of Jesus-related concerns); partly it reflects the letter's position that the focus of the world has moved – Christ is now 'in all' (4.10).

The minimal reference to the earthly Jesus is accompanied by little, if any, reference to the church in Ephesus. Instead, it is the wider, universal Church that interests Ephesians, and specifically the relationship between Christ's achievements and how they benefit the Church; what is true of Christ is now true of the Church.[16] Like him, they are seated in the heavenlies (1.20–21; 2.5–6); Christ gave himself up for them (5.25) and Christ is now the head of the Church (5.23; cf. 1.22; 4.15; also Col. 1.18). In particular, Christ's cruciform death has removed the division between Jew and Gentile (Eph. 2.14), thereby creating one, new humanity (2.15), a new household (2.19) or temple (2.21) of God, with Jesus Christ as the cornerstone (2.20). This Christological-ecclesiological redefinition has some parallels elsewhere in the New Testament (e.g. Acts 15.16–17), but the construal Ephesians gives it is both

---

[15] Andrew T. Lincoln, *Ephesians*, WBC 42 (Waco: Word Books, 1990) xc.
[16] Furnish, *Jesus* 104: '[W]hat the author of Ephesians has to say about Christ cannot be separated from what he says about church.'

very developed and (more significantly) something of an evolution from the historical Jesus' apparent interest only in Israel's fate and restoration (cf. Matt. 15.24; Luke 1.16; 14.21).

At several points in the letter, though, Ephesians does reflect – however incidentally – details and information as to how Jesus was understood. It can draw exemplary value from Christ's death (Eph. 5.25), suggesting that there was at least some familiarity with a Christ story (if not his history), some broader understanding of the way in which Jesus went about his death. Not much is explicitly said about the manner of the death, though, beyond its having a self-giving nature. Likewise, Ephesians can speak of Christ's resurrection (1.20), but it is the theological ramifications of that event, rather than any historical exploration, that concern the author. There may perhaps be an echo of Mark 7.15 in Ephesians 4.29, but if so it is a faint one, and there is no particular attribution to Jesus. Thus, perhaps the most significant appeal to Jesus comes in Ephesians 4.20–21 and the somewhat allusive references both to 'learning Christ' (4.20) and that the truth is in Jesus (4.21). The first phrase is a compact and ambiguous one, thus cautioning against laying too much import on it, but it remains an intriguing expression worthy of some comment. The notion of 'learning Christ' (4.20) seems to equate to the passing on of Jesus tradition; like Colossians 2.6–7, it probably reflects the process of acquiring knowledge about Jesus/Christ, in ways that might inform behaviour and discipleship.[17] While the instruction about Christ may be in the service of conduct and practical living (cf. 4.14–24), it remains the case that the Ephesians are supposedly learning Jesus tradition – and, if geared to discipleship, in a way that goes beyond information about his death. In short, as in Colossians 2.6–7, knowing *about* Jesus Christ seems to matter.

Such a conclusion seems to be confirmed by Ephesians 4.21. The author reminds the Ephesians that they have heard about Christ, presumably as part of the missionary preaching in the city,

---

[17] Lincoln, *Ephesians* 279. He suggests the same process is at work in Acts 5.42.

and akin to the references Paul makes in the uncontested epistles. But as they have also been taught in (or about?) him, it sounds as if knowledge about Christ has been forthcoming after this initial missionary foray; the epistle does not say of what such teaching comprised, but Lincoln's suggestion that it 'involves receiving instruction in the gospel tradition'[18] seems perfectly plausible. If so, while Ephesians itself does not yield much explicit information about Jesus, it equally seems to imply that such information was important to the life and practice of its readers. 'Learning' is about imbibing a particular behaviour (cf. Eph. 4.22–32), and the sense is that Christ – Jesus Christ – is the model upon which such learning is founded.

The rest of 4.21 is similarly intriguing, specifically the statement that 'truth is in Jesus'. Bearing in mind the slightly oblique nature of the phrase, we don't want to place too much weight on it, but equally notable is the fact that the claim is made in respect of *Jesus* – not Christ.[19] This is the only instance in the letter where the name Jesus is present without the Christ/Lord appellation, and it would seem that Jesus – and specifically the earthly Jesus – is being held up as a paradigm of ethical behaviour, perhaps 'in order to stress that the historical Jesus is himself the embodiment of the truth',[20] or that truth is patterned around the earthly Jesus in a way that he captures or encapsulates. Hence, even within the emphasis on the ascended Christ, Ephesians still reveals some interest in Jesus, especially when addressing paraenetic concerns over conduct (4.22–24).

The letter's other slightly ambiguous reference is to Christ's 'descent' (4.9), a concept that begs the kind of interpretative questions raised in respect of 1 Peter 3.18–20; 4.6.[21] The description of the downward journey, in Ephesians, is far less expansive

---

[18] Lincoln, *Ephesians* 280.

[19] Luke Timothy Johnson, *Living Jesus: Learning the Heart of the Gospel* (San Francisco: HarperSanFrancisco, 1999) 114: 'The use of the personal name is striking.'

[20] P. T. O'Brien, *The Letter to the Ephesians*, Pillar New Testament Commentary (Grand Rapids: Eerdmans, 1999) 326.

[21] See Chapter 7 for further discussion.

than the Petrine examples and amounts merely to a descent 'to the lower parts of the earth', with no further indication as what such 'lower parts' might be. It is conceivably a descent into Hades, the realm of the dead,[22] thereby reflecting the belief that Jesus descended to the dead on Passion Saturday, or it could be merely a more general reference to Jesus' death.[23] More probable is the view that Ephesians 4.9 reflects the incarnation; the 'descent' to earth parallels the 'ascent' into the heavens, the latter event being so prominent elsewhere in the epistle (1.20–22; 2.5–6).

Jesus in Second Thessalonians

The Jesusology of 2 Thessalonians can be summarized in fairly brief and succinct fashion. Although Jesus is named reasonably frequently throughout the letter, the references almost exclusively relate to the second, rather than the first coming. Jesus is characterized as being revealed from heaven (2 Thess. 1.7; 2.1) and coming to destroy the 'lawless one' (2.8); he will bring about a punishment of eternal destruction (1.9), but will likewise be worshipped by those who have remained faithful (1.10). Indeed, the occasion for the letter seems to be some kind of misunderstanding on the part of the Thessalonians about the Parousia, with Paul keen to correct their confusion. Therefore one can find little or no reference to the earthly Jesus within 2 Thessalonians. The heightened eschatological interest may parallel the tone of 1 Thessalonians, which I suggested could have resulted from Paul portraying Jesus in fairly apocalyptic terms. But there is nothing in the second epistle necessarily to warrant that connection. In effect, the 'Jesus remembered' of 2 Thessalonians is really the 'Jesus anticipated'.

---

[22] William Bales, 'The Descent of Christ in Ephesians 4:9', *CBQ* 72 (2010) 84–100. He notes that this is the literal sense of the verse, but that it is used metaphorically to speak of Jesus' death.

[23] Gordon D. Fee, *Pauline Christology: An Exegetical-Theological Study* (Peabody: Hendrickson, 2007) 358.

Jesus in the Pastoral Epistles

Few people regard the Pastoral Epistles as useful sources for historical Jesus discovery, because they look on them as fairly late entrants into the canonical collection, and as texts more interested in ecclesial structures and practices than in recollection of Jesus tradition. Their relative lateness may also be of value, however, especially if they are found to attest other (earlier) data and traditions located elsewhere in the canon; if so, they would evidence Jesus material being preserved, taken on and framed as 'secure', potentially for catechetical or creedal purposes. And such creedal fixity need not be in conflict with historical interests; once again, the Pastoral Epistles would be showing Jesus as he was remembered by those who followed after him. But at the same time, it is interesting that the Pastorals do not make any explicit appeal to the Gospel accounts, as the latter could well have been available in some form at the point of composition. This is a notable historical datum in and of itself – the Pastoral Epistles continue the non-Gospel materials' reticence in appealing to Jesus tradition.[24]

It is no surprise, then, that at one level, Jesus 'information' in the Pastoral Epistles is piecemeal and occasional, not unlike the data gleaned from the primary Pauline corpus. We glean some information about him from the constituent texts but need to read between the lines to do so. Jesus is of Davidic lineage (2 Tim. 2.8), is portrayed as a mediator figure (1 Tim. 2.5) and Saviour (2 Tim. 1.10; Titus 1.4; 2.13; 3.6); he is someone who has given himself as a ransom for all (1 Tim. 2.5–6; Titus 2.14), who has been raised from the dead (2 Tim. 2.8) and has thereby abolished death itself (2 Tim. 1.10). The ransom ascription of 1 Timothy 2.6 may reflect the remembrance of the logion of Mark 10.45, commonly regarded as a genuine Jesus saying.[25]

---

[24] So Helmut Koester, *Ancient Christian Gospels: Their History and Development* (London: SCM Press, 1990) 63.

[25] See also the discussion in Chapter 7, on 1 Peter.

Jesus gives testimony before Pontius Pilate (1 Tim. 6.13) and is said to make 'good confession' in so doing. This 'good confession' may be merely the positive answer to Pilate's questioning (cf. Mark 15.2), but that seems a somewhat minimalistic rendering of 'confession'. More broadly, it may serve to highlight Jesus' commitment to, or positive embrace of, his imminent death, and thus act as another mode of encouragement for the audience in their difficulties (as we will encounter in 1 Peter and Hebrews).[26] If so, it may even articulate a more extended call to faithfulness – the confession may represent a testimony to Jesus' whole life enacted during the era of Pilate, rather than just to the actual words spoken during the trial.[27] This would be commensurate with the exhortation in the previous verse (1 Tim. 6.12), whereby the 'confession' made by Timothy seems to incorporate his life lived, rather than just that one particular instance of confession. If so, 6.12 would seem to appeal to the earthly Jesus as a model of behaviour, and not just in his obedient death.

Beyond this, there may also be some detectable emphasis in 1 and 2 Timothy to the words and acts (past, present and future) of Christ, particularly the way in which Jesus' words assume authority. For instance, 1 Timothy 6.3 can speak of the 'sound words' of Jesus; it does not expand upon the content of such words, but the implication seems to be that Jesus' teaching did form, in some way, the content that other teachers were expected to pass on (1 Tim. 6.2–3). First Timothy 5.18 may be a further case in point. The verse cites Deuteronomy 25.4 (as does Paul in 1 Cor. 9.9), but juxtaposes it with a further statement, that a labourer deserves to be paid for his work. This is the same 'text'

---

[26] L. W. Hurtado, 'Jesus' Death as Paradigmatic in the New Testament', *SJT* 57 (2004) 413–33: '[T]he reference to his steadfastness before Pilate certainly makes Jesus' ordeal paradigmatic for the resoluteness called for, and it also functions to underscore Jesus' authority to demand such perseverance of Christians' (424).

[27] Greg A. Couser, '"The Testimony about the Lord", "Borne by the Lord", or Both? An Insight into Paul and Jesus in the Pastoral Epistles (2 Tim. 1:8)', *TynBul* 55 (2004) 295–316 (306–9).

cited by Paul in 1 Corinthians 9.14, one that he accords to Jesus, as we have seen, a citation roughly akin to Luke 10.7. Therefore while it is not named as such, it is possible that 1 Timothy 5.18 is quoting Jesus – or at least appealing to Jesus tradition, akin to Paul's appeal in 1 Corinthians 9.14, as no formal attribution is given – and a dominical logion is being put on the same level as Scripture.

We might also make this claim of Jesus' actions, not just his words. In 2 Timothy 1.8, Timothy is advised not to be ashamed of the witness *about*, or maybe *of* Jesus. On such a reading, it becomes conceivable, perhaps probable, that 2 Timothy 1.8 is best rendered as a subjective genitive – 'the witness of the Lord'. That is, Timothy holds up the example of Jesus – in words and action – as a paradigm for the audience to embrace and follow.[28]

Furthermore, interspersed within the letters are what seem to be liturgical declarations or catechetical/creedal statements (1 Tim. 2.5–6; 3.16; 2 Tim. 2.8, 11–13), each of which could be seen as potted, succinct 'stories' of Jesus.[29] The statements can be quite brief, 2 Timothy 2.8 particularly, though it is notable that in such a pithy summary of the gospel, 2.8 only mentions attributes of the earthly Jesus (i.e. a Davidic descendant and one raised from the dead). In the other creedal formulae, the precise referent points of the confessions are not always so clear. Consider 1 Timothy 3.16 as a typical example. The reference to being revealed in the flesh surely reflects Jesus' birth, and sustains the notion that, for Timothy, Jesus' humanity matters, in that he has entered into the physical world (1 Tim. 1.15). The vindication by, or in, the s/Spirit is more ambiguous, however. It could be seen as a reference to Jesus' baptism, and particularly the Spirit's activity within that (cf. Mark 1.10–11); if so, that would be something of a rarity within the non-Gospel corpus, where there is no explicit mention of that event apart from in

---

[28] See Couser, '"Testimony about the Lord"'.
[29] See, for example, Fowl, *Story of Christ* 155–94.

Acts (though, as we shall see, 1 John 5.6 may possibly allude to it). Alternatively, it may bespeak the resurrection, as that 'event' could equally be said to vindicate Jesus' status (cf. Rom. 1.4).[30] It may even allude to Jesus' vindication as he ascends into the heavenly realm,[31] at which point it is effectively no longer 'earthly' Jesus testimony. Because of the temporal ordering implied by 1 Timothy 3.16, the reference of 'seen by angels' will depend upon what one considers is implied by the previous clause. If it is indeed the resurrection, then the angelic sighting may allude to Jesus' resurrection appearances, but if it is orientated to the Ascension, then some form of angelic encounter in the heavenly places is surely implied.

Conclusion: the Jesus of the Deutero-Paulines

For Colossians, Jesus' bodily incarnation matters, but there is no reference to Jesus' teaching; while it makes much of Christ's physical achievements on the cross, he is now firmly established in the heavenly places (Col. 3.1), and the text celebrates his exaltation and authority. Ephesians echoes the perspective of Colossians, and is arguably even more attuned to the achievements and triumph of the exalted Christ, particularly in respect of inaugurating one new humanity, ensconced in the heavenly realm (2.5–6, 13–22). Both texts seems to know of Jesus tradition, and the importance of its being passed on (Col. 2.6–7; Eph. 4.20). Ephesians specifically casts the earthly Jesus as a focal point of truth (4.21), but there is little in the letter that fleshes out of what such truth might be composed. In the Pastoral Epistles, the appeal is not so much to the history of Jesus – though there are elements of that – but rather to a story of Jesus Christ, particularly remembered in liturgical form.

---

[30] So Edward Adams, 'Paul, Jesus and Christ', in *The Blackwell Companion to Jesus*, ed. Delbert Royce Burkett, Blackwell Companions to Religion (Malden, MA: Wiley-Blackwell, 2011) 94–110 (108).

[31] Fowl, *Story of Christ* 155–74. He reads 1 Tim. 3.16 as exhibiting a negative view on Jesus' earthly existence.

In sum, the Jesus of the Deutero-Paulines is primarily the ascended Christ. Their references to Jesus are therefore fairly infrequent, but when they do occur, they portray a Jesus whose life and especially whose death mattered, and whose earthly existence offered a pattern for those seeking to follow after him.

5

'The sacrificial high priest':
Jesus in Hebrews

In many ways, the ambience or 'feel' of Hebrews is fundamentally different from that of the rest of the NT, making it 'almost certainly the most mysterious text to have been preserved in the NT canon.'[1] Its focus on sacrifice, new covenant, high priesthood and heavenly intercession all contribute to this sense of mystery, while its characteristic mode of introducing scriptural quotations, or its seemingly harsh position on the consequences of apostasy (Heb. 6.4–6; 10.26–31), likewise add to the idiosyncratic character of the letter. This same epistolary distinctiveness is also borne out by its treatment of Jesus. Hebrews's depiction of him as high priest in the order of Melchizedek is core to the letter's overall Christological argument (1.13–14; 5.5–6; 7.1–28), but in a fashion found nowhere else within the canonical testimony.

Yet despite such peculiarity and distinctiveness, despite, as we shall see, the particular nature of Hebrews's portrait, the letter shares with its canonical counterparts a central focus on Jesus. Indeed, one might propose that Hebrews is actually *all* about Jesus – Jesus is the 'hero' of the text, the focal point of its reflection and theologizing, and in a series of comparisons, Jesus is portrayed as one greater than the prophets, the angels, Moses and the Aaronic high priests.[2] The letter's readers are consequently exhorted to fix their attention upon

---

[1] Pamela Eisenbaum, 'Locating Hebrews within the Literary Landscape of Christian Origins', in *Hebrews: Contemporary Methods, New Insights*, ed. Gabriella Gelardini, *BibInt* 75 (Leiden: Brill, 2005) 213–37 (213).

[2] Keith Warrington, *Discovering Jesus in the New Testament* (Peabody: Hendrickson, 2009) 166. Cf. Luke Timothy Johnson, *Living Jesus: Learning the Heart of the Gospel* (San Francisco: HarperSanFrancisco, 1999) 93, speaking of Hebrews: 'At the heart of the argument is the figure of Jesus.'

him amid their present struggles and testing (12.2–3).[3] Deliberately construed or otherwise, it may be no coincidence that the letter is anonymous, serving to remove any focus from the author and instead place it centrally upon Jesus, the author and perfecter of the readers' faith (12.2). Hebrews may be said, then, to function as a quasi-funeral oration, a celebration of the life of its primary character Jesus.[4] Todd Still concludes somewhat succinctly: 'If Hebrews is a mysterious masterpiece, then Jesus is clearly the centrepiece.'[5]

Hebrews has much to say about the significance of Jesus' humanity and its necessity for the efficacy of the sacerdotal atonement project (cf. 2.14–18; 4.14–16; 5.1–10). We might therefore expect the letter to be a profitable source for historical data, particularly in regard to Jesus and his death.[6] Our experience of dealing with Paul, however, and with the 'over-expectation' experienced there in terms of Jesus tradition, should equally caution against similar over-expectation in terms of the epistle's contribution to historical Jesus discussion. Attridge's muted assessment of the portrait of Jesus in Hebrews is therefore somewhat salutary: 'Hebrews devotes little attention to the details of the life of Jesus, citing no dominical sayings nor mentioning any of the deeds of Jesus during his public ministry.'[7]

Several further limiting factors might also be mentioned. First, the epistle's focus is generally more 'future' than 'past' orientated, particularly in its urgings to enter into the heavenly rest (4.11) or proceed beyond the veil (10.19–22); rhetorically speaking, the audience are to look forward rather than back in their pilgrimage journey of

---

[3] It is notable that Hebrews begins the heroes list of chapter 11 with some reservation about 'things seen', but still urges its hearers specifically to *look* to Jesus (12.2).

[4] So Thomas H. Olbricht, 'Hebrews as Amplification', in *Rhetoric and the New Testament: Essays from the 1992 Heidelberg Conference*, ed. Stanley E. Porter and Thomas H. Olbricht, JSNTSup 90 (Sheffield: JSOT Press, 1993) 375–87.

[5] Todd D. Still, 'Christos as "Pistos": The Faith(fulness) of Jesus in the Epistle to the Hebrews', *CBQ* 69 (2007) 746–55 (755).

[6] So suggests Sophie Laws, 'Hebrews, Letter to the', in *Jesus: The Complete Guide*, ed. Leslie Houlden (London: Continuum, 2005) 328–31 (330). She remains, however, relatively sceptical as to what Hebrews contributes to knowledge about the life of the earthly Jesus.

[7] Harold W. Attridge, 'Jesus in the General Epistles', in *The Blackwell Companion to Jesus*, ed. Delbert Royce Burkett, Blackwell Companions to Religion (Malden, MA: Wiley-Blackwell, 2011) 111–18 (116).

discipleship (12.12–13) or within the race set before them (12.1), as they anticipate the city that is to come (13.13–14).[8] Second, the letter is equally infamous for its apparent preference for things heavenly or eternal – akin to Philo perhaps[9] – rather than for the earthly or created entities: the earthly tabernacle, made by hands, is inferior to its heavenly counterpart (9.24), and it is Christ's entry into heaven that renders the atoning work efficacious (9.23–24). Third, while the letter is famously silent on matters of authorship and provenance, the text does offer some clues, and the possibility of a location outside Judah remains most likely, with plausible candidates including Rome (cf. 13.24) or Alexandria (bearing in mind the letter's Philonic similarities). As such, any familiarity with Jesus tradition because of geographical proximity to Judah would seem to be minimal at best. Fourth, the writer and audience do not appear to have been eyewitnesses to Jesus' actions (2.3–4), and any information received has come to both parties at least second-hand. In that sense at least, Hebrews cannot be said to be 'autoptic'.

Yet none of these apparent limitations is insurmountable. While the encouragement in the letter is certainly to keep going in their discipleship and thereby to look forward, such exhortation is regularly premised upon the call to 'remember' or recall their earlier experiences as the grounds for keeping going (10.32–34; 12.3; 13.7). Memory, particularly of their own experience but also that of Jesus, remains a core and fundamental ingredient of the letter's paraenesis. Likewise, the Philonic or neo-Platonic character of the letter can be overstated, and such characterization tends to omit the fact that Hebrews is very interested in divine action in *history*. Indeed, what seems to differentiate Hebrews from Philo is that very fact that something decisive has happened within the human time/space continuum.[10] And in terms of geographical

---

[8] C. M. Tuckett, *Christology and the New Testament: Jesus and His Earliest Followers* (Louisville: Westminster John Knox, 2001) 95–6.

[9] In his recent commentary, Luke Timothy Johnson, *Hebrews: A Commentary*, NTL (Louisville: Westminster John Knox, 2006) 21, avers that Hebrews is the letter Philo would have written had he been a Christian.

[10] See the critique of Ronald Williamson, *Philo and the Epistle to the Hebrews* (Leiden: Brill, 1970) and, more recently, David M. Moffitt, *Atonement and the Logic of Resurrection in the Epistle to the Hebrews*, NovTSup 141 (Leiden: Brill, 2011).

distance and second-hand appropriation of Jesus material, one might easily make the same criticism of the Gospel of Mark. Apparently composed in Rome,[11] by an anonymous author (albeit latterly identified as John Mark), its knowledge of the Jesus tradition was also conveyed through another figure, identified in the tradition at least, as Peter. Moreover, Hebrews claims that the message was given to them by those who had *heard* the Lord (2.3), which – setting aside Paul for the moment – does rather suggest that the foundations of the Hebrews' 'church' were established by those with first-hand testimony of Jesus. The fact that they are so defined also suggests that Jesus narrative formed part of the instruction at the establishment of the church, and that what the 'founders' had heard Jesus say was subsequently communicated to them. Second-hand communication, therefore, need not mean that it was inherently inferior.

Perhaps, then, we are back to the question as to what is ultimately meant by 'history', and the way in which the NT texts seem to articulate 'Jesus remembered'. Rather than merely seeking to cite 'facts' or 'words' that derive from him, Hebrews constructs a narrative (a liturgically geared one perhaps?) that recalls the Passion story and its effect upon the recipients' present situation. Within such narratival construction, within such 'remembering', present concerns and perspectives of course come to bear. Death at the hands of Roman soldiers gets expanded to become the sacrificial Day of Atonement offering of the high priest, and likewise aspects of the characterization of Jesus (such as his sinlessness) are surely more theologically deductive than historically demonstrable. But while the narrative in Hebrews is not 'history' as a reworking of 'historical' events, the writer ensures that it retains at least some 'historical' perspective; the physical death of Jesus is neither lost nor (to a careful reading, at least) eclipsed by the sacerdotal recasting. Hebrews shows the capacity for Jesus' life – and particularly his death – to be understood, proclaimed and remembered in a new context, be that the loss of the sacred space

---

[11] The provenance of Mark is contested, and Rome is only one option, but it would seem a feasible suggestion.

of the Temple or another salient, formative event. But note –
Hebrews recalls that death as the death of *Jesus*, not of the Christ,
not of the Son; Jesus' earthly suffering matters.

As such, perhaps more than any other NT epistle, Hebrews
recalls a 'story' of Jesus – or maybe a story of the 'Son' – that seeks
to make sense of the historical figure in terms of his present and
ongoing significance. Hebrews does not seek to recreate a life of
Jesus, but is, I suggest, commensurate with the broad narrative of
that life. To go further, Hebrews demands that its audience focus
their attention on Jesus and learn from his story; the audience are
asked to consider Jesus (3.1), not just in a reflective fashion, but
as a means of coming to understand him, his character and way
of being, a continual reflection in their life of discipleship, and to
follow after him (cf. 12.2–3; 13.12–13).[12] The statement that Jesus
Christ is the same 'yesterday and today and forever' (13.8) is therefore not necessarily a doctrinal proposal, but is rather a declaration
of the one who is consistently faithful to be worth following after,
the exemplar or model par excellence, whose prior action gives
grounds for present and future obedience. The Jesus whom they
are to model and follow after (13.13) is the same Jesus whose
sacrificial death has opened the way (10.20) and who is now the
source of salvation (5.9), the merciful and faithful high priest
(2.17). As Small notes: 'The earthly Jesus, who suffered and died,
is coterminous with the exalted Jesus who now serves as High
Priest', and therefore 'the modern scholarly distinction between
the "Jesus of history" and the "Christ of faith" does not appear in
Hebrews; both designations "Jesus" and "Christ" are used interchangeably without any apparent difference in meaning'.[13] To put
it another way, Hebrews can use Jesus' name interchangeably,
whether speaking of his earthly activity or his high priestly action,
and there seems no compelling reason to dissent from Filson's
proposal: 'the basic function of the name Jesus is to designate the

---

[12] On the notion that Hebrews has a narrative of Jesus, see Brian C. Small, 'The Use of
Rhetorical Topoi in the Characterization of Jesus in the Book of Hebrews', *PRSt* 37
(2010) 53–69.
[13] Small, 'Rhetorical Topoi' 62.

central figure of the gospel story, the historical figure'.[14] It is this figure that dominates the epistolary content.

Identity: Jesus – the heavenly high priest

While recognizing this continuity between the earthly Jesus and the exalted Son,[15] it is heuristically convenient to distinguish the respective portraits within the letter. The lens that considers the high-priestly achievements of the (pre-existent) Son can be distinguished, even if only artificially,[16] from the ministry and work of the earthly Jesus. Although it is the latter aspect that predominantly interests us, some cursory consideration of the more fuller Christological portrait will help contextualize the more extended discussion of the earthly work. After all, Hebrews itself describes the same 'Son' as both greater *and* lesser than the angels (1.4–14; 2.5–18).

The so-called prologue to Hebrews (1.1–4) launches the reader into the 'letter' without any customary epistolary greetings, instead, from the outset, demarking the identity, role and character of the 'Son', whose activity and function mark the break between the old and new ages (1.1–2). This Son is explicitly identified as Jesus in 4.14, but the attribution is more than implicit by the prior association Hebrews draws between (human) 'sons' and Jesus in 2.6–9; it is this same figure – Jesus the Son – whose entry into the world divides history into two, between the former times and the last days. Within the prologue itself, a sevenfold ascription is made of the Son: he is the heir of all things (1.2) and the agent of creation (1.2), the one who can be said to have made the very 'ages' themselves. The Son is also described as the *apaugasma* of God's glory (1.3), a term that could mean either the 'reflection' or the 'radiance' of such divine glory – early Church writers differed on which option to pursue. The latter suggests more of the

---

[14] Floyd V. Filson, *Yesterday: A Study of Hebrews in the Light of Chapter 13*, SBT 2/4 (London: SCM Press, 1967) 36–7.

[15] Luke makes the same connection, we have seen, and this is further suggestive of Luke's association with, or similarity to, Hebrews.

[16] Hebrews 6.20 illustrates the artificiality: the forerunner beyond the curtain is identified solely as Jesus (6.20) – and not as Jesus *Christ*.

possession of the divine glory, while the former (more limitedly, perhaps) affirms that such glory was encountered in the Son. As a minimum, one might say that, in the Son, Hebrews affirms that the presence of God is actualized or known, particularly as it continues to describe the Son as the divine *character* of God (1.3), what one might term the true divine 'icon', the one who bears God's proverbial 'stamp'. As well as being the agent of creation, the Son also sustains that creation through his powerful word (1.3); after his atoning, high-priestly work (1.3)[17] – the achievement of which is a core theme for the epistle – he is now seated at the right hand of YHWH (1.3, alluding to Ps. 110.1), having assumed a most superior name (1.4).[18] This is the first of several references to Psalm 110 in the epistle, and the psalm's combination of king–priest terminology is exegeted to its fullest extent. The psalm is also, of course, a significant text within other NT documents, and is placed upon Jesus' lips in the Gospel accounts (Mark 12.35–36; 14.62). It may have formed part of early *testimonia* books, but its prominence may also reflect remembrance of it being Jesus' own citation. Darrell Bock, for example, ventures that Mark 12.35–37, and maybe even Mark 14.62, reflect genuine Jesus tradition, and Hebrews's appropriation of the psalm would represent further reflection on the Christological significance of Jesus' claim.[19]

The discussion of Jesus' identity in Hebrews is expressed in several ways. It is achieved in part by the allocation of a series of titles – Son, apostle, high priest – that encapsulate something

---

[17] Bearing in mind the mooted Roman backdrop to Hebrews (cf. the intriguing reference to 'those from Italy' in 13.24), it is possible that Jesus' high-priest designation has a political dimension, challenging the Emperor's role as *Pontifex Maximus*. Such an association is possible, but ultimately impossible to prove, and the high-priestly role is far more driven by the sacrificial (and especially Day of Atonement) context to the letter.

[18] For the suggestion that the Son receives the divine name – i.e. YHWH – see Richard J. Bauckham, 'The Divinity of Jesus Christ in the Epistle to the Hebrews', in *The Epistle to the Hebrews and Christian Theology*, ed. Richard Bauckham, Daniel R. Driver, Trevor A. Hart and Nathan MacDonald (Grand Rapids: Eerdmans, 2009) 15–36 (21–2).

[19] Darrell L. Bock, 'Blasphemy and the Jewish Examination of Jesus', in *Key Events in the Life of the Historical Jesus: A Collaborative Exploration of Context and Coherence*, ed. Darrell L. Bock and Robert L. Webb (Grand Rapids: Eerdmans, 2010) 589–667 (641–2).

of how Jesus is understood within the letter.[20] The titular designation of Jesus as apostle (3.1) is particularly interesting: it is unique to the NT canon and the title is normally given to those sent by Jesus rather than to Jesus himself. But perhaps the most characteristic aspect of Hebrews's portrayal of Jesus is through the mechanism of comparison: the opening two chapters, for example, invoke a lengthy comparison with angels, partly that Jesus is superior to them (1.4–14) and partly that he was temporarily made lower than them (2.5–8) for the duration of his earthly existence.[21] The letter does not offer a reason for the explicit comparison with angels, and it may be that some confusion about Jesus' identity is being corrected, namely that he was being worshipped as an 'angel' or that there was some confusion relating to his designation as 'son of God'. The LXX customarily referred to angels as 'sons of God', so any confusion is understandable, particularly if Jesus tradition applied the appellation to him (cf. Heb. 4.14 – 'Jesus, the Son of God'). More probably, however, the clarification regarding Jesus' (non-angelic) status derives from the overall comparison between the old and new covenant dispensations in Hebrews. The old or former covenant was instituted through angelic mediation – they were the ones through whom Moses received the Law (2.2) – but the mediator of the new covenant is Jesus himself (cf. 12.24). Through the angelic comparison, Hebrews portrays Jesus as the firstborn (1.5–6), the one who is worshipped (1.6), the one who is without end (1.7–12) and who is seated at YHWH's right hand (1.13–14).

Jesus is also portrayed as greater than Moses (3.1–6), a high standing bearing in mind the high repute in which Moses was held in Jewish circles. But perhaps the most distinctive part of Hebrews's portrayal of Jesus lies in the Son's work as heavenly high priest, the one who offered himself, bearing the sins of many (9.28), and who is a high priest in the order of Melchizedek.

---

[20] For a review of Jesus' identity in terms of such titles, see A. Katherine Grieb, '"Time Would Fail Me to Tell...": The Identity of Jesus Christ in Hebrews', in *Seeking the Identity of Jesus: A Pilgrimage*, ed. Beverly Roberts Gaventa and Richard B. Hays (Grand Rapids: Eerdmans, 2008) 200–14 (200–5).

[21] Reading 2.7 temporally – 'for a little while lower' (so NRSV).

This is unpacked predominantly in chapters 7—10, though there is allusion to it in 4.14–16 and 5.1–10. Hebrews 7.1—10.18, often seen as the core of the epistle's doctrinal message, consider a further sequence of comparisons, elucidating, in turn, a better priesthood (7.1–28), a better covenant (8.1–13), a better tabernacle (9.1–10) and a better sacrifice (9.11—10.18). The unit addresses the nature and location of Jesus' sacrificial act, the offering made within the heavenly tabernacle, and his role as the one whose sacrificial self-offering initiates or inaugurates the new covenant (7.27; 9.28; 10.9). Jesus continues to intercede (7.25); he is the guarantee of the better covenant (7.22); and he holds his priesthood eternally (7.24). He has sat down, his sacrificial work complete, but Hebrews can also speak of the future, a time when the Son will once more return, to bring salvation to those who await him (9.28).

Hebrews explicitly credits Christ as having come into the world to do God's will (10.5–9). But such credit is derived from an appeal to Psalm 40.6–8, and specifically a psalm voiced by Christ; Scriptures are put onto the lips of Jesus. Elsewhere in the epistle, Scripture is put in Jesus' mouth (Heb. 2.12–13) and treated in the same fashion as that spoken by God or the Holy Spirit. Hebrews therefore portrays Jesus not only as the one who interprets Scripture, and does so about himself, but also as one who actually speaks the words in the same vein as divine speech. Indeed, Aitken's conclusion seems most plausible: 'we may say that Hebrews portrays Jesus – a cosmic figure now seated in heaven (Heb. 1.3) – as one who performs the authoritative text in a way that makes himself and his experience the authoritative principle of interpretation'.[22] Israel's story is reconfigured around him.

Identity: Jesus – the human 'high priest'

It remains the case, though, that Jesus' humanity is fundamental to the epistle's message and intrinsic to the efficacy of his high-priestly

---

[22] Ellen Bradshaw Aitken, 'Tradition in the Mouth of the Hero: Jesus as an Interpreter of Scripture', in *Performing the Gospel: Orality, Memory, and Mark*, ed. Richard A. Horsley, Jonathan A. Draper and John Miles Foley (Minneapolis: Fortress, 2006) 97–103 (102).

activity. Indeed, one might argue that, of all the canonical non-evangelical testimony (and maybe even including the canonical Gospel accounts), no other NT text places more significance on Jesus' human identity.[23] He is portrayed as one who is able to sympathize with the audience's testing because he himself was tested in every way (4.15), and is able to secure the salvation of his sisters and brothers (2.10–11) because he shares in their very humanity. He is the faithful, empathetic, consummate elder brother, responsible for his siblings, bonded with them (2.12–14) and able to bring about their freedom (2.15).[24] Hebrews emphasizes how Jesus' focus is upon helping humanity, rather than (heavenly) angels (2.16); he makes atonement for the people (2.17) and must therefore be 'human' so to do. Particularly in terms of the presentation of 5.5–10, there is no question that Jesus is not 'a fully self-conscious, thinking, willing human being'.[25]

The human Jesus first comes to the fore in the second chapter of the epistle where, in quoting Psalm 8 LXX, the writer exploits the ambiguous phrase 'son of man' (i.e. human being – 2.6–8) to rhetorically shift focus to Jesus and to the necessity of his humanity. Such a play on the phrase s/Son of m/Man may therefore reflect knowledge of Jesus tradition in which Jesus was associated with that title.[26] The emergence of the title and its origins (or otherwise) with Jesus of Nazareth is a complicated scholarly discussion that is beyond our purview here, and the limited appeal to the title by Hebrews cautions against making any significant assumptions as to this designation. However, it is noticeable both that Hebrews

---

[23] Johnson, *Living Jesus* 94. See further Bart D. Ehrman, *Did Jesus Exist? The Historical Argument for Jesus of Nazareth* (New York: HarperOne, 2012) 116–17, where he includes a long list of references in Hebrews to Jesus' earthly/human activity.

[24] On the fraternal characterization of Jesus in Hebrews, see Patrick Gray, 'Brotherly Love and the High Priest Christology of Hebrews', *JBL* 122 (2003) 335–51.

[25] Bruce L. McCormack, '"With Loud Cries and Tears": The Humanity of the Son in the Epistle to the Hebrews', in *The Epistle to the Hebrews and Christian Theology*, ed. Richard Bauckham, Daniel R. Driver, Trevor A. Hart and Nathan MacDonald (Grand Rapids: Eerdmans, 2009) 37–68 (63).

[26] So Donald A. Hagner, 'The Son of God as Unique High Priest: The Christology of the Letter to the Hebrews', in *Contours of Christology in the New Testament*, ed. Richard N. Longenecker, McMaster New Testament Studies (Grand Rapids: Eerdmans, 2005) 246–67 (253).

makes no further mention of the link (therefore suggesting that it had sourced it from elsewhere), and yet the association with Jesus can be so rapidly drawn in the rhetorical move.

What, then, does Hebrews know of the life of the human Jesus? Bearing in mind the apparent distance – geographical, temporal or human – between the letter and Jesus' ministry, there is perhaps a surprising amount of detail in the letter, more than one might expect. Such detail may not be 'new' or extra to the Gospel accounts, but it may be seen as confirming information also located therein. Hebrews is very interested – and indeed *has* to be so – in Jesus 'in the flesh' (5.7); while the epistle will recount the activity of the heavenly high priest, such heavenly actions only have value or efficacy because of the human activity of the earthly Jesus. Recalling such fleshly existence, Hebrews speaks of Jesus offering up prayers and supplications to God (5.7), and the likelihood is that this reflects the broad contours of the Passion narrative. The prayers are offered up to the 'one who was able to save him from death' (5.7)[27] and there is therefore the possibility that Hebrews is recalling the Gethsemane moment, and specifically a hesitant Jesus, wary of death and hopeful in some way that it might be avoided (cf. Mark 14.34–36). Loud cries accompany the prayers, however, and these could be understood as portraying a more confident Jesus in Gethsemane, or at least one not necessarily *fearful* of his impending death (5.7–8 need not imply any apprehension on Jesus' part).[28] If it is the *intensity* of the experience that Hebrews has in mind, rather than Jesus' uncertainty, it may be that Hebrews reflects the Lucan version of the Gethsemane episode (Luke 22.41–44).[29] Or, in view of the *loud* cries and tears, it may recall tradition of Jesus' words from the cross, even though the explicit

---

[27] On the difficulty of how Jesus' cries were 'heard', but without saving him from death, see Harold W. Attridge, *The Epistle to the Hebrews*, Hermeneia (Philadelphia: Fortress, 1989) 149–50.

[28] Dale C. Allison, Jr., *Constructing Jesus: Memory, Imagination, and History* (London: SPCK, 2010) 417n10, ventures that Heb. 5.7–8 portrays a Gethsemane Jesus halfway between Markan apprehension and Johannine confidence.

[29] Laws, 'Hebrews' 330. This possibility is attractive bearing in mind the suggestion that Luke may have contributed to the authorship of Hebrews, but the disputed textual integrity of Luke 22.43–44 cautions against confidence in such a relationship.

logia are not named, and therefore Golgotha, rather than Gethsemane, is the scene of Jesus' prayers.[30]

Whatever the specific event, Hebrews underscores the depth and reality of the suffering Jesus endured in his death, and ascribes some formational or pedagogical efficacy to the experience; Jesus *learnt* obedience through such suffering (5.8) and was perfected by such experience (5.9).[31] This perfection terminology is an important theme within Hebrews, and it is striking that the one who is sinless (4.15) still awaits 'perfection' (5.9); the term probably has the sense of 'completion', that Jesus was completed through his obedience to suffering. Hence Jesus' humanity matters, not only for his capacity to empathize with the suffering of humanity but also because it is fundamental to how Sonship is given expression. Hebrews thus 'daringly suggests that the human Jesus grew progressively into the full stature of being God's Son',[32] that there was an increasing manifestation or presence of God within Jesus as his life ensued. In Hebrews, Jesus emerges as a 'Son of God who was perfected as Son precisely through his humanity'.[33]

In terms of events in the life of the earthly Jesus, it is, then, his death that Hebrews finds of most interest. Through his death, he has beaten the one who exercises power in death – that is, the devil (2.14). But other detail is still forthcoming. Hebrews knows of Jesus' Judaic lineage (7.14) and makes no effort to hide or ignore such information, however difficult it makes the epistle's subsequent argument. Indeed, the very fact that the letter deals with the lineage question – and works to remove it from being a significant stumbling block to Jesus' high-priestly characterization – suggests that such a datum was well recognized and known to the audience. To put it another way, Jesus' Judaic lineage fulfils the criterion of embarrassment; it would have been far easier for Hebrews just

---

[30] Christopher Richardson, 'The Passion: Reconsidering Hebrews 5.7–8', in *A Cloud of Witnesses: The Theology of Hebrews in its Ancient Contexts*, ed. Richard Bauckham, Trevor Hart, Nathan MacDonald and Daniel Driver, Library of New Testament Studies 387 (London: T&T Clark, 2008) 51–67.

[31] On the important theme of perfection in Hebrews, see David Peterson, *Hebrews and Perfection*, SNTSMS 47 (Cambridge: Cambridge University Press, 1982).

[32] Johnson, *Hebrews* 54.

[33] Johnson, *Hebrews* 56.

to 'invent' a person that fitted the bill in terms of Levitical – or Zadokite – qualification and then to apply Melchizedekian qualification at that point, or even to make no mention of the lineage at all. The fact that this does not happen therefore suggests that Jesus was remembered for being of Judaic lineage and that that was an important part of its testimony.[34] The acknowledgement that such information was 'evident' (7.14) also points to its being an established piece of information within early Church circles.

It is hard to discern whether Hebrews evinces further knowledge of Jesus tradition. The letter makes much of Jesus' testing (2.18; 4.15; 5.7–8), and the encouragement this should give to the audience in their sufferings, but the locus for such testing tends to be at the occasion of his death (cf. 2.17–18). Likewise, the reference in 4.15 is somewhat allusive and may merely reflect the writer's wish to show Jesus as a fully empathetic human being. At the same time, Hebrews may also have in mind the temptation narratives as part of this paraenesis; Hebrews does recognize that the devil is beaten (2.14) – commensurate with the Synoptic account (especially Luke) that the temptation narrative anticipates Jesus' victory over the devil in his Passion (Luke 4.13). One other possible reference occurs in Hebrews 2.3. While the referent of the phrase is ambiguous, the declaration that the Lord announced *salvation* is intriguing. Salvation tends to be a more future- than present-orientated concept in Hebrews (cf. 9.28),[35] and it may reflect a more general statement about the whole salvation event, particularly in view of the use of speech in Hebrews to illustrate God's activity in respect of humanity. However, it is not impossible that some reference to Jesus speaking about salvation matters (Luke 19.10 perhaps?) formed part of the (spoken) discourse for which Jesus was remembered during his earthly ministry.

In terms of his life, then, it is Jesus' Passion with which Hebrews seems most familiar, and the letter's references to him are generally confined to that particular locus. The event or physical experience

---

[34] It also sits well with the notion of Davidic kingship.
[35] See Scott D. Mackie, *Eschatology and Exhortation in Hebrews*, WUNT 2.223 (Tübingen: Mohr Siebeck, 2007) 100–1.

of Jesus' death is alluded to in Hebrews 12.3–4, part of a comparison between the respective suffering on his part and on that
of the audience. The latter, it seems, have experienced some form
of suffering (10.32–34), but not yet to the point of shedding blood
(12.4); Jesus, by contrast, has seemingly shed blood, in accordance,
I suggest, with his cruciform death (12.2). While the majority of
the letter's references to the shedding of blood are in service
of the sacrificial imagery being conveyed, and while there is no
explicit reference to the mode of Jesus' crucifixion, the comparison
being drawn in 12.2–4 implicitly suggests that Hebrews thought
that Jesus' death involved some form of bloodshed (i.e. that it
was more than just a hanging by a rope until death arrived).[36]
Hebrews 12.3 is also notable for its suggestion of Jesus experiencing hostility from sinners. Because of the parallel with 12.4 (sin/
hostility/Jesus compared with sin/blood/audience), such hostility
is presumably that experienced as part of Jesus' death. The identity of the 'sinners' is a moot point: it could be a generic human
designation (i.e. differentiating him, the sinless one (4.15; 7.26),
from the rest of sinful humanity), and bearing in mind the letter's
atonement thinking elsewhere, that is a likely scenario. But also
bearing in mind the letter's thoroughgoing Jewishness, it is possible that 'sinners' designates Gentiles, thereby referring to Jesus'
death at the hands of the Roman authorities (cf. 1 Cor. 2.6, 8). If
so, then it is similarly possible that the exhortation to lift weak
knees and be healed (Heb. 12.12; alluding to Isa. 35.3) may reflect
or echo the Jesus tradition that his legs were not broken as he was
found to be already dead (John 19.32–33).

Perhaps the most significant aspect of the letter's Passion testimony concerns the location of Jesus' death outside the city gate
(13.12). William Lane concurs that 13.12 is 'an implicit reference
to the historical event of Jesus' death on Golgotha',[37] and such a
suggestion seems highly plausible; it was, after all, common practice for crucifixion to happen outside the populated part of a city,

---

[36] See the similar argument for Paul in Chapter 3.
[37] William L. Lane, *Hebrews 1—8; Hebrews 9—13*, 2 vols, WBC 47A–47B (Dallas: Word, 1991) 2.541.

and such a location also accords with the Johannine siting of Jesus' death (John 19.16–18; cf. also Mark 15.2–22). Both texts emphasize the outward trajectory from Jerusalem, and the leaving behind of the city confines. Some have suggested that the reference in 13.12 is driven by the Day of Atonement reference (cf. Lev. 16.27),[38] and such imagery is relevant up to a point; but equally there is no reason not to believe that Hebrews knows of and reflects 'historical' tradition, and merely exploits the Yom Kippur coincidence of that association for paraenetic purposes. After all, there is a fundamental distinction between the death of Jesus (outside the camp) and that of the animals on the Day of Atonement (where they actually die inside, but their carcasses are subsequently taken outside). Such dissimilarity would suggest that history has not been conformed to the Levitical account, but rather reflects the remembered reality of Jesus' death. The ambiguous reference to the altar (13.10) may also be a metonym for the Golgotha crucifixion.[39]

We might press the historical reflection even further, specifically in three related directions. First, it is feasible that Hebrews 13.11–14 recalls tradition regarding Jesus' own cross-bearing activity.[40] John's Gospel notably has Jesus carrying his own cross (John 19.17), different from the Synoptic account where Simon of Cyrene fulfils that function (Mark 15.21 pars). While the resolution of that tension will remain a historical quandary, the Johannine emphasis on Jesus controlling his own destiny is certainly upheld by Jesus' own cross-bearing mantle. Hebrews shares John's 'Jesus-in-control' perspective – the 'active' high-priestly role Jesus assumes surely demands that that be the case. It also demands that others follow him 'outside the camp' and bear the abuse he bore (13.13). The precise imagery of 13.12–13 remains contested, particularly the phrase 'outside the camp', but it surely includes some reference to Jerusalem, and therefore the exhortation for others to (however symbolically) replay the death-bound journey of Jesus outside

---

[38] Laws, 'Hebrews' 330; for an alternative view, see David M. Allen, 'Why Bother Going Outside? The Use of the Old Testament in Heb 13.10–16' (forthcoming).

[39] Marie E. Isaacs, 'Hebrews 13:9–16 Revisited', *NTS* 43 (1997) 268–84 (280).

[40] Lane, *Hebrews* 2.543.

the city. The 'outsideness' may also recall the parable of the vineyard, and specifically Matthew 21.39/Luke 20.15.[41] Within the parable, the son is sent into the vineyard (note the frequent designation of Jesus as Son par excellence; Jesus the Son also learnt obedience through suffering – cf. Heb. 5.8), but is thrown outside the vineyard (symbolically Jerusalem) and then killed outside – the same ordering that Hebrews ascribes.

Second, Hebrews's portrayal of the crucifixion, albeit tangentially so, seems historically credible. It depicts crucifixion as a public activity, as something that bore 'shame' (12.2). Whereas such a reference might also pick up the cultural shame of a worthy one who faced imminent death, there seems no reason not to view it as addressing the very shameful nature of the event itself. Hebrews is interested in the historical 'event' that is the crucifixion, and seeks to preserve its shame-bearing or shocking aspect. The exhortation to follow Jesus outside the camp also, I suggest, retains that public, shameful, shame-bearing dimension; the full force of the event is captured.[42] While the exhortation is delivered with some rhetorical or homiletical flourish, as we might surely expect from the preacher to the Hebrews, the exhortation requires knowledge of the public, shameful death that Jesus experienced for it to work.

Third, this exhortation to follow Jesus 'outside' the camp (13.13) and to leave behind the security and sanctity of Israel's holy places, probably reflects an exhortation to embrace those on the outside, those on the fringes of society.[43] If this is an allusion to Jesus' (similar) interest in those on the fringes, it is surely an implicit one, but the ethos of Hebrews remains towards those on the outside. The letter's lack of a distinctive, ethical injunction is often critiqued, and its paraenesis is commonly seen as rather generalized. But that may be a misreading of it: in terms similar perhaps to those of James, Hebrews may be seen as constructing

---

[41] See Attridge, *Epistle* 398.

[42] A. Katherine Grieb, 'Outside the Camp: *Imitatio Christi* and Social Ethics in Hebrews 13:10–14', in *Staying One, Remaining Open: Educating Leaders for a 21st-Century Church*, ed. Richard J. Jones and J. Barney Hawkins (New York: Morehouse, 2010) 109–23 (116).

[43] See further Grieb, 'Outside the Camp'.

a social existence of marginalization, a 'not conforming' to the way of the world.[44] While not being directly credited to Jesus, two factors suggest that there is some patterning or allusion to the earthly Jesus operative here. First, Hebrews exhorts its readers to model their lives on the behaviour or identity of their leaders (13.7, 17); they are to mimic those in authority over them. There is the sense, though, as we have seen, that Jesus is their leader par excellence, and the appeal of 13.7 probably includes him within its broader purview. After all, the next verse bespeaks Jesus (13.8), not, as has often been observed, in terms of an unchanging Christology but rather as a leader figure whose exemplar is consistent, steady and constant. It is the *pistis* – the faithfulness – of the leaders that believers are to model, and it is Jesus' faithfulness to which they should primarily aspire (cf. 3.2, 6). Second, the marginality discourse to which Hebrews commends its readers, one that attends to those in prison (10.34; 13.3), to those on the fringes of society (10.33) and to the stranger (13.2), is distinctive. Such a disposition sits particularly well with the Lucan portrayal of Jesus and it is further suggested that the 'life of Jesus' (however faintly sketched in the letter) forms a framework for the ethic that Hebrews espouses.

The other 'event' of Jesus' life on which Hebrews (surprisingly) does not draw more is the resurrection. There are some hints in the epistle that suggest Hebrews knows of the resurrection tradition, notably 13.20, though many have contested whether that reference is indeed original to the text. Likewise, the claim that Abraham received Isaac back from the dead (11.19) suggests a reading of that narrative that has been informed by the resurrection tradition. The reference to Jesus' prayers being 'heard' (5.7) may also be an oblique pointer to the resurrection. But generally speaking, Hebrews has been viewed as reluctant to exploit the resurrection tradition, with the cross and exaltation instead being the key points of interest. That said, recent scholarship has begun

---

[44] See Knut Backhaus, 'How to Entertain Angels: Ethics in the Epistle to the Hebrews', in *Hebrews: Contemporary Methods, New Insights*, ed. Gabriella Gelardini, *BibInt* 75 (Leiden: Brill, 2005) 149–75.

to challenge such assumptions, with some suggesting that the resurrection 'holds a central place in the explanation of Jesus' atoning work in Hebrews'.[45]

Throughout the epistle, and particularly in his earthly work, Jesus is held up as a faithful and merciful high priest (2.17), and this twofold designation summarizes Hebrews's Jesusology *in nuce*. His mercy is shown through his capacity to empathize with the recipients' situation, as one who had been tested in every way. He can meet them in their 'time of need' (4.16), and believers can be partners or partakers of him (3.14). But Jesus is also the truly faithful one – he stands at the climax of the list of those who acted 'by faith' (11.1—12.2) – and he models paradigmatically what it means faithfully to carry out what God had called him to do (10.5–9). In a letter where the possibility and consequence of apostasy are set forth, where the example of faithlessness is offered (3.7—4.11), Jesus comes forth as the one who is supremely faithful (10.23), who did not fall away and who has successfully gone beyond the curtain; he is 'one who trusts in God and is trustworthy before God'.[46] Indeed, it is possible to read Hebrews 12.2 as saying that Jesus is the 'pioneer of faithfulness', the one who both inaugurates and defines what being faithful comprises. Held up for such exemplary faithfulness, particularly in his suffering, Jesus' obedience unto death is a foundational aspect of such fidelity; aligning him with the faithful of the past (Heb. 11.1—12.2), Hebrews presents its readers with a Jesus who is the model of faithful living,[47] and it is thus hard to say that the NT epistles have *no* role for Jesus' life.

Moreover, bearing in mind the situation of the readers as a people suffering some form of pressure, and who have previously done so, Jesus' example as one who *endures* may be significant. Within the epistle, the verb (*hupomeno*) is used four times, twice of Jesus (12.2, 3) and twice of the audience (10.32; 12.7). Of Jesus, Hebrews recalls how he endured the cross (12.2), and it may be,

---

[45] Moffitt, *Atonement* 296.

[46] Still, 'Christos as "Pistos"' 754.

[47] See also Bertram L. Melbourne, 'An Examination of the Historical-Jesus Motif in the Epistle to the Hebrews', *AUSS* 26 (1988) 281–97.

as suggested above, that 12.3 reflects his endurance at the hands of sinners who put him to death.[48] But it is equally possible, particularly bearing in mind the shared verb, that the hostility he bore parallels that experienced by the audience. That is, the retelling of the experiences of the audience (10.32–34) may reflect that which Hebrews (and its readers) knew of Jesus' own experience, and his 'modelling' of what it meant to faithfully endure paralleled their own experience of similar circumstances. Such an association is certainly only implicit, but the common verbal idea invites it, and it opens up the possibility that the readers knew more of Jesus' earthly experience than the letter actually tells us.

Conclusion: the Jesus of Hebrews

Anyone hoping to mine Hebrews for extended biographical information about Jesus will be disappointed, for such pondering is not the epistle's agenda. One might well expect, for example, Hebrews to appeal to the Temple incident as Jesus 'evidencing' the demise of the sacrificial system,[49] but the epistle remains silent on any such claim. Likewise, we might have anticipated some comment on Jesus' engagement with, or response to, the high priesthood or the efficacy (or otherwise) of the sacrificial system, but again the epistle offers nothing in this regard.

But that does not mean that Jesus – human or otherwise – is not central to the epistle; indeed, quite the reverse. Jesus remains pivotal to the whole narrative retelling of Hebrews. Israel's story is reconfigured around the one who is hero par excellence, and other figures of the Jewish tradition are accommodated to him (cf. 12.1–3). Isaac becomes received back from the dead (11.19), while Moses is identified as bearing the reproach of Christ (11.26) and is patterned according to him. The story of Israel gets reworked in the light of the Jesus tradition, and Jesus becomes the focal

---

[48] L. W. Hurtado, 'Jesus' Death as Paradigmatic in the New Testament', *SJT* 57 (2004) 413–33 (422–3), thus opines that the portrayal of Jesus' death in Hebrews reflects the situation of the believers; his death is both 'redemptive and paradigmatic'.

[49] Though the issues are different: for Hebrews, the issue is the inefficacy of the sacrificial system; for the Gospels, the system has been abused.

point or pivot about which Israel's story is reinterpreted and fulfilled. In a text focused around the Jewish Scriptures, and one in which such Scriptures are interpreted in the light of Jesus, he becomes the fulfilment of the story, the one who inaugurated the new covenant and thereby rendered the old covenant 'old'.

The 'Jesus remembered' in Hebrews is a Jesus in which both 'divine' and 'human' meet, co-exist and flourish. Jesus is depicted as one who is both worshipped and an empathetic elder brother, and as one who is simultaneously heavenly priest seated at the right hand of God and fellow pilgrim along the way. Jesus is presented as one who is uniquely empathetic, whose humanity matters, who can identify with his fellow sisters and brothers in their weakness and testing. To put it another way: 'the book of Hebrews moves easily between the poles of the faith and obedience of Jesus on the one hand and the worship of Jesus on the other with little sense of any tension between them. And it does so with designations such as Son, and images, such as Jesus' suffering and temptation, that come straight from the story of Jesus himself.'[50]

---

[50] Marianne Meye Thompson, 'Jesus and His God', in *The Cambridge Companion to Jesus*, ed. Markus N. A. Bockmuehl, Cambridge Companions to Religion (Cambridge: Cambridge University Press, 2001) 41–55 (54).

6

'The remembered teacher': Jesus in James

Martin Luther's so-called 'epistle of straw' has come in from the cold in recent years. There is an emerging interest in the letter, in both Church and academy alike, and a fresh attention, therefore, to its wisdom character and to its focus on right action or 'ortho-praxy'. While the inevitable comparisons with Paul on questions of justification still linger – rightly or wrongly – the epistle is increasingly heard on its own terms, and for its own particular and distinctive witness within the canonical testimony. Within the NT corpus, it has a particular interest in liberation theology (its attention to the poor, e.g. – 2.1–9, 14–16), but the text also exhibits other characteristic and distinctive features: it has much to say, for example, on the role of the tongue (3.1–12), and notably recounts the regular practice of healing within a local church context (5.13–16). Following on from the similar re-evaluation of the Pauline corpus, a 'new perspective' on James is emerging, one that enables the hearing of the text as another representative view (alongside Paul, Peter and John) of the supposed senior figures of the early Church.

This rediscovery of James, however, has tended to bypass questions relating to the identity of Jesus Christ and/or the portrayal of Jesus within the epistle. Such neglect is under-standable, up to a point, for as we will see, the letter's explicit references to Jesus and/or Christ are few and far between. James has therefore come to be seen as characteristically *disinterested* in Jesus, and we notice a consequent lacuna in the scholarly treatment of Jacobean Jesusology or Christology. With appar-ently so little upon which to comment, scholarly books on New Testament Christology often lack any entry on the letter of

James.[1] John Reumann, for example, charged with exploring the Christology of James, compares it with the task of working with a series of blank pages, noting the absence of any 'kerygmatic Christology about the meaning of Jesus' death and resurrection'.[2] In short, the epistle simply makes no mention of Jesus' death (the central, era-marking datum for both Paul and Hebrews), let alone his life, deeds or ministry. Yet at the same time the letter possesses a number of parallels or allusions to Jesus' teaching, probably more so than any other NT text, and we therefore sense that the voice of Jesus is still somehow heard, even if he himself is not explicitly named. Indeed, the scale of these allusions makes the lack of formal reference to Jesus, and the absence of any attribution of the teaching to him, all the more surprising. This (apparent) disparity warrants further investigation, suggesting that the treatment of Jesus in James is actually more nuanced and sophisticated than people have often tended to think.

The epistle of James, the 'historical James' and the 'historical Jesus'

For reasons that will soon become clear, some clarification as to the source of the letter has significant implications for what we think the text might have to say regarding Jesus. The epistle itself identifies its author as 'James' (Jas. 1.1). The lack of any other further clarification as to who he is (beyond being a servant of God and of the Lord Jesus Christ – 1.1) would suggest this (implied) figure is intended to be the so-called James the Just, brother of Jesus[3] and the one subsequently identified as 'bishop'

---

[1] Frank J. Matera, *New Testament Christology* (Louisville: Westminster John Knox, 1999), and C. M. Tuckett, *Christology and the New Testament: Jesus and His Earliest Followers* (Louisville: Westminster John Knox, 2001), would be two recent examples.

[2] John Reumann, 'Christology of James', in *Who Do You Say That I Am? Essays on Christology*, ed. Mark Allan Powell and David R. Bauer (Louisville: Westminster John Knox, 1999) 128–39 (135).

[3] We will not get into questions of whether this is Jesus' brother or half-brother. For further discussion of such matters, see Richard J. Bauckham, 'The Family of Jesus', in *Jesus Amongst Friends and Enemies: A Historical and Literary Introduction to Jesus in the Gospels*, ed. Chris Keith and Larry W. Hurtado (Grand Rapids: Baker, 2011) 103–25.

of Jerusalem within the tradition. To be known solely as 'James' suggests a figure sufficiently well known to be identified just by his first name (consider the modern equivalents of, say, Elvis or Madonna), and on such a basis James the Just is really the only conceivable candidate. Scholars continue to debate whether this James might be the legitimate author of the letter or whether the designation is pseudonymous, and contrasting positions are subsequently adopted. Peter Davids, for example, avers that 'from the literary point of view the implied author is James, brother of Jesus',[4] but this rather depends upon how one defines 'literary point of view'. While, as we shall see, James reflects and passes on much Jesus tradition and wisdom, thereby secondarily establishing its own particular 'Jesus portrait', the text itself makes no fraternal claim. For the sake of what is to come, we will work on the basis that James the Just is in some way associated with the letter (however minimally or pseudonymously), if only to test out how that impacts, or otherwise, on its depiction of Jesus. Who or what, then, is the Jacobean Jesus?

It is worth restating at the outset that James's own self-designation is somewhat minimal. The text itself purports to derive from nothing more than a 'servant' of the Lord Jesus Christ (1.1), and no fraternal relationship with Jesus is implied. Similarly salient for our purposes is the epistle's very limited explicit mention of Jesus, be that in terms of his earthly ministry or Christological role/function. If the letter was connected with Jesus' brother, however figuratively, one might well expect 'James' to exploit that fraternal familiarity and contain more specific reference to Jesus.[5] But in explicit terms at least, it simply does not do so. Many have thus speculated that the text is an ideal forum for interfaith dialogue, as its more ethical bent provides fertile ground for a number of faith traditions,

---

[4] Peter H. Davids, 'James and Jesus', in *The Jesus Tradition outside the Gospels*, ed. David Wenham, Gospel Perspectives 5 (Sheffield: JSOT Press, 1985) 63–84 (66).

[5] Indeed, the lack of explicit reference to Jesus poses questions as to the potential pseudonymity of James. If 'James' is merely a literary appellation, one might expect more reference to Jesus to justify or support the claims to 'authorship'.

without generating points of difference over potentially divisive Christological claims.[6]

Indeed, James mentions Jesus explicitly just twice.[7] The first reference (1.1), as we have seen, is a fairly generic one, and presents Jesus in lordly, Christological terms – both titles are used. It does, though, position Christ almost in parallel to God (i.e. 'servant (lit. 'slave') of God and of the Lord Jesus Christ'), and such parallelism may have implications for how *kurios* is understood elsewhere in the epistle. That is, when James speaks of 'Lord', does he understand God or Christ (or even both at the same time)? The Jesus reference of James 1.1, though, clearly transcends 'history', and there is no implication of any knowledge of the earthly or historical Jesus; it is Christology pure and simple. At the same time, James evidently regards Jesus as *Lord* and views him in a way that approximates to his readers' regard of YHWH; the fact that James can also claim to be a 'slave' of this Jesus is a radical redefinition of Jewish monotheism, within a text that is generally understood to be very 'Jewish' in flavour. The designation of Jesus as Christ also shows that he was interpreted as a messianic figure within what seems to be a Jewish community (cf. the reference to the 'twelve tribes' in 1.1).

James 2.1 – the second (and final, explicit) Jesus reference – is more intriguing. A number of exegetical possibilities exist as to its rendering, and these caution against any overconfidence or certainty regarding interpretative decisions, but 2.1 may be making a direct appeal to Jesus as one who embodies the ethical positions found in the epistle. Like 1.1, 2.1 locates him within Lord/Christ terminology, but the context for the designation is more contested. A cursory comparison of contemporary translations shows the variations in rendering:

- NRSV: 'do you with your acts of favouritism really believe in our glorious Lord Jesus Christ?'

---

[6] That said, James's self-designation as 'servant of the Lord Jesus Christ' (1.1) clearly demarks to whom his loyalty lies.

[7] Such minimalism is a potential argument against pseudepigraphy; one might expect more reference to Jesus the brother if it was indeed a pseudepigraphical text.

- TNIV: 'believers in our glorious Lord Jesus Christ must not show favoritism'
- NASB: 'do not hold your faith in our glorious Lord Jesus Christ with an attitude of personal favoritism'

The NRSV turns the phrase into a question, and assumes that the audience has been showing favouritism of some sort. The TNIV is a declarative statement and makes no such assumption. The NASB is a negative imperative, and hints at the possibility of some act of favouritism on the readers' part. Such syntactical differences apart, however, it is notable that all three translations render the phrase as an 'objective genitive', implying that faith is placed *in* Jesus Christ.

On such a reading, James 2.1 may merely reflect the belief – or otherwise – of the readers in Jesus, and the consequences for such belief in terms of partiality and favouritism.[8] Following Jesus and showing partiality are simply incompatible. At the same time, however, we have seen the debates within Pauline studies regarding the variant renderings of *pistis Christou*, and these suggest that we have here another such instance, but this time with a Jacobean bent. It is possible, and arguably more likely, that the phrase is a subjective genitive, and should instead be understood as akin to 'show no partiality as you hold the faith/faithfulness of our glorious Lord Jesus Christ';[9] that is, Jesus is portrayed as one who is faithful, or whose faithfulness is exemplary. There are several reasons in support of such a reading. First, it is not obvious from elsewhere in the letter as to why James's readers would be exhorted to put their faith *in* Jesus; there is no Passion or messianic

---

[8] See Scot McKnight, *The Letter of James*, NICNT (Grand Rapids: Eerdmans, 2011) 174–80.

[9] On the exegetical discussions of 2.1 and in support of the subjective genitive, see Bruce A. Lowe, 'James 2:1 in the Pistis Christou Debate: Irrelevant or Indispensable?', in *The Faith of Jesus Christ: Exegetical, Biblical, and Theological Studies*, ed. Michael F. Bird and Preston M. Sprinkle (Peabody: Hendrickson, 2009) 239–57; Wesley Hiram Wachob, *The Voice of Jesus in the Social Rhetoric of James*, SNTSMS 106 (Cambridge: Cambridge University Press, 2000) 64–6. For a contrasting perspective, cf. McKnight, *James* 176–80; Richard J. Bauckham, 'James and Jesus', in *The Brother of Jesus: James the Just and His Mission*, ed. Bruce Chilton and Jacob Neusner (Louisville: Westminster John Knox, 2001) 100–37 (133).

characterization of Jesus that would warrant such a faith; and even allowing for the possibility that some of the Jacobean references to Lord refer to Jesus, they wouldn't necessarily require an exercise of faith in him. James has Abraham believing (*episteusen* – the same root verb) *God*, not Jesus (2.23; cf. 2.19). Second, and relatedly, the rest of James 2 – and especially the passage *célèbre* of Abraham and Rahab (2.14–26) – conceives of *pistis* as faithfulness (action/activity), as much as the placing of faith *in* someone. On such a reading, James 2.1 is alluding to a story of Jesus that appeals to him as one whose actions in regard of the poor are exemplary, as someone who paradigmatically did not show partiality (2.1; cf. 2.9). In short, the subjective genitive option does have explanatory power in ways that other options do not yield, setting Jesus as the standard of one who had faith in, and acted faithfully towards, God.[10]

Some may respond that, even if 2.1 were a subjective genitive, it contributes little to the epistle's picture of Jesus, in that James does not explicitly exploit the connection and fails to relate it particularly in terms of earthly Jesus practice. It is other Old Testament figures – Abraham, Rahab, Elijah and Job – who are affirmed for their exhibition of faith,[11] and we might expect a more explicit appeal to Jesus if he were occupying this exemplary function. However, the location of the reference at 2.1 is surely significant, particularly bearing in mind how the first chapter of James is often seen as a kind of table of contents for the epistle. If the latter is the case, then 2.1 sets the scene for the rest of the discourse, a quasi-statement of purpose that is outworked particularly in 2.1–13, but potentially extends throughout the rest of the letter. Perhaps it is best to live with the ambiguity of the phrase, and recognize that James may be referencing Jesus as both the object *and* the exemplar of faith.[12]

---

[10] Lowe, 'James 2:1', makes this argument.

[11] Ian G. Wallis, *The Faith of Jesus Christ in Early Christian Traditions*, SNTSMS 84 (Cambridge: Cambridge University Press, 1995) 175–6.

[12] This seems to be the approach of Luke Timothy Johnson, *Living Jesus: Learning the Heart of the Gospel* (San Francisco: HarperSanFrancisco, 1999) 87, who after translating 2.1 as 'the faith of our glorious Lord Jesus Christ' continues 'faith is most intimately connected with Jesus, *either as its source or as its object*' (my emphasis).

The other factor is the description of Jesus as 'glorious' (2.1), an interesting designation bearing in mind the lack of any other reason elsewhere in the letter to describe Jesus in such terms (particularly in view of James's silence on the resurrection). It could be linked to the Hebrew notion of *kabod* (glory) – that is, the one who manifests what God essentially 'is' – or it may reflect Jesus' present exalted state;[13] James offers little further guidance. But as the only two specific mentions of Jesus occur in 1.1 and 2.1, it is possible that Jesus' glorious status (2.1) echoes the high standing accorded to him in 1.1, and thereby also forges a link back to the twelve tribes, the addressees of the letter (1.1). If so, and if the glory ascription is James rendering some form of messianic credentials upon Jesus, then the question arises whether James has in mind some tradition about the restoration of Israel, and the possibility that such an idea permeated Jesus' teaching.[14] Or to put it another way, the two parallel references may be James's way of saying that one could be a follower of Jesus and still remain foundationally within Judaism; James – and the 'Jesus' he (re-)presents? – could be seen as promoting some form of Jewish Restoration Movement, echoing the Matthaean Jesus' own interest in Israel's restoration (Matt. 10.5–6; 19.28–29; note how, in 19.28, the Son of Man judges the twelve tribes while seated in glory). The epistle, after all, exhibits no apparent interest in Gentile matters, and remains a fundamentally Jewish text.[15]

Beyond James 1.1 and 2.1, there may be other references to Jesus, albeit indirectly so. The ambiguous mention of the 'excellent name' that is being blasphemed (2.7) could be that of Jesus,[16] particularly bearing in mind how 2.1 sets up the concept, but there is no pressing requirement for that to be the case. Likewise, the

---

[13] McKnight, *James* 178–9.

[14] Wachob, *Voice of Jesus* 69n27, makes the association between 1.1 and 2.1, and hints at the possible implications for the historical Jesus proclaiming the restoration of Israel. On Jesus' proclamation of Israel's redemption, and the association with the twelve tribes, see E. P. Sanders, *The Historical Figure of Jesus* (London: Penguin, 1993) 184–7.

[15] See further Patrick J. Hartin, 'James and the Jesus Tradition', in *The Catholic Epistles and Apostolic Traditions*, ed. Karl-Wilhelm Niebuhr and Robert W. Wall (Waco: Baylor University Press, 2009) 55–70 (65–7).

[16] Reumann, 'Christology' 132.

referent of 'Lord' (4.15) is ambiguous, but there is no contextual reason to think that Jesus is specifically in view. The near coming of the Lord (5.8) may have Jesus in mind, and if so it echoes the Jesus tradition of Matthew 24.42–44 (which was also located in 1 Thess. 5.2), but this is only a possibility. More enticing is the *kurios* reference of James 5.16, occurring within the pithy 'healing' discourse of 5.14–16. The unit is significant of itself for its testimony to the practice of healing within the early Church, and the lack of any need to justify such practice. It is merely presented as a given, with the accompanying instructions – the 'how to do so' – seeming to be more James's concern. Significantly for our interests, the Lord is invoked as the one who will raise up the sick. While it is 'Lord' rather than Jesus who is explicitly specified here, and while Elijah is specified as the exemplar in this regard, the association with healing is intriguing: if indeed Jesus is understood as the subject of Lord, then this resonates with Jesus enacting his own ministry of healing, associating such healing with the forgiveness of sins (the 'elders' of the Church carry on Jesus' ministry in the same way that James carries on Jesus' teaching).[17] Although Acts 3.2–8 makes a similar connection, James would be notable in this regard, as the other NT letters make barely any use of the Jesus/miracle tradition (though cf. Heb. 2.3–4).

James and the Jesus tradition

Were the Jacobean Jesus merely just about locating specific references to Jesus' name, then even with the most optimistic application of 2.1, we would surely end up with a fairly limited picture, a faint portrait at the very best. However, James's remembrance of Jesus goes beyond such limitations, in that the epistle shares a lot of 'teaching' attributed to Jesus elsewhere within the Gospel accounts. Even a cursory reading of the epistle by someone familiar with the Synoptic material, and thus having their 'Jesus radar' on, will quickly identify points of comparison and similarity, and 'no

---

[17] Cf. Bauckham, 'James and Jesus' 135: 'Just as Jesus had healed the sick during his ministry, so he continues to do in his activity as exalted Lord.'

one who has read James carefully can avoid the impression that this letter breathes the air of the Sermon on the Mount'.[18] Indeed, discussion of allusions to Jesus tradition in James is not a new phenomenon within scholarly research, with the recognition of such matters going well back into the nineteenth century. As such, it is not so much *whether* or not James recalls and reappropriates Jesus logia, but *how* much it does so, and what significance or implication we might draw from it.

Trying to categorize or quantify the allusions to earlier tradition is a complex and contested task, however, what Luke Timothy Johnson terms 'an invitation to a hazardous and necessarily tentative examination'.[19] James generally weaves source material into his own letter without reference to its origin; there is no formal attribution to Jesus, nor any designation of such teachings as in some way dominical logia. Therefore we can only really surmise whether, upon encountering Synoptic parallels, the source is thought to be Jesus of Nazareth himself or (apparently added) non-Jesus material.[20] Yet awareness of such hazards need not limit the exercise, particularly if we acknowledge the nature of the Gospels' own claims; they are seeking to remember Jesus within their own context, rather than being texts whose layers we can peel away to get to the 'real' Jesus. Thus, while debates about the full extent of the Jacobean parallels and their significance will continue, it is hard to avoid the conclusion that a number of them do exist. And while it is *possible* that such parallels merely derive from common sources unrelated to Jesus, the sheer number of 'would-be coincidences' makes that option somewhat unlikely. After all, in the Gospels at least, the material is associated with Jesus, and thus '[i]t is quite possible that some of these sayings and injunctions were known to James as sayings

---

[18] Johnson, *Living Jesus* 88.

[19] Luke Timothy Johnson and Wesley Wachob, 'The Sayings of Jesus in the Letter of James', in *Brother of Jesus, Friend of God: Studies in the Letter of James*, ed. Luke Timothy Johnson (Grand Rapids: Eerdmans, 2004) 136–54 (136).

[20] Johnson and Wachob, 'Sayings' 136. Such a perspective may derive much from Johnson's own perspective on the relative value of the historical Jesus quest; see further Johnson, *Living Jesus*.

of Jesus'.[21] Furthermore, the sheer volume of the parallels to the Jesus tradition warrants taking seriously the fact that such parallels are more than just accident, but rather form the foundation of how the Jacobean Jesus is shaped, particularly as we might argue that 'each major paragraph in the epistle contains one or more allusion ... and that in every paragraph the allusion(s) supports the main point'.[22]

Let us consider a few examples of such parallels,[23] noting that the allusions manifest themselves in different ways, with some being more specific than others. For example, James 1.2–4 bears a strong thematic similarity to Matthew 5.11–12 (cf. Luke 6.23, 31) and the vindicatory aspect of testing and persecution. Likewise, James's exhortation to ask a generous God for wisdom (1.5; cf. 4.2–3) is thematically similar to the Sermon on the Mount exhortation to 'ask and it shall be given' (Matt. 7.7). While the Matthaean example lacks the wisdom context found in James, it remains the case that, in both instances, the exhortation is to ask God in the expectation that what is asked for will ultimately be forthcoming. Probably the closest James/Jesus link, however, and one with some strong lexical similarity, is James 5.12/Matt. 5.33–37, and almost all scholars would see some form of allusion or appropriation operative here.[24] Nowhere else are oaths forbidden in the Hebrew Bible or the New Testament, and while the verbs are not the same, the context is similar in both instances – the exhortation to refrain from swearing an oath is followed by a positive affirmation to do something 'in the immediate future'.[25] Johnson poses the question of which tradition is earlier (assuming that neither James nor Matthew knew each other), and concludes both that Matthew is

---

[21] Helmut Koester, *Ancient Christian Gospels: Their History and Development* (London: SCM Press, 1990) 75.

[22] Davids, 'James and Jesus' 70.

[23] For a suggested list of parallels/allusions, see Davids, 'James and Jesus' 66–7.

[24] Bauckham, 'James and Jesus' 118, for example, argues that this is the only allusion to Jesus tradition in the epistle. (Though note that this is because of his definition of what constitutes an allusion; he still conceives of the letter as exhibiting a core Jacobean presentation of Jesus.)

[25] Johnson and Wachob, 'Sayings of Jesus' 141.

secondary, and that 'the form of Jas 5.12b may be closer to Jesus' original saying'.[26]

But it is perhaps the unit of James 2.1–11 that most encapsulates the Jacobean appropriation of Jesus' teaching. I have already suggested that 2.1 sets forth Jesus as the paradigmatic expression of faithfulness, and the subsequent pericope probably contains at least three specific allusions to Jesus' teaching.[27] The 'feel' of the Synoptic tradition permeates the whole paragraph, particularly in its support for the poor.[28] James 2.5 forms perhaps the closest parallel to Jesus testimony (cf. Matt. 5.3; Luke 6.20) and, for some commentators, represents a more 'accurate' record of Jesus' witness than the Matthaean or Lucan equivalent.[29] The question of each author's sources is a difficult one to resolve, but the parallels between the three texts are significant: all associate the poor with the receipt of the kingdom, and thereby specify that God's kingdom is ultimately for the poor. As such, Johnson concludes that James 2.5 is 'an early, widely known and exploited saying of Jesus'.[30] He further suggests that the Jacobean representation is closer to the Matthaean perspective than the Lucan one (i.e. God does not 'bless' the situation of the poor in the James/Matthew discourse, but does so in Luke);[31] James ensures the inclusion of the poor within the community of faith – therefore exhibiting no partiality – rather than showing a particular preference for the poor (so Luke).

James 2.8 (cf. Matt. 22.39; Mark 12.31; Luke 10.27) continues the link with Jesus tradition. Its quotation of Leviticus 19.18 is the only formal OT citation in the letter, and a case may be made that the whole unit of 19.11–18 permeates the epistle of James

---

[26] Johnson and Wachob, 'Sayings of Jesus' 142.

[27] James 2.5 (Matt. 5.3; Luke 6.20); Jas. 2.8 (Matt. 22.39; Mark 12.31); Jas. 2.10–11 (Matt. 5.19, 21).

[28] On the passage generally, and its appropriation of Jesus rhetoric, see Wachob, *Voice of Jesus* 59–193.

[29] Cf. James B. Adamson, *The Epistle of James*, NICNT (Grand Rapids: Eerdmans, 1976) 109–10.

[30] Johnson and Wachob, 'Sayings of Jesus' 149.

[31] Johnson and Wachob, 'Sayings of Jesus' 150: 'In no sense does James suggest that God's kingdom belongs to the socio-economically poor as a reward for their earthly poverty.'

(and maybe to being James *in nuce*).[32] The text is also, of course, an important one in the Synoptic portrayal of Jesus, both in terms of the particular saying placed on Jesus' lips (Matt. 22.39; Luke 10.27) and in the narrative characterization of Jesus as one who effectively 'lives out' the text. Dale Allison suggests that Leviticus 19 is a 'popular intertext' for other contemporary literature,[33] but the common combination of Leviticus 19 material found in both the Sermon on the Plain (especially Luke 6.27–42) and in the letter of James makes the case for Jacobean reuse of a tradition elsewhere associated with Jesus (and maybe even going back to Jesus himself) all the more plausible.[34] We might suggest, therefore, that James is implicitly claiming the Jesus model for his discourse on the poor, something the Synoptic Jesus likewise models in terms of both words and action. James 2.8 alludes to the (faithful) model of Jesus (cf. 2.1), partly by reflecting the poverty-choice that the incarnation exemplified,[35] partly by embracing the actions and teaching of Jesus, the one who embodies the royal command of Leviticus 19.18. Combining both aspects, 'James has drawn both on Jesus' saying and on the kind of teaching to which Jesus himself was indebted.'[36]

We might note a couple of other, salient observations. First, the discourse on wealth/poverty is the first, or primary 'issue' addressed in the epistle, and is linked to Jesus; this is interesting bearing in mind that the Synoptics render the poor as the focus of Jesus' first beatitude (Matt. 5.3; Luke 6.20). Second, James's appropriation of Jesus tradition shows the capacity for Jesus' teaching to be taken and reapplied in ways that were germane to the particular local context. The precise wording and context have changed – James

---

[32] Luke Timothy Johnson, 'The Use of Leviticus 19 in the Letter of James', *JBL* 101 (1982) 391–401. He makes the following connections: Lev. 19.12/Jas. 5.12; Lev. 19.13/Jas. 5.4; Lev. 19.15/Jas. 2.1, 9; Lev. 19.16/Jas. 4.11; Lev. 19.17/Jas. 5.20; Lev. 19.18/Jas. 5.9.

[33] Dale C. Allison, Jr., *Constructing Jesus: Memory, Imagination, and History* (London: SPCK, 2010) 370–2.

[34] Allison, *Constructing* 380–1.

[35] So Ralph P. Martin, *James*, WBC 48 (Waco: Word Books, 1988) 74: 'The Lord of glory once entered on the human scene, and came not as might be expected in all the regalia of might and majesty but in the lowly garments of a beggar and was refused.'

[36] Bauckham, 'James and Jesus' 119.

is not giving a sermon on the Mount or on the Plain – but the content is recognizably consistent with the material delivered in the two Synoptic scenarios. Jesus tradition was not so fixed that it could not be reworked in a fresh situation or milieu.

We could list further possible parallels in the subsequent verses (Jas. 2.13 – cf. Matt. 5.7; Jas. 2.14–16 – cf. Matt. 25.35–36), or point to similar allusions in the later chapters of the epistle (Jas. 4.10 – cf. Matt. 23.12; Luke 14.11). But for the present, it suffices to draw some broader conclusions. These types of comparison are forged against the Synoptic testimony, and therefore assume such knowledge in order for the comparison to function (as there is no direct attribution to Jesus). But the vast majority of the shared material occurs within the Sermon on the Mount/Sermon on the Plain, and the close proximity of the sayings suggests that Jesus tradition circulated in block form rather than as isolated sayings. Whether James's material is closer to the Matthaean or Lucan traditions, or whether it represented a further community of its own, will continue to be a matter of debate, but the key suggestion remains that James was familiar with a block or corpus of Jesus tradition, rather than just disassociated logia.

It is, of course, possible that James also contains *agrapha*, namely sayings not found elsewhere in the Gospel record, and these may supplement our knowledge of the Jesus tradition. We cannot prove how 'genuine' they may be, but James 3.18 or 4.17, for example, both sound not unlike the kind of utterance that the Jacobean Jesus might have said.[37] And as soon as we begin to identify Jesus tradition within James in terms of logia or sayings, it opens up the possibility of there being other ways by which Jesus is presented within the epistle. It is possible, for example, that the exhortation to resist the devil such that he flees (4.7) refers back to the temptation narrative (Matt. 4.1–11; Luke 4.1–13); the letter itself is themed around the notion of testing (cf. Jas. 1.2–4),[38] and the parallel instruction in James 4.7 relates to submission to God, in effect the threefold response Jesus gives to the devil (Matt. 4.4, 7, 10).

---

[37] Davids, 'James and Jesus' 69.

[38] The term *peirasmos* carries both English senses of 'trial' and 'temptation'.

Such exhortation unto resistance, however, is a relatively common feature of Jewish narrative,[39] and James does not make any formal link to Jesus. Less likely is the possibility that the reference to the death of the 'righteous one' (Jas. 5.6) alludes to the Passion; the phrase is more likely to be a reference to the abuse of the poor, perhaps alluding to the Cain and Abel narrative,[40] or it could bring to mind the death of James the Just (Righteous) himself.

The Jesus behind the Jacobean text

The parallels between James and the Synoptic Jesus teaching are of interest/value, and I have suggested that it is difficult to avoid the conclusion that James does not somehow have the pattern of Jesus in mind as the one whose faithfulness was marked out by deeds, and specifically in respect of the poor. While James doesn't explicitly place Leviticus 19.18 on Jesus' lips, the implication is that he was associated with it, and sought to live out its ethical demand. What, though, does this mean for James's broader presentation of Jesus?

We have, of course, to be somewhat cautious about trying to get behind the canonical text to (re)construct the Jesus behind it. This has been the strategy or *telos* of the Historical Quest over the last couple of centuries, as its practitioners have sought to remove the evangelists' overlay of material and arrive at the real Jesus of Nazareth. It inevitably generates questions about the criteria we use to remove such an overlay, and debates continue as to the legitimacy and efficacy of the exercise. But James's case may be somewhat different, or rather the text itself may invite further consideration of the kind of Jesus it is seeking to remember. Bearing in mind the number of parallels I have identified, it seems

---

[39] It may, for example, be a citation of *T. Naph.* 8.4, though this also has echoes of the temptation narrative with its mention of wild animals and attendant angels – so Craig A. Evans, 'Exorcisms and the Kingdom: Inaugurating the Kingdom of God and Defeating the Kingdom of Satan', in *Key Events in the Life of the Historical Jesus: A Collaborative Exploration of Context and Coherence*, ed. Darrell L. Bock and Robert L. Webb (Grand Rapids: Eerdmans, 2010) 151–79 (161).

[40] See John Byron, 'Living in the Shadow of Cain: Echoes of a Developing Tradition in James 5:1–6', *NovT* 48 (2006) 261–74.

logical to infer that Jesus is being remembered for his sayings, for his teaching and for the type of character he represented. There is a corresponding silence on the cross and resurrection, no mention of Jesus' death, and such silence constructs a portrait of Jesus as more of a teacher or sage, someone remembered for his teaching more than his deeds. As I have noted, within historical Jesus debates, scholars tend to take polarized views as to whether Jesus was an apocalyptic figure announcing the end of the world or whether he was a prophet/sage offering a critique of his society. N. T. Wright labels the respective views the *Schweitzerstrasse* and *Wredebahn*, named after the approaches' historic proponents,[41] and the Jacobean Jesus would very much seem to be travelling on the latter road. There is some expectation of a judgement and Parousia (cf. 5.7–8), and James certainly polarizes friendship with world and friendship with God (4.4), but the 'feel' of the letter is far from apocalyptic, it has to be said – James is not really interested in any particular event of Jesus' life, but rather in the social teaching that he brought forth and symbolized.

For James, therefore, and for the communities addressed by the epistle, the Jesus remembered is one whose teaching mattered. Jesus is clearly more than a teacher – as the high regard of 1.1 and 2.1 dictate – but 'Jesus as teacher' is core to James's epistolary presentation. He embraces Jesus tradition and re-presents it for his own interests; to remember Jesus is to continue in and uphold his teaching in the context that James now addresses. Thus, James becomes a wisdom teacher in the Jesus mould, one who appropriates Jesus teaching to the extent that he almost becomes the voice of Jesus, one who is continuing with Jesus' ministry. This suggests a high view and recognition of Jesus as teacher, as someone to model or imitate, and it also concurs with the significance James elsewhere accords to the role of teacher (3.1). Indeed, James may have in mind – and reflect – Jesus' own declaration about having one teacher (Matt. 23.8), and his suspicion of other so-called teachers (Matt. 23.1–8).[42]

---

[41] N. T. Wright, *Jesus and the Victory of God*, Christian Origins and the Question of God 2 (London: SPCK, 1996) 3–82.

[42] McKnight, *James* 269.

But what sort of teacher is the Jacobean Jesus? Here Richard Bauckham's characterization is helpful.[43] He proposes that James functions as wisdom teacher, and one who – like Jesus – is counter-cultural in his teaching. James, Bauckham suggests, disavows conventional wisdom, the type that consists of how to 'get on' on in life; instead, it promotes a radical take on Torah (2.10), challenges social conventions and structures (1.9–11; 2.1–9; 5.1–5), focuses on a merciful, compassionate God (1.5; 2.13; 5.11) and has a particular focus on the renewal of Israel as God's people (1.1; 2.23; 4.4). Such wisdom teaching is commensurate with that attributed to Jesus within the Gospels, and Bauckham concludes: 'James's wisdom corresponds to the major characteristics and points of focus and emphasis which give the Synoptic teaching of Jesus its distinctiveness.'[44]

James and the historical Jesus

What value does this have for historical construction or for data regarding the earthly Jesus? At one level, one might say that the very negation of any attention to Jesus' life renders James somewhat worthless as a historical Jesus source, and that even to speak of historical Jesus concerns within the epistle is anachronistic, for the text apparently presents itself as essentially uninterested in Jesus' life. But that perhaps misses the point when it comes to formulating James's Jesusology, or when attempting to frame the Jacobean Jesus. It is a text that – in Christological formulation at least – remains fairly minimalist, but our analysis has suggested that the epistle is replete with Jesus tradition, with connections across many parts of the letter, and that there is a particular allusion to Jesus as one who lived out a life of faithfulness. In this sense, then, James is a case in point for the exercise in which we are engaged; it actually gives us a picture of how the earthly Jesus was remembered, a picture that is less bothered about the Jesus of the 'past', and more concerned with the ongoing preservation

---

[43] Bauckham, 'James and Jesus'.
[44] Bauckham, 'James and Jesus' 130.

and application of Jesus' teaching within the present context(s). And furthermore, it is a historical datum that James remembers Jesus in this fashion; just as we noted how Paul chose to remember Jesus in a way that minimizes direct allusion to him, James does likewise, carrying on the Jesus tradition in its own particular fashion, utilizing Jesus' teaching but without naming it as such. Dunn's summation of Paul's and James's use of Jesus tradition is worth restating: Jesus' teaching is 'absorbed into the ethical teaching of Paul and James, so that it has become an integral part of their own paraenesis without any sense that particular exhortations would only be authoritative if explicitly addressed to Jesus'.[45]

To put it another way, the frequent parallels between James and the Gospels require some explanation, and that becomes the charge laid before historians, to explain and interpret the given evidence, thereby giving some 'explanation' for the data encountered. Our analysis would seem to show that James has taken the Jesus testimony of Luke 6.40, 47 at its word – that is, the ultimate way to remember Jesus the teacher and to celebrate his life is for the disciple to become like his teacher, to inhabit his teaching and to act upon it accordingly. James has done as the Lucan Jesus has suggested, but for him to 'accredit' the teaching to Jesus, to ascribe it to him, would be to miss the very point of the exercise, as would be any attempt to recall aspects of Jesus' life. Instead, the absence of any material being attributed to Jesus, it seems, is intentional: James remembers Jesus by donning his garb and presenting his teaching in a way that is distinctive, contextual and relevant to the Jacobean audience, while still remaining 'distinctively Jesus'.[46] To put it another way, 'James's rhetoric uses the Jesus tradition to

---

[45] James D. G. Dunn, *Jesus, Paul, and the Gospels* (Grand Rapids: Eerdmans, 2011) 40.

[46] There are potential parallels here with 2 Peter and Jude. It has been argued that Peter's use of Jude – without attribution – affirms Jude as a figure within the apostolic community, as someone to be 'quoted' – see Gene L. Green, 'Second Peter's Use of Jude: Imitatio and the Sociology of Early Christianity', in *Reading Second Peter with New Eyes: Methodological Reassessments of the Letter of Second Peter*, ed. Robert L. Webb and Duane Frederick Watson, Library of New Testament Studies 382 (London: T&T Clark, 2010) 1–25. Does James's use of Jesus tradition, and its adoption of a (apparently) familiar Jesus character, likewise function as a mark of respect to that figure?

communicate his own voice' and therefore continues 'the thrust of Jesus' mission'.[47]

A helpful modern term to describe this process is that of 'emulation'. Just as a computer emulator takes the image of an original system and places it in a new or different system context, so James takes Jesus' teaching and relocates it afresh, assuming it for himself and his particular situation.[48] As such, James sets forth the possibility of *some* access to the figure of the historical Jesus, even if not on the terms that the historical Jesus project would normally desire. It also follows that we should not get overly concerned about getting back to or reconstructing the historical Jesus. The testimony of James is that the first-century 'Questers' went about historical remembrance in several ways; while preserving Jesus tradition through a more biographical approach was certainly desirable (as the Gospel genre shows), it was equally possible to recall and reappropriate Jesus tradition within new and different situations.

And this 'non-biographical' remembrance still has historical bite. James's construal is, of course, his own re-presentation, but that is true of all accounts of the earthly Jesus (Gospel and non-Gospel); and the volume of allusions to Jesus' teaching invites the conclusion that, through James, we may be able to perceive the contours of the sort of person he 'remembers'. If so, James's Jesus is someone who appeals to the Scriptures, quoting from them where appropriate (cf. Lev. 19), but more generally interweaving them into the discourse. Jesus is a wise teacher who addresses the concerns of contemporary Israel, and is one who is particularly attentive to the poor and matters of social justice. We might well agree with Hartin: 'the thought of this letter is in harmony with

---

[47] Hartin, 'James and the Jesus Tradition' 70. He rightly points out that, while James has made the interpretation and teaching his own, the assumption is that the hearers will be 'reminded of Jesus' voice behind the advice' (61).

[48] McKnight, *James* 26–7, offers a similar parallel with the world of computing, comparing James's use of Jesus to a 'wiki' approach: the view that you take given/established material, but allow for it to be taken forward by subsequent developers. McKnight concludes: 'we stand on sure footings when we conclude that James has made Jesus' teachings his own'.

Jesus' own reassessment of Judaism . . . Through this letter, the reader comes into close contact with Jesus' message, his central vision and the heritage of Judaism.'[49] We might wonder, therefore, whether Jesus himself 'encouraged' others to share and pass on his teaching and expected others to continue his ministry (cf. Matt. 28.19–20).

One final point is worthy of mention. At the beginning of the chapter, we commented on the relationship between the epistle of James and the historical figure of James the Just, brother of Jesus. We noted that the letter does not exploit the fraternal relationship, but that there is the implication of some relationship to James the Just, however pseudonymous. In our subsequent discussion, we have ventured that the text regularly alludes to Jesus' teaching, and rearticulates a not insignificant amount of it. Therefore, if James the Just *was* in some way the 'source' of the letter, he would seem to have become quite familiar with Jesus' teaching, perhaps even being 'among the first disciples who accompanied Jesus and learned his teaching, at least for a significant part of Jesus' ministry'.[50] If that were the case, and it is, of course, just one hypothesis,[51] it would offer a different portrait of Jesus' relationship with his brother than the Gospels are normally thought to present.

Conclusion: the Jacobean Jesus

We might wish that James had been more explicit in his adoption of the Jesus-persona, and given formal citation to Jesus' life and teaching. But as we have noticed already, the NT writers generally seem to eschew such an explicit appeal, and one can only imagine the contested furore of an epistle claiming Jesus' authorship, however pseudonymously stated! Instead, while the Jacobean Jesus may be

---

[49] Hartin, 'James and the Jesus Tradition' 55.

[50] Bauckham, 'James and Jesus' 109. See also John Painter, *Just James: The Brother of Jesus in History and Tradition*, Studies on Personalities of the New Testament (Minneapolis: Fortress, 1999).

[51] The epistle's late attestation in the tradition and its absence from early canonical listings would be counter-arguments in this regard.

a construct of sorts, it retains an integral coherence – Jesus is one who challenges social convention, one whose teaching alludes to scriptural testimony and one who issues a call to faithful orthopraxy as much as to right belief. The letter also suggests that Jesus was remembered as someone who did not show favouritism, who modelled faithfulness, who had a special regard for the poor and who critiqued landowners' abuse of their workers. James's silence on Jesus actually turns out to be very loud.

7

'The model Christian': Jesus in 1 and 2 Peter and Jude

If Hebrews and James offer different and distinctive portraits of Jesus when compared with that of Paul, can the same be said of the two Petrine epistles and the letter authored by Jude? How does the Petrine Jesus compare to the Pauline or Jacobean personifications? Generally adjudged to be later texts, perhaps even dated to the second century, 1 and 2 Peter, along with Jude, are commonly grouped together, partly because of their (apparently) shared author, Peter, and partly because of the material common to the epistles. Although separated canonically by the Johannine letters, Jude remains generally associated with, and treated alongside, 2 Peter, as the two epistles exhibit substantial common material and imagery. Indeed, most scholars think that Jude was a source for 2 Peter, and that the Petrine author has taken Jude's material and reworked it within a fresh context and milieu.

The precise chronology and ordering of the texts, however, is beyond our interest here; my concern is instead to consider the particular portraits of Jesus that the texts yield, especially given that, within the canonical choir, 2 Peter and Jude are frequently forgotten and disregarded. But that may be to the Church's detriment. Perhaps more than any other of the texts we have discussed thus far, this corpus of epistles (and especially 1 Peter) present Jesus as the ideal model to follow, and this is arguably the key contribution of this portion of the NT corpus in terms of their application of Jesus tradition. The term Christian is found in only three places in the NT, and one of them is here (1 Pet. 4.16; cf. Acts 11.26; 26.28), suggestive, perhaps, of a portrayal of Jesus as one to be followed, modelled and obeyed.

Jesus in 1 Peter

As 1 Peter purports to be authored by a figure identified as 'Peter' (1.1), it would not be unreasonable, I suggest, to expect the first Petrine epistle to provide a fruitful discourse for information and data about the earthly Jesus. The further identification of Peter as 'an apostle of Jesus Christ' (1.1), and the subsequent lack of any more immediate information, would seem to associate this 'Peter' with the figure known by that name within the Synoptic tradition, someone portrayed therein as a close associate and follower of Jesus. One might call him the 'historical Peter'. As this historical Peter is seemingly identified as an apostle by Paul (Gal. 2.7–8), and is portrayed as the leading figure of the post-Easter community in Acts (cf. Acts 1.15), there seems to be no reason to believe that he is anyone other than the *Petros* of 1 Peter 1.1.[1] If so, then we might reasonably expect to find no shortage of references to Jesus within the epistolary text.

Such an expectation, however, warrants some immediate qualification. Many contemporary scholars doubt that Peter is the 'author' of the letter, commenting, for example, that the letter's literary quality is not commensurate with the Galilean fisherman Peter is elsewhere described as being. The letter actually claims to be written down by the scribe Silvanus (5.12), so linguistic arguments alone are not necessarily persuasive, but for many people the letter still remains essentially pseudepigraphical – that is, written by someone else in Peter's name. The evidence of the text itself is intriguing: the writer of the letter – for convenience, we will call him 'Peter' – claims to be a 'witness' to the sufferings of Christ (5.1), and this might suggest a more personal frame of reference to the epistle's retelling. But two factors militate against this. First, within the Synoptic accounts, Peter seems to absent himself from the Passion sufferings of Jesus, and they do not

---

[1] This statement makes no claim about the historical Peter's actual association with the letter (as author or otherwise), but only establishes the implied relationship between 'text' and historical figure.

portray him as an 'eyewitness' in that sense; if anything, the opposite is the case, with the Markan account of the Passion removing Peter from any direct observation of the events (Mark 14.66–72; 15.40). Some have suggested that 1 Peter 5.1b and 'Peter's' sharing in the glory to be revealed is a reference to the Transfiguration (cf. Mark 9.2–8),[2] but any such association is minimal and there seems no grounds to make it except if we were seeking corroborative evidence that the historical Peter authored the epistle. Second, the term 'witness' (1 Pet. 5.1) probably carries the sense of bearing testimony to – or proclaiming – Christ's suffering, giving 'witness' to its significance for the lives of others (rather than implying that Peter was an eyewitness to the events described). That option seems plausible, bearing in mind the letter's broader concern of evaluating the efficacy of the suffering presently being borne by its readers (cf. 4.1). As Eugene Boring pithily surmises: '"witness" is something the author does in the letter, not something he did at the 30 CE crucifixion'.[3] Likewise, the audience themselves are definitely not witnesses of Jesus; they are said to have never seen him (1.8).

More significant, though, than the evidence of 1 Peter 5.1, is that 1 Peter simply does not seem to interest itself greatly in recounting the broader content of Jesus' life.[4] This is not to say that Jesus has no significance for 1 Peter – that would be a major misreading of the letter – but rather it is merely to note that its appeal to Jesus' life and teaching are relatively limited, and that there is none of the personal interaction or commentary that one might expect Peter to yield. Just as where we observed that Paul did not use Jesus tradition or dominical teaching to support his position when he might have done so, Peter is similarly silent

---

[2] See, for example, Edward Gordon Selwyn, *The First Epistle of St. Peter: The Greek Text* (London: Macmillan, 1946) 30–1.

[3] See M. Eugene Boring, *1 Peter*, ANTC (Nashville: Abingdon Press, 1999) 168.

[4] Boring, *1 Peter* 201: 'Scenes from the life of Jesus play a minimal role in this story. It is important to the author that Jesus lived, that his life was righteous, and that he suffered unjustly for the sake of others without threatening retaliation.'

when pertinent opportunities arise.[5] There is no appeal, for example, to the temptation narrative of Jesus, a notable omission bearing in mind the testing (*peirasmos*) that the audience have been experiencing (1.6; 4.12). As Peter links the suffering of Christ with that of the audience (1 Pet. 4.1–2), we might have expected the temptation tradition to be alluded to in some fashion.

Overall, therefore, questions of authorship and/or pseudonymity actually distract from considering the letter's characterization of Jesus. For despite the limited biographical references and the lack of any explicit dominical citation, Jesus remains as central to 1 Peter as he is to Hebrews, but he is 'central' in a particular, Petrine way. Jesus is held up in exemplary fashion, but with his sufferings being the paradigmatic aspect of such exemplary status (2.21). In sum, Peter 'does not call his audience to imitate specific details of Jesus' teachings or works but rather to the general arc of his life, specifically his suffering and his death'.[6]

As such, Jesus' identity is unpacked at various points of the epistle, but through allusions rather than systematic biographical exposition.[7] As the Christ, Jesus is clothed in terms of pre-existence (he 'is' before the creation of the world – 1.20), and his entry into the world marks the end of the ages (1.20). Jesus is resurrected from the dead (1.3), described as God's Son (1.3), the audience's shepherd and guardian (2.25) and indeed as their chief shepherd who will appear once more (5.4). He is portrayed as sinless (1.19; 2.22–23), as a paradigm of Christian behaviour, someone whose

---

[5] This can lead to cyclical thinking within scholarship more generally. The lack of Jesus tradition in 1 Peter confirms (prior) suspicions as to authorship, but this in turn reduces the expectation that there would be any Jesus material encountered within the letter. At the risk of generalizing, there is not the same 'embarrassment' at 1 Peter's silence on Jesus' life/teaching as we encounter with Paul. We suspect this is due to the consensus view that 1 Peter is pseudonymous.

[6] Clifford A. Barbarick, 'Milk to Grow On: The Example of Christ in 1 Peter', in *Getting 'Saved': The Whole Story of Salvation in the New Testament*, ed. Charles H. Talbert, Jason A. Whitlark and Andrew E. Arterbury (Grand Rapids: Eerdmans, 2011) 216–39 (234).

[7] Cf. Frank J. Matera, *New Testament Christology* (Louisville: Westminster John Knox, 1999) 183: 'this letter says a great deal about the sufferings of Christ, but it never identifies Christ for its audience . . . *First Peter assumes that its audience already knows who Christ is*' (my emphasis).

example the readers are called to imbibe and embrace (2.21). Peter's exhortation is notably explicit in this regard – Jesus' sufferings are the example to follow, and, bearing in mind our discussions thus far, 1 Peter 2.21 is quite unusual for its direct application of the model of Jesus. Rarely, if ever, before have we encountered so *direct* an exhortation to mimic Jesus' actions, to 'follow in his steps'. Paul, for example, seeks to imitate Jesus in his sufferings (cf. Phil. 3.10), but he does not issue so explicit a directive to follow after the suffering Jesus. Peter, however, closely aligns his readers' experience with that of Jesus. Those who bear the name of Christ – note how Peter actually describes his audience as 'Christians' (4.16) – share in the sufferings of Christ (4.12–14); their response in suffering is likewise to be the same response as that of Jesus. Peter describes Jesus as a rejected one (2.4), but rejected as a 'living stone' (2.4); the readers are similarly described as living stones in the following verse (2.5), and it would seem that they too are to experience such rejection. Jesus is described as sinless (cf. 2.22–23), 'not in a theoretical or abstract way, but concretely'[8] so; his action – or inaction – in suffering is the path that Peter's readers are summoned to follow.

In his commentary on 1 Peter, Eugene Boring offers an outline of 1 Peter's narrative world, one aspect of which considers the Petrine understanding of the impact of Jesus' life.[9] Jesus Christ was manifest at the end of the times (1.20) and lived a life that Peter describes as 'righteous' (3.18). However, the reference to Jesus here is a little ambiguous, and it is unclear as to how such righteousness is manifest. Does it encapsulate Jesus' life *in nuce*? Or is it a reference to a particular event (such as Jesus' death)? Is it even a statement about Jesus' *life* at all? Elsewhere Peter notes that Jesus 'committed no sin' (2.22; cf. Heb. 4.15?), and this could correlate with 3.18 in that regard. However, the context of 1 Peter 2.22 is Jesus' Passion suffering, and thus the

---

[8] J. Ramsey Michaels, 'Catholic Christologies in the Catholic Epistles', in *Contours of Christology in the New Testament*, ed. Richard N. Longenecker, McMaster New Testament Studies (Grand Rapids: Eerdmans, 2005) 268–91 (278).

[9] Boring, *1 Peter* 188–90.

sinless disposition could well be just focused on that aspect of his life.

Indeed, it is surely the case that Jesus' Passion is of primary interest for Peter; the description of Jesus as a rejected stone (2.7) suggests a familiarity with the Passion narrative and the handing over of Jesus to his death, but the key passage is surely 1 Peter 2.22–25. Strictly speaking, Peter's subject here is Christ rather than Jesus, but the implication is of an earthly example (2.21), and since the letter never uses the name 'Jesus' without the Christ appellation, in that sense 'Jesus Christ' effectively functions as a name within the epistle. While the context to the suffering is Jesus' death (2.24), it is the suffering that Jesus endures *during* his death and his response to it (rather than the death per se) that interests Peter and that forms the *imitatio* paraenesis (cf. also 4.1; 5.1). Hence his 'sinlessness', or righteousness/blamelessness (3.18; 1.19), is not so much an ontological or doctrinal statement (cp. Heb. 4.15), rather a paraenetically geared declaration of Jesus' obedient and sinless response to suffering – a response Peter's readers are to embrace and exemplify (2.21). Jesus is presented as an active sufferer – like Paul, Peter portrays Jesus as obediently embracing his death.[10] The audience is to respond with similar demonstrations of obedience, directed to Jesus; they are to be obedient to Jesus Christ in the same way that he was previously obedient in his suffering (1.2).

Much of 2.22–25 is dependent upon Isaiah 53,[11] and the Servant Song material has been applied with paraenetical flourish. Peter's portrayal of Jesus' death in such terms may therefore be solely dictated by the Isaianic material, and need not have any direct relevance to its 'actuality'. It is possible, though, that Peter is reflecting Synoptic tradition here. Jesus' cry of 'Father, forgive them' (Luke 23.34) would offer a specific thematic parallel, but that text

---

[10] Dale C. Allison, Jr., *Constructing Jesus: Memory, Imagination, and History* (London: SPCK, 2010) 432.

[11] The intertextual exchange is partly direct quotation (1 Pet. 2.22 – Isa. 53.9; 1 Pet. 2.24b – Isa. 53.5), partly allusion (1 Pet. 2.23 – Isa. 53.7; 1 Pet. 2.24a – Isa. 53.4; 53.12; 1 Pet. 2.25 – Isa. 53.6).

is itself contested tradition. The Roman soldiers' mocking of Jesus (Matt. 27.27–31/Mark 15.16–20) might be another possibility, although the Synoptic texts comment only on the soldiers' actions and not actually on Jesus' response. As to the historical reality of what is claimed in 1 Peter 2.21–22, it is difficult to say more, but there is no significant reason to deny the essential verisimilitude of the Petrine discourse at this point. Elsewhere, of course, one might find points of difference between the Petrine Jesus and the Synoptics' Jesus – the general political conformity Peter encourages (2.11–17) sits less easily with the more radical Jesus portrayed in other parts of the Gospel accounts (the Temple cleansing, for example – Mark 11.15–18). But Peter and the Gospels seem far more in tune in their presentation of Jesus' death.

What 1 Peter 2.21–25 does illustrate well, though, is our earlier comments about the expectations of historical construction, namely that the presentation of events is always mediated through a particular lens (theological, confessional or otherwise) and is thus always encountered in perspectival fashion. In effect, we can only speculate on the historical actuality of the crucifixion scene, and artists, filmmakers and playwrights have sought to do so – one thinks particularly of the Mel Gibson film *The Passion of the Christ* or of the Passion Plays presented every ten years at Oberammergau. Whatever presentation they offer is still imbibed with unavoidable interpretative gloss, and 1 Peter is no different. The text is not doing history for history's sake per se, but rather sets out a narrative to imbibe and ultimately follow after (2.21). The picture of Jesus given in 2.22–24 is of an exemplary figure, a righteous sufferer whose obedience to God in his suffering was accompanied by a refusal to mistreat or threaten those causing his suffering. And that is surely the point. This is how Jesus was remembered and celebrated, how Jesus was identified, and we assume Isaiah 53 was utilized because it made 'sense' of the remembrance of Jesus for 'Peter' and/or his audience. Peter's reference to the locus of Jesus' death is illustrative of this. Bearing in mind the apparently widespread knowledge of the Passion narrative (in broad scope, perhaps, rather than necessarily its fine detail), it would seem implausible for Peter to have been unaware of the tradition ascribing Jesus' death to crucifixion. The epistle, however, records that Jesus' suffering occurred on a tree, rather than on a cross;[12] just as with Acts (5.30; 10.39; 13.29) and Paul (Gal. 3.13), the arboreal 'relocation' of Jesus' death captures the imagery of Deuteronomy 21.22–23 and the curse that would fall upon the one who hung from the tree.

While Jesus' suffering remains Peter's primary area of interest, the epistle also seems to draw on a dominical sayings tradition and, in similar fashion to James, echoes Jesus material within its own paraenesis. The extent (and concentration) to which it does so is less than that of the Jacobean epistle, and the volume of Jesus echoes within 1 Peter is certainly contested.[13] But David Horrell rightly surmises how commentators generally 'agree . . . that there are some places where 1 Peter echoes sayings from the gospel tradition, with the clearest examples coming from the Sermon on the Mount'.[14] Indeed, one can identify parallels between the Gospel tradition and 1 Peter with relative ease. Peter's declaration that good works cause others to give glory to God (2.12) recalls Matthew 5.16, while the encouragement to rejoice in suffering for Christ's sake (1 Pet. 4.13–14) probably echoes the final Matthean beatitude and its declaration regarding the blessings and reward that arise from persecution (Matt. 5.11–12; cf. also Luke 6.22); a similar perspective is shared in 1 Peter 3.14 and Matthew 5.10. We might make a case for similar echoes in 1 Peter 2.19–20 (cf. Luke 6.32–34), 1 Peter 3.9 (Luke 6.28) and 1 Peter 3.14 (Matt. 5.10; Luke 6.22).[15]

Perhaps the most contested allusion is whether Peter knows of the Markan ransom logion (Mark 10.45; cf. Titus 2.14) and

---

[12] Though a number of English translations still preserve 'cross' rather than 'tree' in 1 Pet. 2.24.

[13] The different summations of Robert H. Gundry, 'Further "Verba" on Verba Christi in First Peter', *Bib* 55.2 (1974) 211–32, and (the more minimalist) Ernest Best, '1 Peter and the Gospel Tradition', *NTS* 16.2 (1970) 95–113, while somewhat dated now, still demonstrate the variance one encounters in this area.

[14] David G. Horrell, *1 Peter*, NTG (London: T&T Clark, 2008) 35.

[15] See, for example, Helmut Koester, *Ancient Christian Gospels: Their History and Development* (London: SCM Press, 1990) 66. He avers: 'We must, therefore, conclude that 1 Peter has access to a collection of sayings that was related to or identical with Matthew's special Jewish-Christian source.'

represents it in 1 Peter 1.18. The legitimacy of the Markan claim itself is contested, and the verse is a *crux interpretum* as to whether the Jesus of history himself understood his death in terms of a suffering servant. Now, it is not our job here to adjudicate on whether 10.45 is indeed genuine Jesus teaching, and therefore what he might have understood by it; instead, the mooted allusion illustrates the difficulties we face when trying to discern if/when Jesus tradition is being utilized. The similarities between Mark and 1 Peter are well established, notably in their common interest in Deutero-Isaiah (especially Isa. 53), and Peter certainly understands Jesus' death in ransom terms (1 Pet. 1.18, perhaps 2.24). However, there is no *pressing* reason to think that he is dependent on Jesus tradition for so doing. The appeal to ransom/liberation tradition could equally draw on Old Testament imagery (e.g. the ransoming of Israel from Egypt – Exod. 6.6; Deut. 7.8), or may be merely a convenient contemporary motif to express the work of Christ in his death.

We should also make mention of 1 Peter 3.19–20 and the nature of Christ's proclamation to the imprisoned spirits. We have seen a similar reference in Ephesians 4.9, but the Petrine example is more developed and, as a result, more intriguing. In context, the passage appears to be associated with some form of baptismal liturgy (cf. 1 Pet. 3.20–21), but the specific 'event' being described remains famously ambiguous, with even Martin Luther, not usually known for his lack of confidence, proverbially shrugging his shoulders as to the particular event being described: it 'is a strange text and certainly a more obscure passage than any other passage in the New Testament. I still do not know for sure what the apostle means.'[16] The event has no parallel in the Gospel accounts, and it remains a point of scholarly contention as to exactly what 'event' Peter is portraying. It may be the descent into Hades on Passion Saturday, or the activity of Christ in the time of Noah, or it may even reflect

---

[16] Martin Luther, *Luther's Works: The Catholic Epistles*, trans. Martin H. Bertram (St Louis: Concordia, 1967) 113.

the Ascension.[17] In view of the heaven-entry language of 1 Peter 3.22, the third option seems the most likely, with the spirits addressed being fallen angels. Everything is made subject to Christ (3.22). However, the letter's subsequent reference to the gospel being proclaimed to the dead (4.6), customarily linked with 3.19–20 but not necessarily addressing the same situation,[18] probably references tradition of a descent to the dead/Hades. Peter has no explicit subject for the proclamation, but bearing in mind the parallels with 3.19–20, it seems not unreasonable to view Jesus as the agent of the action. Both options, of course, reflect more a 'Christ' activity than one pertaining to Jesus' earthly life (and indeed Peter makes 'Christ' the subject of the action – Jesus is not mentioned). But they remain, either way, developments of the Jesus tradition in areas not covered by the Synoptic testimony.

Jesus in Jude

Formerly described as the 'most neglected book of the New Testament',[19] attention to Jude in recent years has demonstrated how its intricate appropriation and usage of Old Testament and pseudepigraphical material actually warrants no such lack of neglect.[20] A further factor in its reintegration might well be its particular interest in Jesus: Jude cites Jesus at least 6 times in only 25 verses, which is a very good average by any account! At the

---

[17] On the paragraph generally, see William J. Dalton, *Christ's Proclamation to the Spirits: A Study of 1 Peter 3:18—4:6*, AnBib 23 (Rome: Pontifical Biblical Institute, 1965); R. T. France, 'Exegesis in Practice: Two Samples', in *New Testament Interpretation*, ed. I. Howard Marshall (Carlisle: Paternoster, 1997) 252–81.

[18] For a persuasive argument for differentiating the two events, see David G. Horrell, 'Who Are "the Dead" and When Was the Gospel Preached to Them? The Interpretation of 1 Pet 4.6', *NTS* 49 (2003) 70–89.

[19] Douglas J. Rowston, 'The Most Neglected Book in the New Testament', *NTS* 21 (1975) 554–63.

[20] Cf. Robert L. Webb, 'The Use of "Story" in the Letter of Jude: Rhetorical Strategies of Jude's Narrative Episodes', *JSNT* 31 (2008) 53–87: 'While Jude is a short letter in comparison with the other NT letters, it is unusually rich in its use of story drawn from the Jewish scriptural tradition. In fact, one might be hard pressed to find a NT letter in which concentration is as high as that found in Jude' (55).

same time, the letter purports to be from a brother of James (v. 1); bearing in mind James's putative association with James the Just, and therefore by fraternal extension with Jesus, 'Jude' likewise becomes a brother of Jesus, and we encounter the same lack of explicit relationship to Jesus akin to the question of James.[21]

The six agreed references to Jesus in Jude (vv. 1 (x2), 4, 17, 21, 25) are fairly standard. In each of them, Jesus is consistently described as Jesus *Christ*, potentially a means of differentiating this Jesus from any other. Jesus is also portrayed as merciful (v. 21), Lord (vv. 4, 25) and, of particular interest, as 'Master' (v. 4), suggestive perhaps of one who is the ruler of the household (and thereby establishing a new royal family identity).[22] This familial imagery may have resonance with 'brother Jude', and is certainly not inimical to it, but it is implicit at best, and, just like James, Jude does not exploit the fraternal relationship or offer any reflection on Jesus' earthly life. It does acknowledge that Jesus had apostles (v. 17), and this may be a reference to the immediate post-Easter generation, but there is nothing in the verse itself to demand that.

There is one further possible reference to Jesus within Jude's epistle. In most contemporary translations of Jude 5, the salvation of Israel out of Egypt, and the destruction of those who did not believe, is attributed to the work of the 'Lord', an unsurprising designation perhaps. Some early manuscripts, however, have 'Jesus' – rather than 'Lord' – as the subject of that activity, a very difficult reading in that it transposes Jesus' work back into exodus times. There may be other similar instances to this elsewhere

---

[21] The canonical ordering of the Catholic Epistles would seem to concur with the fraternal designation, as James and Jude – the two 'brothers' – bookend the corpus and give it designated authority. Second Peter's heavy borrowing of Jude may also contribute to its authority, and perhaps testify to the seniority of the historical Jude within the early Church – see further Gene L. Green, 'Second Peter's Use of Jude: Imitatio and the Sociology of Early Christianity', in *Reading Second Peter with New Eyes: Methodological Reassessments of the Letter of Second Peter*, ed. Robert L. Webb and Duane Frederick Watson, Library of New Testament Studies 382 (London: T&T Clark, 2010) 1–25.

[22] See Richard J. Bauckham, *Jude and the Relatives of Jesus in the Early Church* (Edinburgh: T&T Clark, 1990) 302–7.

in the NT (we think of 1 Cor. 10.1–9 or Heb. 11.26, where 'Christ' is somehow involved in exodus/wilderness remembrance), but Jude 5 is distinctive in that it is *Jesus* who is the named agent, rather than Christ. Adjudicating as to what is the original/best reading of Jude 5 is beyond our scope here,[23] but it would seem to be a possible reading within the manuscript tradition. And if we were to embrace it, it would suggest that Jude's Jesus has evolved significantly, to become a cosmic figure whose activity is closely associated with that of YHWH, and who is operative pre-incarnation. This is a high Jesusology indeed.

Jesus in 2 Peter

Whereas the first Petrine epistle laid significant emphasis on Jesus' suffering, and especially on the suffering he endured in his death, 2 Peter pursues a somewhat different avenue in terms of its presentation of Jesus. This is not the only point of distinction between the two texts, which differ in a variety of ways, including the identification of their respective authors (1 Peter = *Petros*; 2 Peter = *Sumeon Petros*), the source material they use (we note 2 Peter's heavy borrowing from Jude) and the generic flavour of the content (the distinctive valedictory address mode adopted by 2 Peter). The majority of scholars also find 2 Peter to be a late text, probably the latest in the New Testament canon, and therefore a pseudonymous epistle rather than one 'authored' by the historical Peter.[24] Perhaps the most important difference between the two Petrine letters for our purposes, however, is their particular eschatological interests. Where 1 Peter emphasizes Jesus'

---

[23] For a view supporting the 'Jesus' reading, see Philipp F. Bartholomä, 'Did Jesus Save the People out of Egypt? A Re-examination of a Textual Problem in Jude 5', *NovT* 50 (2008) 143–58; also Jerome H. Neyrey, *2 Peter, Jude: A New Translation, with Introduction and Commentary*, AB 37C (London: Doubleday, 1993) 61–2. For a contrasting view, see Bauckham, *Jude and the Relatives of Jesus* 307–12.

[24] Though, for example, note that Keith Warrington, *Discovering Jesus in the New Testament* (Peabody: Hendrickson, 2009), attributes both letters to Peter. Second Peter speaks of itself being a second letter (3.1), and 1 Peter is the obvious intended predecessor, but that need not imply they are from the same hand.

efficacious suffering as an example for his readers' present distress, 2 Peter (and especially chapter 3) is orientated more to presenting Jesus Christ as one who will return as judge (2 Pet. 3.3–10, 13). Indeed, much of 2 Peter 3 revolves around those scoffers who are rejecting the concept of the Parousia (3.4), and Peter's robust responses to them (3.8–10). The scoffers may even be querying the very occurrence of the (first) Jesus event – that is, speculating that nothing has changed since the advent of creation (3.4). Any Petrine usage of Jesus tradition to justify the coming of the Day of the Lord may therefore be serving double usage: as well as reminding the hearers as to the imminence of the Parousia, it may also be indirectly referring them to the impact of Jesus as the one who proclaimed such an event. In Jesus Christ, something has 'happened' (cf. 1.16–18).

That all said, because of its putative late dating, 2 Peter rates very low compared to other NT texts in terms of yielding historical Jesus testimony (and that is saying something, bearing in mind the reticence we have already encountered!). While the letter does seem to reflect knowledge of the Synoptic Gospels and/or Paul, in terms of following or knowing Jesus, some have observed how 'neither the life of Jesus nor his death and resurrection play any role in the exhortation'.[25] Coupled with this, we also see a very high or developed Christology in the epistle, with Jesus and God treated in almost equivalent terms (1.1),[26] Jesus reigning over an eternal kingdom (1.11) and portrayed as Lord and Saviour (1.11; 3.2, 18).

Now, as noted above, the letter is evidently concerned more with Jesus' return than with his earthly life and teaching. So much is certain. Yet its presentation of the figure of Jesus nonetheless

---

[25] Pheme Perkins, 'Christ in Jude and 2 Peter', in *Who Do You Say That I Am? Essays on Christology*, ed. Jack Dean Kingsbury, Mark Allan Powell and David R. Bauer (Louisville: Westminster John Knox, 1999) 155–65 (156).

[26] Ruth Anne Reese, *2 Peter and Jude*, The Two Horizons New Testament Commentary (Grand Rapids: Eerdmans, 2007) 179, describes 1.1 as 'one of the clearest statements in the New Testament' of Jesus' divine credentials. She notes, though, how in the very next verse Jesus is also distinguished from God (1.2).

remains of interest, and we still encounter particular takes on the Jesus tradition within the letter. Jesus' identity matters within the epistle, and while the Jesus of 2 Peter surely transcends his earthly existence, it is at least that, and does not exclude it. Ruth Reese seems to capture this broad portrayal, surmising that the 'epistle gives attention to numerous aspects of Jesus' person. His life on earth is considered along with his saving works and the gifts that he gives to those who follow after him.'[27] On what grounds can Reese make this assertion?

The first significant extended reference to Jesus occurs in 1.16–18, which, on the surface at least, appears to allude to the events of the Transfiguration. If there is indeed a connection, then it becomes the 'one clear reference in the general epistles to an episode of the life of Jesus reported in the synoptic gospels'.[28] Where 1 Peter appealed to being an eyewitness of Jesus' sufferings, 2 Peter takes a contrasting view, claiming to have witnessed Jesus' majesty (1.16), as part of a mountaintop divine revelation (1.17–18). The epistolary description of the event is articulated in theophanic terms, and bears a number of parallels with the Gospel portrayal of the Transfiguration (Mark 9.2–8). They share the common mountaintop setting, the presence of Peter and others with Jesus,[29] and the experience of something visual being encountered (this is implied in 2 Peter by Jesus' reception of glory and honour (1.17), though the description remains somewhat allusive). Some evangelistic features are absent from the Petrine record (notably the accompanying figures of Moses and Elijah), and Peter does not actually specify that Jesus is 'transfigured' (cf. Matt. 17.2; Mark 9.2), but the 'feel' of the Petrine retelling surely implies some connection between the respective accounts. The ascription of glory to Jesus seems to draw more on the Lucan account (Luke 9.32), although '2 Peter does not seem to

---

[27] Reese, *2 Peter* 181.
[28] Harold W. Attridge, 'Jesus in the General Epistles', in *The Blackwell Companion to Jesus*, ed. Delbert Royce Burkett, Blackwell Companions to Religion (Malden, MA: Wiley-Blackwell, 2011) 111–18 (115).
[29] Note how Peter moves from first person singular to first person plural at 1.16.

follow any particular synoptic version, but contains elements found uniquely in each of them.'[30] Indeed, the retelling of the event essentially differs between the Synoptics and Peter. But the similarities are sufficient to suggest that Peter has the Transfiguration in mind, and that the grounds for confidence in following after Jesus are premised upon an 'earthly' event.

The other important potential locus of Jesus tradition is 2 Peter 3.8–10 and Peter's refutation of the scoffers' perspective on the Parousia. It is possible that the section has several echoes of Jesus tradition within it, and specifically draws on his parabolic eschatological teaching. Peter's rebuttal is strong, defending the imminence of the Parousia, partly on temporal grounds (the thousand years/one day comparison – 3.8), partly in terms of the patient promise of the Lord (3.9), partly by the unexpectedness with which the event will occur (3.10a). The material in all three instances is associated with 'the Lord', but without specific clarification as to whether YHWH or Jesus is implied. It is, of course, possible that Peter here understands Lord as YHWH, particularly bearing in mind the prior reference to the creation and flood narratives (3.5–6), but in those verses 'God' is explicitly identified and named (cf. likewise 3.12), and earlier on in the chapter (3.2) 'Lord' is surely a reference to Jesus (3.2). Hence, there is a strong possibility that 3.8–10 reflects the same identification, and that the Lord is understood to be Jesus.

What, then, are the implications of the three Lord-related statements of 3.8–10? What Jesus connection might they have? The last example is the clearest one, and appears to include a couple of allusions to Jesus' teaching. In the Synoptic record (Matt. 5.18; 24.35; Luke 16.17; 21.33), heaven and earth are said to pass away; this is akin to 2 Peter 3.10, even if, technically speaking, the Petrine example only has heaven 'passing away' (the earth is said to dissolve with fire). The Gospel parallels lack the predictive or prophetic element that 2 Peter includes, but the case for a Jesus allusion is stronger by the association of the Day

---

[30] Neyrey, *2 Peter* 173.

of the Lord with thief-in-the-night imagery (3.10; cf. Matt. 24.43). The association is not an exact one (in 2 Peter, the Day comes likes a thief, whereas the Matthaean Jesus compares the thief to the Son of Man – Matt. 24.44), but the eschatological context is common to both texts. We have also seen Paul utilize such imagery (1 Thess. 5.2, 4); Neyrey avers accordingly that the 'phrase in 3.10 is identical with that in 1 Thess 5.2, and possibly dependent upon it', and ventures further that 'there seems to be a tradition dating back to Jesus which compares the Parousia to the coming of a thief'.[31]

There is less reason to link the two statements of 3.8–9 to Jesus, however. The first declaration regarding millennial time (3.8) is a citation of Psalm 90.4, and the subsequent statement about the Lord's patience (1 Pet. 3.9) may be no more than a general, theological statement. There is no obvious Synoptic parallel to which 3.8–9 might be compared. But the Lord is still invoked in both statements, and it is absent from the Psalm citation; therefore it is just possible, for example, that 2 Peter 3.8 reflects a tradition that Jesus was remembered for voicing the kind of idea expressed in 2 Peter 3.8/Psalm 90.4.

Conclusion: the Jesus of the Petrine epistles/Jude

Of the three texts from the Petrine 'school' it is 1 Peter that yields the richest and most rounded portrait of Jesus. He is *the* pattern for Peter's audience, a model for them in their suffering and distress, 'the foundation for the community's new life'.[32] Jesus' actions in his suffering contribute significantly to the exemplary presentation, but the 'event' of Jesus also matters (even if the 'event' is essentially the death and resurrection of Jesus, rather than other aspects of his life). The portrait that Peter offers of the earthly Jesus is one mediated and informed by the audience's situation;

[31] Neyrey, *2 Peter* 242; see also David Wenham, 'Being "Found" on the Last Day: New Light on 2 Peter 3.10 and 2 Corinthians 5.3', *NTS* 33 (1987) 477–9.
[32] Barbarick, 'Milk' 238.

in view of their suffering it is that aspect of Jesus' life that comes to the fore.[33] It is therefore perhaps the 'most pastorally sensitive' depiction of Jesus that we encounter within the New Testament record.[34]

By contrast, 2 Peter and Jude have less to say about Jesus, and particularly his earthly existence. The appeal to the Transfiguration (2 Pet. 1.16–18) is a notable one because of the absence of any similar comparison elsewhere within the non-Gospel material, but there is little else said directly about the historical figure of Jesus. Instead, akin to the Deutero-Pauline corpus, they testify to the Christological development of perceptions about Jesus, casting him as on a par with YHWH and spoken of in terms almost indistinguishable from those used for God.[35] Jesus of Nazareth is not completely subsumed within such a development, but the letters are more interested in his second rather than in his first advent.

---

[33] So Earl Richard, 'The Functional Christology of 1 Peter', in *Perspectives on First Peter*, ed. Charles H. Talbert, NABPR Special Studies Series 9 (Macon: Mercer University Press, 1986) 121–39: 'he wishes to discuss suffering, not the death or life of Jesus, and so . . . he focuses upon that precise element of the Jesus tradition' (133).

[34] Matera, *New Testament Christology* 184.

[35] Cf. Perkins, 'Christ in Jude and 2 Peter' 156: 'Thus Jude and 2 Peter raise the possibility that by the end of the New Testament period, Jesus is perceived as Lord, recipient of divine power, and future judge.'

8

'The apocalyptic Son of Man': Jesus in the Johannine letters and Revelation

Perhaps more than any of our texts under discussion, the Johannine corpus poses the most significant questions regarding the identity of the historical Jesus. The texts themselves – the three epistles attributed to John and the book known as Revelation – are commonly grouped together because of their position at the end of the New Testament. They are also often associated because of their apparent shared figure of 'John', even if only Revelation actually refers to anyone by that name.[1] More pressing for our concerns, however, are the issues relating to the portrayal of Jesus within the respective texts, and particularly the limited scope of such a portrayal. Revelation, for example, is more concerned with matters heavenly than earthly, and Jesus of Nazareth can seem to be subsumed by symbolic imagery of the heavenly Lord. Likewise, 3 John does not actually mention Jesus at all, and possesses only one fairly incidental reference to Christ (3 John 7). The reference is intriguing though, in that it relates to the support owing to those working in the cause of Christ, a similar topic to the discussion found in 1 Corinthians 9.14. The Johannine example, however, lacks any appeal to a dominical saying akin to that found in the Corinthian discourse.

Jesus in 1 John

In terms of Jesus reference in the Johannine epistles, then, it is 1 John that carries the most interest. The text purports to be from

---

[1] The Johannine epistles and Revelation are grouped together for heuristic convenience, with no implication as to their authorship, provenance or audience.

someone who was present with Jesus, someone who has experienced the Christ event first-hand and someone who justifies their message on the basis of such exposure (1 John 1.1–3). The epistolary prologue sets the scene for the discourse to come. In the Greek text, the object of what was 'seen, heard and touched' is in the neuter gender – rather than the masculine one – and this would normally suggest an encounter with a concept or idea, rather than with a human person. This seems improbable, though, in the context of 1.1–3: the sensory language is evocative of an experience of, or an encounter with, a person, rather than with an inanimate idea or concept – 'touch' surely implies a personal or physical encounter with an individual. Thus, although the letter may be addressing some docetic tendencies among its opponents, thereby laying particular emphasis upon the physicality of what they have experienced, John's tactic is still to point to physical experience and engagement, rather than just to a myth or story. While very little is said explicitly about Jesus' life, his humanity (and especially the writer's *experience* of it) matters. As Moody Smith concludes: 'With the possible exception of Hebrews (2.14–18; 4.14—5.10), in no New Testament book besides the Gospels are the reality and character of the historical figure of Jesus as a human being more important than in the Johannine epistles, particularly 1 John.'[2]

John's multi-sensory encounter is described as occurring 'from the beginning' (1 John 1.1). The expression probably echoes both the Genesis account of creation (Gen. 1.1) and the Fourth Gospel's logos-centred prologue (John 1.1), but in its epistolary context here, it relates to the new beginning that has been inaugurated by Jesus. *He* is the new beginning – the *arche*, to use the Greek term – and Jesus/*arche* becomes a key frame of reference for John's analysis; the term is 'pregnant with 1 John's conception of the

---

[2] D. Moody Smith, 'The Historical Figure of Jesus in 1 John', in *The Word Leaps the Gap: Essays on Scripture and Theology in Honor of Richard B. Hays*, ed. J. Ross Wagner, Christopher Kavin Rowe and A. Katherine Grieb (Grand Rapids: Eerdmans 2008) 310–24 (314).

historical figure of Jesus',[3] and 'the one from the beginning' becomes almost the equivalent of a name for Jesus in John's eyes (cf. 1 John 2.13–14; though 3.8 adopts a different, non-Jesus sense). The letter is therefore replete with the notion of carrying on the tradition begun with Jesus. John speaks of passing on what they have heard from *him* (1.5); while the identity of this figure is not explicitly identified, it is hard to think that it could be anyone but Jesus. It is clear that Jesus had come in the flesh (4.2), and that this has generated an era-marking moment in the mind of the community. Accordingly, it is the last hour – and they now await Jesus' return (2.18, 28). In the meantime, they are to 'walk' as Jesus 'walked' (2.6) – they are to 'walk his walk' – suggesting (as with 1 Peter, though less explicitly perhaps) that Jesus' earthly life/example mattered to John and his readers, and therefore that they knew something as to the manner of such a 'walk' that encompassed more than just his death.[4] That said, the manner of Jesus' death is particularly exemplary; John's readers are to follow his example by laying down their lives for each other (3.16).

Elsewhere in the epistle, Jesus is portrayed as Son (1.3; 1.7; 3.23) and Christ (2.22; 5.1), and notably as the righteous one (2.1), perhaps some form of titular phrase (cf. Acts 3.14; 7.52; 22.14; though probably not so in James 5.6). Much of John's Jesusology may derive from the particular situation/opponents he is addressing: it seems that the letter is responding to the notion that Jesus did *not* come in the flesh, and that Jesus was therefore not the Christ. John robustly responds to this, contending that Jesus is indeed the Christ (1 John 2.22), and belief in Jesus' Christological status makes the believer a child of God (5.1). In asserting Jesus' Christological credentials, John focuses on his achievements: Jesus has destroyed the devil (3.8), his death has brought about cleansing from sin (1.7), was the atoning sacrifice (2.2), and he has become the saviour of world (4.14). But these declarations are not especially distinctive – at least not when compared to other parts of

---

[3] Smith, 'Historical Figure' 312.
[4] John Painter, *1, 2, and 3 John*, SP 18 (Collegeville: Liturgical Press, 2002) 177–8.

the NT – and it is another aspect of its depiction of Jesus that sets 1 John apart from its canonical peers. There is in 1 John something quite distinctive about the *present* relationship – we might call it the 'present presence' – of Jesus to the Johannine group. Jesus is their advocate before the Father (2.1) and obedience to him is fundamental to community conduct (2.3–6). The Jesus proclaimed is the same Jesus who is encountered within the Johannine community – they have fellowship with him (1.3). As Attridge concludes: 'It is not the Jesus of sacred memory that is important, but the Jesus who is present to the community of his disciples.'[5] Thus, while John is clear that something has happened 'in the beginning' – the Jesus event, in the past – the impact of that event remains into the present.[6]

The letter is also replete with a number of connections to, or echoes of, the Fourth Gospel. While these may be derivative from the evangelical tradition, and perhaps 'secondary' in that regard, they nonetheless contribute to the epistle's own portrait of Jesus and supplement the overall (canonical) portrait. Bearing in mind the importance of Jesus' identity in the epistle, and the significance of right Jesusology, it is probable that the community had some access to Jesus tradition and to the Gospel material, and it is difficult to read 1 John without the Gospel echoing in the background.[7] In both texts, Jesus' enfleshed humanity matters, and we see correspondences between them as a result. For example, 1 John 3.23 restates the love commandment of John 13.34, implying, as with the Gospel, that it is an instruction given to them by Jesus. First John 2.7 may also be a play on, or reworking of, John 13.34. The epistle claims that the commandment is actually an old one that they have had 'from the beginning' (1 John 2.7), the same phrase

---

[5] Harold W. Attridge, 'Jesus in the General Epistles', in *The Blackwell Companion to Jesus*, ed. Delbert Royce Burkett, Blackwell Companions to Religion (Malden, MA: Wiley-Blackwell, 2011) 111–18 (112).

[6] Thus, the observation of Smith, 'Historical Figure' 316, that Jesus' 'pastness is crucially important', could be seen as missing the 'presentness' of Jesus within the community.

[7] This is not to imply that 1 John postdates the Fourth Gospel (it may well precede it), but rather merely to note their shared 'feel' or flavour.

that is used in the prologue to demark the Jesus event (1 John 1.1), the dawning of the new era. Second John 5 seems to confirm this suggestion: the commandment to love one another (John 13.34) is described as 'old', rather than new, one they have had since the beginning. There may even be echoes of Synoptic material in 1 John, with 3.15 a possible parallel to Matthew 5.22.

Perhaps the letter's most intriguing Jesus reference, though, is the symbolic allusion to Jesus coming by water and blood (5.6). The reference continues the letter's frequent efforts to underscore the importance of Jesus' humanity, but the phrasing suggests something more than just anti-docetic commentary. The verse has what de Boer calls a 'polemical stamp',[8] in that – distinctively so in the letter – it reveals a key point of distinction between the community and their opponents, who, it seems, were propagating the idea that Jesus came only in water. The dual reference to blood and water could have sacramental connotations, but John does not exploit that connection if that were the case. Alternatively, it may reflect the mixture of blood and water that emanated from Jesus' side in the Passion sequence (John 19.34),[9] but this view struggles then to make sense of the association with the Spirit (1 John 5.6–8). An alternative possibility is that 5.6 portrays Jesus as a baptizing figure, with water and (salvific) blood the agents of his baptizing power.[10] This connects with the Gospel account where Jesus is said to be baptizing (John 3.26, though cf. 4.1–2), but it is still only one possible explanation of what is an infamously elusive point of reference. A more plausible possibility is that water and blood represent the contours of the Jesus narrative, namely the journey from baptism to cross;[11] this would be a rare and interesting reference to Jesus' baptism within the non-Gospel testimony, though it is notable that John's Gospel does not include

---

[8] Martinus C. de Boer, 'Jesus the Baptizer: 1 John 5:5–8 and the Gospel of John', *JBL* 107 (1988) 87–106 (88).

[9] Raymond Edward Brown, *The Epistles of John*, AB 30 (Garden City, NY: Doubleday, 1982) 579–80.

[10] De Boer, 'Jesus the Baptizer'.

[11] Attridge, 'Jesus in the General Epistles' 112.

the baptismal event. If this option is the best fit, then this would mark out the broad pattern of how Jesus was remembered. It also concurs with the Spirit being the one who confirms Jesus' status before John the Baptist – Jesus is the one on whom John recognizes the Spirit dwelling (John 1.32–33). It would be a rather indirect way of placing it, but the human testimony to the Son (5.9) might recall John the Baptist's declaration about Jesus. The s/Spirit is also connected with Jesus' death – he is said to give up his spirit at the moment of death (John 19.30).[12]

Conclusion

In sum, Jesus is central to the life of John's community. For John, what we think about Jesus matters; it matters for membership of the community and seems to have been a defining marker for such membership. We might argue that Jesus is therefore central to the Johannine community – not only in terms of belief in him but also in terms of obedience to that which he taught or espoused.

Jesus in 2 and 3 John

The other two Johannine epistles have much less to say about Jesus. As I have noted, 3 John is effectively silent on the subject, but the second epistle is slightly more forthcoming. It identifies Jesus as the Father's Son (v. 3), but also raises some other points worthy of note. In similar terms to its predecessor, 2 John seems to address the issue that Jesus has not come in the flesh (v. 7). Reaffirming the actuality of the 'incarnation' becomes a focal point of the letter, and anyone who might deny the event is described as the Antichrist (v. 7; cf. 1 John 2.22); it may be that this is the issue that is dividing the community, perhaps the element of some early docetic tendency. More intriguingly, perhaps, 2 John 9 alludes to the 'teaching of Christ', and the

---

[12] Terry Griffith, *Keep Yourselves from Idols: A New Look at 1 John*, JSNTSup 233 (Sheffield: Sheffield Academic Press, 2002) 162.

necessity of preserving and holding on to it. The epistle does not expand on what such teaching entails, and, of course, the content relates specifically to *Christ* rather than to *Jesus*. But nevertheless it suggests a couple of possibilities. If it is teaching *about* Christ, then some kind of narrative about him has emerged, and this might well include something pertaining to Jesus' ministry, or at least to his coming in the flesh (v. 7). Alternatively, it may personify Christ as the teacher, and, if so, it seems probable that Jesus' teaching would be one aspect of that. After all, as noted above, 2 John 5 restates the commandment they have had from the beginning, namely to love one another, a probable allusion to John 13.34. If so, it would characterize Jesus as an authoritative teacher, one whose teaching is to be preserved and upheld. Thus, however 'teaching of Christ' is to be understood, the implication is that some aspect of Jesus tradition is to be maintained and upheld within the addressed community.

Jesus in Revelation

Perhaps more than any other NT book, Revelation is customarily viewed as exhibiting 'little interest in the earthly life and ministry of Jesus of Nazareth'.[13] The language, imagery and appeal of the Apocalypse draw heavily on the Jewish Scriptures (particularly Ezekiel and Daniel), rather than deriving from any explicit appeals to Jesus' earthly life. David Aune encapsulates this view well, noting how 'the name "Jesus Christ" . . . is not primarily in the Johannine Apocalypse the name of a historical figure, but of the Lord and Saviour of the Christian Church'.[14] As the book points towards the consummation of history – however imminent or futurist – rather than to the events of first-century Galilee, expectations of

---

[13] Ian Boxall, 'Jesus in the Apocalypse', in *The Blackwell Companion to Jesus*, ed. Delbert Royce Burkett, Blackwell Companions to Religion (Malden, MA: Wiley-Blackwell, 2011) 119–26 (119).

[14] David E. Aune, 'Stories of Jesus in the Apocalypse of John', in *Contours of Christology in the New Testament*, ed. Richard N. Longenecker, McMaster New Testament Studies (Grand Rapids: Eerdmans, 2005) 292–319 (316–17).

any reference to the historical Jesus will rightly be somewhat muted. While Jesus is found speaking in the Apocalypse, it is actually the voice of the risen Lord that we hear (cf. 1.17–20) rather than that of the earthly Jesus. As such, just like Colossians perhaps, Revelation can be said to be very Christological in its exposition but far less Jesusological (at least in the way that we have defined the terms thus far).

Questions of provenance and authorship also dampen any great expectation as to historical Jesus insights. The Asia Minor milieu to which the letters are addressed is somewhat detached from the Palestinian context of Jesus' ministry. And while some have considered the 'John' of Revelation to be John, son of Zebedee, and therefore someone potentially close to the earthly Jesus, there is no textual ground to substantiate such an assertion. Revelation lacks the eyewitness claim that could be attributed to either of the Petrine epistles, and 'John', if anything, seems to separate himself from the Twelve within Revelation's discourse (cf. Rev. 21.14). 'John' the character is actually a fairly minor one within the Apocalypse as a whole, and it is the exalted Jesus Christ who assumes centre stage. Moreover, if there is any interest in Revelation's historical points of reference, this tends to be related more to the historical occasion and context for the text,[15] rather than to biographical recollection of the earthly Jesus.

So do we merely give up? Because of this (apparent) disinterest in the historical Jesus, and because of the very nature of apocalyptic material – as opposed to the Gospel genre – it is tempting to disavow Revelation from having anything significant to say about the earthly Jesus and how he was remembered. At the risk of stating the obvious, the risen Lord riding out on a white horse (cf. Rev. 19.11–16) is simply of a different ilk from that of the Markan Jesus apprehensively awaiting arrest in Gethsemane (Mark 14.35–36). Furthermore, by the very nature of the apocalyptic

---

[15] On this topic, see A. J. P. Garrow, *Revelation*, New Testament Readings (London: Routledge, 1997) 66–79.

genre, any references to Jesus will be somewhat ambiguous, and to expect otherwise is to misunderstand the coded imagery in which apocalyptic material is characteristically shrouded. It is not what Aune calls 'realistic narrative',[16] and it is therefore that much harder to get at any historical referent, however imprecise that may be. We have therefore to read between the lines, in the same way, for example, that we read between them in Paul's letters, but the symbolic language of the apocalyptic material makes that task even harder. The sheer diversity of the figurative imagery – one like a son of man (or Son of Man?) coupled with the rider on the white horse, the enthroned lamb combined with the child of Revelation 12 or the bright morning star (22.16) – also complicates and enlarges the picture of Jesus under discussion.

But perhaps seeking to determine data about the earthly Jesus from Revelation is the wrong question to ask, or is the wrong way of going about the task in hand. Instead, having established the Apocalypse's central focus on the exalted Lord, we might want to start from that premise and work backwards so to speak, drawing out connections or continuity between the earthly Jesus and the risen Christ, ones that help shed some light on how Jesus was remembered by those who followed after him. Brian Blount seemingly pursues this option, contending that Revelation's

> risen Christ is ... a natural follow-up to the earthly Jesus; both are provocative figures who demand a discipleship willing to bear a cross. While Mark's Jesus asks his disciples to take up their crosses and follow, John's Christ demands that they witness to the same testimony to which Jesus testified, the very declaration of lordship that took Jesus to his own cross.[17]

That is, the Jesus of Revelation is certainly the exalted Jesus Christ – but remains still connected to, or in continuity with, the

---

[16] Aune, 'Stories' 292.
[17] Brian K. Blount, *Revelation: A Commentary*, NTL (Louisville: Westminster John Knox, 2009) ix.

earthly Jesus. As such, Jesus becomes portrayed as a prophetic figure; he is both the content of the Apocalyptic message and the one responsible for its delivery (Rev. 1.1). The particular historical reality of that which Jesus resisted is not specified, but the 'feel' of Revelation points to a memory of Jesus as one who was actively challenging and prophetic in his conduct.

Now, such an approach to Revelation's Jesusology certainly necessitates some back reading or analysis to arrive at this position, but it seems invited by the various allusions throughout the Apocalypse to the life of Jesus of Nazareth. For Revelation does indeed retain some reference to the earthly Jesus, and these references provide a not insignificant contribution to the overall portrait of Jesus Christ found within the book. The description of Jesus in terms of the Lion of the tribe of Judah (5.5), and as a descendant of David (22.16; cf. 5.5), suggests some awareness of Jesus' lineage, and the text seems to know of some events from within Jesus' life. It is aware of the cross (11.8) and of the resurrection (1.5), and that Jerusalem is the location of such events (11.8). The notion that the Lamb was slaughtered (5.12) also suggests that the *manner* of Jesus' death was likewise well remembered. The slightly oblique reference to the Lord's Day (1.10) may perhaps refer to Sunday as the known day of the resurrection story. More generally, Revelation offers further evidence of the Twelve as a discrete unit (21.14), and one distinct from other apostles, who can be named but not necessarily included within that grouping (cf. 2.2; also 18.20). Revelation 12.1–5 may have some recollection of the birth of Jesus, and perhaps the sense that he was born in difficult and challenging circumstances, but the reference here is allusive at best, and it is difficult to draw anything particularly concrete from it. After all, it is Jesus' death, rather than his birth, that seems to interest the author of Revelation, and it is the Passion of Jesus that John ultimately exploits. It is a victorious death, one that has atoning value; the death at the hands of Roman authorities becomes a death of victory (5.9–10). Revelation 16.17 may therefore forge a possible link to, or remembrance of, Jesus' words on the cross (cf. John 19.30), the seventh angel's climactic declaration that

'It is done' perhaps equivalent to Jesus' final assertion that 'It is finished.'[18]

More securely, perhaps, the Apocalypse also describes Jesus paradigmatically as the faithful witness (1.5; cf. 3.14), the firstborn from the dead (1.5), and the ruler of the kings of the earth (1.5). His death is described as efficacious and liberative – it achieves something (1.5–6). There may also be a further allusion to Jesus tradition in 1.5: the doxology connects Jesus' motivation ('the one who loved us') with his sacrificial death and its vicarious effect.[19] This embrace of Jesus' loving action seems to address Jesus' life in more than just the bare minimum act of his death, and may have in mind a more general remembrance of Jesus' character and demeanour.

The mention of Jesus' being a 'faithful witness' (1.5) may also function likewise. The reference is an intriguing one, and the attribution assumes something of a paradigmatic aspect in the whole Apocalypse (cf. 3.14), with Antipas, too, held up as a model follower through his personification as a faithful witness (2.13). Such faithful witness or testimony probably points to the death of Jesus, and to his faithful testimony at his death – probably in his trial or in his conduct leading up to his crucifixion. It seems likely, therefore, that Revelation knows something of the tradition regarding Jesus' conduct at his death, and of the trial scene narrative that occasioned it. As such, it is not just that John the Seer recollects Jesus' death, or that he ascribes it efficacious, atoning significance (though that is certainly the case – 1.5; 5.9). Rather, it is the *mode* of the death that matters – the act of witness – that particularly matters for John, and that contributes to his picture and recollection of Jesus. The active resistance and testimony to the truth, which Jesus patterned in his trial and

---

[18] Stephen S. Smalley, *The Revelation to John: A Commentary on the Greek Text of the Apocalypse* (London: SPCK; Downers Grove: InterVarsity, 2005); in relation to the climax of Rev. 16, he ventures: '[i]f it be asked when that occurred, the answer must be in the life and ministry, and death and exaltation of Jesus' (413).

[19] Cf. Aune, 'Stories' 301: 'the phrase "the one who loved us" is striking, for it refers to the motivation of the historical Jesus to sacrifice his life on behalf of others'.

death, is the very response John demands from those who hear this testimony. Just as in 1 Timothy 6.13, where he witnesses before Pontius Pilate, Jesus is recalled for his faithful testimony, at the point of greatest persecution and imminent death. Such an appeal to Jesus as a model exemplar is also reminiscent of 1 Peter and Jesus' obedience and faithfulness outlined there. Later on in Revelation, the call is issued unto the endurance of the saints, that they may keep hold of the faith (*pistis*) of Jesus (Rev. 14.12); it is quite possible that Revelation has in mind there the faithfulness of Jesus, specifically his own activity as faithful witness in suffering unto death. There is thus some exemplary function operative here. Jesus is the paradigmatic faithful one, whose faithfulness in testing operates as an example to those who are being similarly tested (cf. 6.10, and the cry 'how long?').

There is also some narrative patterning – or re-patterning – within Revelation's portrait of Jesus. Jesus is named 14 times – 2×7 – within the Apocalypse, and such mathematical play surely matters within a text replete with numeric significance. Jesus is also re-orientated into the heavenly arena. He is the pre-existent one (22.13); he sits on the throne of God (3.21; 7.17). Much of this Christological exposition is focused on titles, with Jesus Christ described as Lord, Son of God, Lamb on the throne (7.17), the First and the Last (22.13), King of Kings and Lord of Lords (19.16). The portrait of the Son of Man figure, though, in Revelation 1.12–20 is one of the more intriguing elements, and perhaps summarizes the Apocalypse's picture of Jesus *in nuce*, and is arguably the one tied most closely to memories of the earthly Jesus. It is tempting to view the Son of Man appellation here as evidence that the earthly Jesus assumed that title for himself, but the very apocalyptic context of the narrative (and the broader debates within historical Jesus studies as to the titular use of the phrase) cautions against jumping to that conclusion. The description of the figure draws heavily on Daniel 7, and the character is described as one like the Son of Man (1.12; cf. Dan. 7.13, 10.5–6). However, Revelation's portrait of the figure also draws on imagery taken from the Danielic Ancient of Days, particularly with the reference to hair of white wool (Rev. 1.14; Dan. 7.9). As such, the Son of

Man and Ancient of Days imagery becomes intertwined, and within Revelation's Christological portrait the distinction gets blurred; both aspects – human and heavenly – morph into the one figure.[20] But the fact that Son of Man terminology is included at the outset of the Revelation account at least opens up the possibility that the earthly Jesus was indeed remembered as one who upheld the designation 'Son of Man'.[21]

We might make two further points in this regard. First, the Gospel accounts give no information as to Jesus' physical description, an interesting omission on their part. It is notable, then, that Revelation does include such physical description – and has its own purposes for so doing. The portrait it yields (1.13–16), however, is visually symbolic and intertextually evocative, and makes no historical claim; the genre of the Apocalypse and the nature of the imagery surely necessitate that. As such, it is interesting that while the Jesus remembered by the early Church took little or no account of what Jesus actually looked like, subsequent Christian traditions have sought to depict Jesus through visual art in a variety of ways and means, often in contested fashion. Second, the heavenly placement of Jesus, I suggest, is part of Revelation's attempt to portray Jesus as both heavenly and human and to indicate that the heavenly aspect is in continuity with, or builds upon, traditions or remembrances of the earthly Jesus. We arrive therefore at interesting connections between Jesus and Christ, ones that potentially shed light on the corporate memory of Jesus. It is an interesting connection, for example, that the opening dictum of the Apocalypse is a beatitude, a form of address associated with Jesus, and one with which he is portrayed as beginning his teaching discourses (such as the Sermon on the Mount).[22] The particular phrasing here may recollect Luke 11.28.

---

[20] So Charles H. Talbert, 'The Christology of the Apocalypse', in *Who Do You Say That I Am? Essays on Christology*, ed. Jack Dean Kingsbury, Mark Allan Powell and David R. Bauer (Louisville: Westminster John Knox, 1999) 166–84.

[21] The reference to Jesus' face shining may recall the Transfiguration, where Jesus is similarly portrayed with shining visage (Matt. 17.2) and with dazzling white clothing (Matt. 17.2).

[22] Though there are of course other parallels – the book of Psalms, in its received form, begins with a beatitude blessing.

One other aspect of the portrayal of Jesus is the extent to which Jesus, or Gospel, tradition is embedded in the Revelation account. As with both James and 1 Peter, the extent to which such allusions are found credible varies from interpreter to interpreter, and we must be careful of overstating the imposition of Jesus tradition, particularly when the text makes no explicit connection.[23] A number of possible examples exist, however, and they become more persuasive when Revelation actually connects them with the portrait of Jesus himself. Revelation 1.7, for example, seems to echo Matthew 24.30, with their shared imagery of all the tribes of the earth wailing at the coming of the Son of Man. The language is reasonably close, and Revelation 1.7 also prefaces the extended description of the Son of Man/Jesus figure (Rev. 1.12–20). Likewise, Revelation 3.5 places in the mouth of the exalted Son the promise that he will confess the audience's name before the Father, akin to the same declaration made by Jesus in Matthew 10.32 (cf. also Luke 12.8). Just a couple of verses before (Rev. 3.2), the same exalted Son (of Man) promises to come like a thief in the night (cf. also Rev. 16.15), such that people might be ready to receive him, in terms reminiscent of Matthew 24.42–44.

Other possible Apocalypse allusions to Synoptic tradition lack the contextual association with Jesus, but may still be said to have value. There is a possible echo of Luke 12.36–37 in Revelation 3.20 (the appeal to the master knocking, such that he may come in and eat), and the subsequent verse (Rev. 3.21) also shares some common imagery and language with the Lucan Gospel (Luke 22.28–30). Revelation 11.2 recalls Luke 21.24, while the Jesus/Gethsemane tradition that 'those who take the sword die by the sword' (Matt. 26.52) seems to be picked up by Revelation 13.10. It is possible that the marriage supper of the Lamb proclaimed in Revelation 19.9 has in mind Jesus' parable of the

---

[23] M. Eugene Boring, 'Narrative Christology in the Apocalypse', *CBQ* 54 (1992) 702–23 (715n16), notes the following possible connections: 1.3/Luke 11.28; l.3b/Matt. 26.18; 2.7 etc. (7x)/Matt. 11.15, etc.; 3.3 and 16.15/Matt. 24.43 par.; 13.11 (16.13; 19.20)/Matt. 7.15; 18.24/Luke 11.50 par.; 19.7/Matt. 5.12 par., but terms it 'not an impressive list'.

wedding banquet (Matt. 22.1–14). The grounds for making the connection are not always secure, however, and it is difficult to say with any degree of confidence that these were thought to be dominical logia.[24]

Much of this discussion suggests that the shape of Revelation's Jesus, and its presentation of the victorious Jesus Christ, is driven by the concerns and situation of its hearers. As Eugene Boring puts it: 'The story of the Christ who conquered/died is to become the story of the Christian who is called to die/conquer.'[25] Jesus was opposed and affronted, just as those who now follow after him are similarly being opposed and affronted. As such, Revelation offers an insight into *how* Jesus was remembered, how portraits of Jesus could be accommodated and contextualized within the milieu of the community who sought to remember him; it models the emergence or development of Jesus tradition among those seeking to follow after him. This does not mean that the identity of Jesus in the Apocalypse lacks historical referent; rather, it suggests that there was sufficient flexibility as to how the memory of Jesus might impact among the present community addressed by the text.

Conclusion: the Jesus of Revelation

While we glean little biographical detail from Revelation as to the earthly Jesus, the Apocalypse nonetheless yields a picture of him that has its foundations in the remembrance of his earthly life. Revelation manifests the full outworking of Jesus' transition from historical figure to the One established in the heavenly arena as recipient of worship and adoration (Rev. 1.5–6). The references to Jesus' earthy life are allusive and infrequent at best, but their presence, however minimal, indicates a continuity between the earthly Jesus and the exalted Lord.

---

[24] See further Richard J. Bauckham, *The Climax of Prophecy: Studies on the Book of Revelation* (Edinburgh: T&T Clark, 1993) 92–117.

[25] Boring, 'Narrative Christology' 716; see also L. W. Hurtado, 'Jesus' Death as Paradigmatic in the New Testament', *SJT* 57 (2004) 413–33 (424–6).

Revelation refuses to leave Jesus merely as a figure of history, but instead portrays him as one who is encountered in the present: the Son of Man stands in the midst of the seven lampstands (1.13), suggestive of a Jesus figure who is very much present to the churches currently experiencing distress. Revelation, I might suggest, deconstructs the foundations of the historical Jesus project, in that it refuses to confine interest just to the earthly Jesus. While not retelling Jesus' life – at least not in the way that Gospels do – Revelation's portrayal of Christ gives a window onto Jesus, and the remembrance of him by those seeking to imitate his faithful witness. As Boxall surmises: 'the Apocalypse's vision of the enthroned Lamb confronts the reader with the extraordinary claim that one of the human race, the crucified and risen Jesus, is worthy of the worship due to Israel's god alone.'[26]

---

[26] Boxall, 'Jesus in the Apocalypse' 125.

9

Conclusion: the canonical Jesus

In the previous seven chapters, we have focused on the various constituent texts of the New Testament, specifically the non-Gospel material, in an attempt to consider how each text, or group of texts, goes about presenting the figure of Jesus of Nazareth. We have done so with a particular historical interest, namely to glean how the respective texts might inform our understanding of the historical Jesus, but we have also sought to explore the way in which each text presents its own characteristic depiction of Jesus' identity. We now turn to revisit these portrayals, in an attempt to see how they contribute to the overall canonical rendering of Jesus, and to discern both the commonalities and differences between their respective approaches. This takes us back to our introductory discussion of the concept of the canonical Jesus. In using the term, we do not (necessarily) mean the Jesus defined by creedal faith, or constructed by doctrinal or systematic instruction, or the canon in the sense of an imposed rule of systematic belief (important concepts though they all may be). Instead, we mean 'canonical Jesus' to be that combination of the potentially diverse and varied portraits of Jesus yielded by the canonical texts, and specifically by the non-Gospel material, and the way in which Jesus' earthly life is woven into that tapestry.

The non-Gospel material and the earthly Jesus

It is a repeated axiom of NT scholarship that the non-Gospel material yields very little biographical information on Jesus of Nazareth, with comparatively little appeal made to Jesus to support or endorse apostolic teaching. Paula Fredriksen's frank statement encapsulates this perspective:

If all we had were the Epistles, we would know precious little about Jesus of Nazareth: not where or whom he taught, little about his activities and his teaching, scarcely anything about the circumstances of his death – precisely that information that the evangelists are concerned to relate.[1]

As far as historical Jesus interests are concerned, the non-Gospel texts are commonly reduced to being a postscript to the (primary) evangelistic accounts, a window onto the common life of the Church, rather than offering a locus for consideration of who Jesus is/was.

In one sense, our analysis has not disproved this perspective. We have found there to be some significant reticence to speak of Jesus, or to allude to his teaching, particularly from those writers – Paul, Acts, Peter – whom we might have expected to be more vocal in this regard. At key, formative occasions and debates within the non-Gospel texts, at particular instances when Jesus' teaching could have provided very helpful 'support' for the position being taken, no such appeal is made, and their silence is consequently rather loud. But at the same time, our study has also queried the extent of such 'silence', or at least sought to give the non-Gospel material a 'voice' within discussions as to the person and character of the earthly Jesus. While the evangelistic accounts clearly remain the primary texts for explicating the person of Jesus and his identity, and while the concerns of the particular congregations are the focal topic of the non-Gospel texts, we have suggested that Jesus tradition and Jesus formulation continued to be a not insignificant aspect of the NT testimony. It may be that the references are more subtle or nuanced; it may be that details of Jesus' life are not substantively alluded to; and it may be that the various canonical texts pursue different approaches and strategies as to how they go about the exercise of remembering Jesus. But Jesus' teaching and Jesus tradition continue to permeate the epistolary corpus, even as the historical Jesus expands to the Christ of faith, even as traditions regarding the 'Jesus of Faith' are recalled and passed on to other congregations beyond the eyewitness apostolic community.

---

[1] Paula Fredriksen, *Jesus of Nazareth, King of the Jews: A Jewish Life and the Emergence of Christianity* (New York: Knopf, 1999) 98.

In short, the figure of the earthly Jesus mattered to the non-Gospel writers, perhaps not in the terms some historians might wish/expect him to, but he matters nonetheless. We find reference to his coming (1 John 1.1–3), to his teaching (1 Cor. 7.10; 9.14), to events of his life (Acts 2.22–24), to his death (1 Tim. 6.13; 1 Peter 2.22–25) and to his character (Heb. 4.15) and conduct (Rev. 1.5). In James and 1 Peter, we find his teaching taken over and re-presented to the churches and congregations; in Paul, we find some quite substantive detail about the narrative of his death; in Acts and Hebrews, we find the founding and inception of churches to be geared around retellings of Jesus' story. The level of interest varies between the texts of course, and we access it in more second- than first-hand terms, but it is 'interest' nonetheless and is of sufficient volume to inform the NT's portrait of the earthly Jesus.

And this should not probably be a surprise to us, after all. Our understanding of a figure is commonly informed by how those who follow go about remembering and recalling his or her actions. We understand people not just by what they say/do, but by what others say about them, often posthumously; their 'reception history', so to speak, comprises a core part of their identity.[2] We have only to be present at a handful of funeral orations or eulogies to appreciate that fact, as speakers invariably reflect on the character, significance and achievements of a person, as much as retelling their deeds and actions. Of course, if our concern were solely about the effect Jesus had on those who had encountered him, then we would be in a position of some weakness, as there is real doubt as to whether any of the non-Gospel writers had actually ever 'met' the earthly Jesus. They are witnesses to Jesus tradition rather than *eyewitnesses* of it. But one might say the same of the Gospel writers themselves,[3] and it still seems plausible to speak of the impact Jesus had on people, however mediated or vicariously that impact occurred. The non-Gospel texts certainly tell us more about the people who

---

[2] See Dale C. Allison, Jr., 'The Historical Jesus and the Church', in *Seeking the Identity of Jesus: A Pilgrimage*, ed. Beverly Roberts Gaventa and Richard B. Hays (Grand Rapids: Eerdmans, 2008) 79–95, esp. 93–5.

[3] Even taking into account the conclusions of Richard J. Bauckham, *Jesus and the Eyewitnesses: The Gospels as Eyewitness Testimony* (Grand Rapids: Eerdmans, 2006).

followed after Jesus and sought to proclaim, worship and remember him. But through them we also glean access to Jesus; he impacted upon those responsible for the texts, and their commitment to him does not happen in historical isolation.[4]

The plurality of the canonical Jesus

As a minimum, our analysis has revealed the diversity of the images of Jesus located under the canonical umbrella, the way in which his identity is named and expressed in a variety of fashions. The contrasts manifest themselves in different ways and for different reasons. For example, the particular portrait of Jesus is commonly linked to the situation of the addressees, often as they experience some form of persecution (notably 1 Peter, Hebrews and Revelation). Some texts mention Jesus more than others – Hebrews has him as the central character, whereas he is barely named in the epistle of James (though remains absolutely integral to the 'effect' of the epistle). Some remain almost completely silent in terms of Jesusology (3 John). First John can focus almost exclusively on the notion that Jesus has come (i.e. 'in the beginning'), while 2 Thessalonians is really only interested in his coming again. And then there are those texts that tend more towards Christological exploration than to Jesusological, Colossians and Ephesians being particularly prominent in this regard.

The plurality is manifest in other ways. We have seen different aspects of Jesus portrayed – Jesus the wisdom teacher in James, Jesus the model of obedience in 1 Peter, Jesus the suffering exemplar whom Paul seeks to replicate. Some non-Gospel texts – notably James – require a sifting behind the text to reveal the depth of reflection on Jesus tradition (and the apparently avowed desire to continue Jesus' teaching under a different guise in a new context); others, however, such as Hebrews, seem perfectly happy to pass on Jesus tradition and name it explicitly as such (Heb. 2.3–4;

---

[4] In effect, this is the strategy adopted in Chris Keith and Larry W. Hurtado, *Jesus among Friends and Enemies: A Historical and Literary Introduction to Jesus in the Gospels* (Grand Rapids: Baker Academic, 2011). By engaging with figures with whom Jesus interacted, we gain a window onto Jesus, and onto how he was remembered and recalled.

cf. 1 Cor. 11.23–25). For some texts, notably the Pauline corpus, we find ourselves caught in a wide-ranging maximalist/minimalist debate as to the extent of its interaction with Jesus material. And then we encounter variation even within the Pauline corpus itself; Paul's direct citation of Jesus tradition is located primarily in 1 Corinthians, and we have had less need, for example, to engage with Philippians (the Christ-hymn of 2.5–11 aside).

Different pictures of Jesus therefore emerge, or rather the identity of Jesus is teased out in different ways. The canonical Jesus is no monochrome Jesus. Some may find such plurality or diversity unsatisfactory, and desire more of a unified portrait. After all, there is one Jesus of Nazareth – on that the Gospels, the non-Gospel material surely agree – and integrity and coherence would seem to aspire to some kind of correlation between the respective accounts. But the diversity of the canonical portrait remains, and we suggest that the Church is the richer for it. Of course, the canonical Gospels also present pictures of Jesus in different ways – sometimes ascetic, sometimes eating and drinking, sometimes confident about his mission, sometimes more apprehensive. Part of that reasoning is to bring out the rounded picture of Jesus and his identity; while we cannot categorically say such descriptions are equally 'historical' there is no reason to think they were not so, and thus they reveal a diverse non-monochrome remembered Jesus. The non-Gospel texts contribute to this diversity, both deepening the memory of Jesus' identity and cautioning against making Jesus in a particular image, the grand accusation famously levelled by Albert Schweitzer over the claims of the First Historical Jesus Quest.

Hence, with Dunn, though coming at the matter from a different angle, the non-Gospel presentation recognizes that remembrance of Jesus – and the recalling of tradition about him – derives from a position of faith of, or from the 'faith impact' on, each particular community.[5] Paul, James, Hebrews, John et al. all stand in a tradition of interpreting Jesus, of remembering him and his significance

---

[5] James D. G. Dunn, *A New Perspective on Jesus: What the Quest for the Historical Jesus Missed* (Grand Rapids: Baker Academic, 2005) 57.

for them – interpretation is present from the very outset of Jesus' death, and is manifest across the NT testimony, whether evangelical or epistolary, narrative or apocalyptic. Dunn also speaks of the 'characteristic Jesus'[6] and lists a number of factors, derived from the Gospels, that make this figure distinctive, or that contribute to the contemporary impression of him. We might add that the NT texts complement, expand and confirm this 'characteristic Jesus', doing so in ways that particularly draw out how we might respond to him.

But does this 'canonical Jesus' mean that one ends up with what Joseph Hoffman terms a 'historicized' Jesus – that is, that the earthly Jesus is created on a 'needed' basis, a theological necessity that is required to support the establishment of a canonical rule of faith?[7] Hoffman calls this approach the 'canonical-historical Jesus', averring that the early Church composed a story of the human Jesus to fit their presenting beliefs, and that a historical overlay is superimposed onto their pre-existing faith commitments. We would suggest that this is not the case. While Hoffman's titular phrase sounds similar to the one we have coined, our approach has been somewhat different, and we have tried to avoid thinking of 'canon' as either an imposition upon or onto the biblical texts, or as merely contributing to the creation of an 'approved story' (though we recognize that the term can have that dimension to it).[8] Instead, we have worked from the premise that these constituent representations of Jesus provide testimony of how he impacted upon diverse congregations and communities, and they have been gathered together under the umbrella we now call 'canon'. And non-Gospel portrayals have a particular validity in that 'the image of Jesus is *assumed* more than *consciously* constructed'[9] – that is, the non-Gospel texts lack any sense of being theological creations to

---

[6] Dunn, *New Perspective on Jesus* 69–77.

[7] R. Joseph Hoffmann, 'Epilogue: The Canonical-Historical Jesus', in *Sources of the Jesus Tradition: Separating History from Myth*, ed. R. Joseph Hoffmann (New York: Prometheus, 2010) 257–65.

[8] Hoffmann, 'Epilogue' 265.

[9] Luke Timothy Johnson, *Living Jesus: Learning the Heart of the Gospel* (San Francisco: HarperSanFrancisco, 1999) 80.

support a particular perception of Jesus. As we have seen, there is too little said about Jesus in the non-Gospel texts for that to be the case. Instead, memory of the human Jesus is merely woven into the various accounts, and the reader can access that memory/ portrait accordingly. The canonical Jesus may be more than historical (if by historical we mean pure history untainted by the theological reflection), but it is at least 'historical' in requiring a particular context and milieu by which the reader can be exposed to both what can be discerned about the figure and also how that figure has been remembered and celebrated.

The characteristics of the canonical Jesus

As a minimum, perhaps, we have suggested that the NT writers were actually more aware and more interested in Jesus' life than has often been thought. But in order to do so, we have drawn a number of comparisons with the Gospel accounts, and in that sense, we have been dependent upon the Gospels for some form of confirmation or validation. The discussion of James would be a case in point: we can only engage with its re-presentation of Jesus' teaching if we are aware of Sermon on the Mount/Plain tradition found in the Synoptics. However, bearing in mind that several of the non-Gospel accounts are likely to be independent of the Gospel tradition – Hebrews most probably, but possibly Revelation – do they have the potential to supplement the evangelical perspective on Jesus? And within the diversity we have encountered, are there any commonalities, any ways in which the non-Gospel texts are consistent in their Jesusology? What can we say about the way in which the non-Gospel writers remembered Jesus? Let us draw some broader conclusions:

1 *Jesus' humanity matters.* We obviously derive this message from the Gospel record as well, but the non-Gospel material substantiates and confirms it. While they may yield varying amounts of detail as to of what his humanity was composed, the fact remains that Jesus' humanity is central. Jesus' earthly life is an integral part of Paul's story of Christ, while Hebrews

emphasizes Jesus' full humanity and affinity with his (human) sisters and brothers (Heb. 2.12–14). Revelation builds its argument around Jesus' earthly, faithful witness (Rev 1.5; 3.14), while 1 John recognizes the 'beginning-ness' that Jesus' human existence inaugurated (1 John 1.1–3).

2 As a result, the non-Gospel material shows – however indirectly or circumstantially – that *Jesus' life and ministry were a key component of the kerygmatic preaching of the early Church,* and tied to the foundation of churches. The letters, notably of Paul, James, Peter and Hebrews, all assume Jesus knowledge in order for their arguments to be made, and commonly allude back to the content of the preaching as part of the epistolary discourse (Gal. 3.1; Heb. 2.3–4; 1 Cor. 2.2). The speeches of Acts likewise also tie their missional message to the life and ministry of Jesus of Nazareth (Acts 2.22–23; 10.36–41).

3 The third principle follows on from the second. Because the appeal to Jesus tradition is often indirect, because it is commonly made through the medium of allusion rather than through direct citation or narrative retelling, *we need to know about Jesus tradition or Jesus' life in order to make the connections, and to hear them as Jesus 'allusions'.* It is fair to say that the writers of James and Peter, in particular, assume that their audiences possess the foundations of knowledge about the earthly Jesus and can make the connections accordingly. In that sense, if the aim of our exercise is to use the non-Gospel material to shed light on the events of the life of Jesus, then we cannot venture too much further forward. Generally speaking, they do serve something of a confirmatory aspect – a 'this event did happen' perspective – and we normally need the Synoptic testimony to make the connection. At a stretch we could construct a Passion narrative of sorts from the Pauline/Deutero-Pauline corpus,[10] but such creations are exceptional; for Jesus' teaching to be reheard (as in James), we would normally have some prior reason for associating it with Jesus.

---

[10] Dale C. Allison, Jr., *Constructing Jesus: Memory, Imagination, and History* (London: SPCK, 2010) 392–403.

4 It would seem that the non-Gospel material portrays Jesus as one who is – in some way – *accessible in the present*, and not (just) a figure reduced to the past. He is remembered, but is also present and active within such remembrance (cf. 1 John 1.3). We might say that followers of Jesus were interested in the earthly Jesus (and preserving traditions about him), but integral to that process was its 'present' dimension; the texts remember Jesus not as a figure who merely died but as someone who they understood 'to be alive today, a celestial Lord to whom they (would) daily turn in prayer and other acts of worship'.[11] The liturgical extracts or catechetical formulae of the Pastoral Epistles (1 Tim. 2.5–6; 3.16; 2 Tim. 2.8; 2.11–13) also point in that direction, linking the (hi)story of Jesus with the present worshipping life of the gathered church. Similarly, Paul, Luke and James seem to have some freedom to shape their presentation of Jesus' teaching to fit their particular needs and interests.[12] There is sufficient 'flexibility' in the Jesus tradition to apply it to the local context; none of Paul's citations of Jesus' teaching exactly mirrors the form found elsewhere in the Synoptics. Michael Bird's summary is apposite:

> the Jesus material that survived the attrition of time was that which was continually relevant to the primitive Jesus movement in terms of community praxis for the new age. In fact, the more radical and subversive Jesus' teachings were going against the grain of the Greco-Roman ethos, the more likely they were to be embedded in communal practice as visible affirmations of Christian identity.[13]

5 It would seem that *much of the Jesus tradition we have encountered refers to the Passion narrative* and to discussion of Jesus' death. This is of course commensurate with the Gospels, all of

---

[11] Birger Gerhardsson, *The Origins of the Gospel Traditions* (Philadelphia: Fortress, 1979) 43.

[12] Cf. Allison, *Constructing* 377: 'Early Christian literature leaves the definite impression that his followers were uninterested in parrot-like verbatim memorization.'

[13] Michael F. Bird, 'The Purpose and Preservation of the Jesus Tradition: Moderate Evidence for a Conserving Force in its Transmission', *BBR* 15 (2005) 161–85 (166).

which culminate in Jesus' Passion and devote a proportionally high amount of content to that event. That is not to concur with Kahler's famous dictum that Mark's Gospel is a Passion narrative with an extended introduction, but merely to remark that the whole of the New Testament – Gospel and non-Gospel – shares a focal interest in Jesus' death. At the same time, it is also not to ignore our findings that often it was the manner or character of Jesus' death that the non-Gospel texts explore; it was not just that he died, but *how* he did so. Revelation points to the faithful witness aspect of his death, 1 Peter to his active embrace of suffering. Paul emphasizes the obedience with which Jesus went to his death. Thus, it is difficult to agree with Hoffman's assertion that 'there is simply no evidence that the early Christians were concerned about whether Jesus had really lived or died'.[14] That Jesus died, and how/why he did so, is central to the historical Christ event and to the manner of Jesus worship/imitation that this birthed. Romans 4.25, for example, is evidently a theologically geared reflection upon the death of Jesus, namely that he was handed over for human trespasses. But that was the very Jesus, or the very death, that Paul 'remembers'.

6 As such, it is only really in Paul and James, and to a lesser extent 1 Peter and Revelation (and therein, it has to be said, in more oblique fashion), that one finds substantial reference to Jesus' teaching. There is some broader non-Gospel characterization of Jesus as teacher – Acts 1.1–9 articulates the continuity with Luke's Gospel portrait as teacher, while James seems to assume and re-present Jesus' teachings in a new guise, under his own name – but it remains a relatively minor characteristic of the canonical Jesus.

7 Perhaps, though, the prevailing image of the canonical Jesus is *his presentation as an exemplary figure*. In Acts, the apostles are portrayed as doing and acting like Jesus; within its narrative, Peter, Paul, Stephen and Philip are all pictured in terms that

[14] R. Joseph Hoffmann, 'On Not Finding the Historical Jesus', in *Sources of the Jesus Tradition: Separating History from Myth*, ed. R. Joseph Hoffmann (New York: Prometheus, 2010) 171–84 (180).

Luke had used of Jesus. Paul likewise models his own ministry on the story and sufferings of Christ (Phil. 3.10), patterning himself in terms and imagery similar to that of Jesus, and carrying the death of Jesus in his body (2 Cor. 4.7–12). Albeit more implicitly, James presents Jesus as the paradigmatic faithful one (Jas. 2.1), a figure whose attitude towards the poor his addressees should replicate. Revelation holds out Jesus as the faithful witness whose example is to be followed (Rev. 1.5; 3.14), while Hebrews portrays him as the faithful witness par excellence (Heb. 12.1), whose example its readers are to embrace as they follow him outside the camp to bear the abuse he endured (13.13). Most explicitly, perhaps, 1 Peter urges its readers to follow in Jesus' steps (2.21) and embrace his example of one who demonstrated active obedience in his suffering (2.22–25).[15]

But why not more?

A frequent feature of our discussion has been engaging with the expectation that the non-Gospel material should make more appeal to the life and teaching of the historical Jesus. Whether it is Luke's reluctance to refer back to Jesus tradition in Acts, or Paul's apparent lack of interest in explicitly citing Jesus to support his position, or even the (for some) disappointing lack of personal insight onto Jesus from 1 Peter, the consistent feature of the discussion has been the expectation that the particular NT author really should have said more about Jesus of Nazareth. Craig Evans's summation of this apparent reticence is representative of the scholarly consensus: '[I]t is surprising that the Jesus tradition has so little to say about several pressing problems and disputes in these early communities, as we see them discussed and debated in the book of Acts and in many of the New Testament letters.'[16]

On the one hand, though, the reticence to cite Jesus tradition may in fact inspire some historical confidence: if Jesus tradition

---

[15] Cf. Bird, 'Purpose' 177: 'One observes in the NT that the example of Jesus is a constituent element of ethics for the believing community.'

[16] Craig A. Evans, 'Seeking the Identity of Jesus: A Pilgrimage', *Modern Theology* 27.1 (2011) 212–14 (214).

were merely created or constructed to suit the needs of the early Church, then we might well expect to find more evidence of it, particularly in those situations (such as the Council of Jerusalem) where it would prove to be most 'useful' or 'applicable'. The relatively limited nature of the testimony, therefore, actually gives confidence, when we do encounter it, to conclude that it attests genuine or reliable tradition. Moreover, there is very little evidence of Jesus tradition being constructed to justify any post-Easter position. Indeed, we have seen how Paul actually cites Jesus tradition only then to *qualify* it (cf. 1 Cor. 9.14); there is no sense in which it is his trump card, quite the reverse. Once again, Strange's reminder of the Jesus strategy of Acts is helpful: 'It is significant ... that there is virtually no evidence in Acts that Luke wrote his Gospel in order to enshrine the authoritative teaching of Jesus for the church.'[17]

But on the other hand, perhaps this silence also encourages us either to rephrase the question or to come at the matter from a different angle. The lack of interest in certain aspects of the life/teaching of Jesus can be considered as a historical datum in its own right, a matter to be explored/explained, rather than an embarrassment to be assuaged. Just as in our discussion of Paul's reticence to allude to Jesus explicitly, exploring the (relative) silence for its own sake can actually yield insight on how Jesus was remembered by his immediate followers. After all, the non-Gospel writers are not alone in this more allusive mode of referring to Jesus tradition: there is a similar reticence on the part of the Apostolic Fathers who, even with the Gospels apparently available to them, reference them (and Jesus' teaching) only indirectly.[18] To put it another way, the non-Gospel texts caution us against placing undue weight on historical Jesus questions, or at least to avoid an overemphasis on the way in which they are framed (i.e. attempting to get back to the 'real' Jesus through the mechanism of some form of historical reconstruction, and by applying criteria as to what is 'genuine' or not).

---

[17] W. A. Strange, 'The Jesus-Tradition in Acts', *NTS* 46 (2000) 59–74 (69).

[18] Peter H. Davids, 'James and Jesus', in *The Jesus Tradition outside the Gospels*, ed. David Wenham, Gospel Perspectives 5 (Sheffield: JSOT Press, 1985) 63–84 (69).

For if, as I have suggested, Jesus is central to the non-Gospel enterprise, then we must take seriously the way in which those same writers sought to remember him, rather than superimposing modern (or even postmodern) expectations about how the non-Gospel writers should do so. The non-Gospel texts reveal how they remember Jesus and recall his teaching and character, and worship him as risen, ascended Lord; but they do so not by mechanical citation of teaching or biographical detail, but rather through the more indirect appeal to the prevailing example of a life faithfully lived and followed. The 'Jesus remembered' is certainly framed in a way that appealed to sayings, deeds, stories and events (as the Gospel accounts clearly demonstrate), but the NT writers also demonstrate the importance of other parts of Jesus' 'historical' identity – his character, his nature, quite simply what people made of him and how he impacted upon them. Of course, the Gospel tradition enables the more overtly biographical mode of recollection to occur, and the preservation (both inside and outside the canon) of that oral tradition in written form testifies to its ongoing significance for the life of the Church. But it is not the *only* way in which Jesus was remembered, not the *only* way in which Jesus' memory was upheld. In almost all of the texts we have considered, we have identified the presentation of Jesus as an exemplary figure, one whose earthly life gave some form of pattern or example. It is *this* 'historical Jesus', a Jesus in whom faith is placed and to whom worship is offered, one whose identity is outworked, remembered and modelled; it is this Jesus to which the non-Gospel material contributes.

Furthermore, the non-Gospel texts may even show the aims of the historical Jesus project to be in some sense wrong-headed or misplaced. In the same way that modern historians have grappled with differentiating the historical Jesus from the Christ of faith, in the same way that contemporary readers of the NT texts struggle to separate the resurrected Jesus from the figure who, by the majority of accounts, was also a historical, bodily figure, I suggest that the NT writers experienced the same tension or challenge. To put it another way, the historical Jesus questers of the first century (to apply that title anachronistically!) seem to have faced similar problems to their modern (and postmodern?) counterparts in finding a way of remembering Jesus that was not coloured by theological reflection or faith commitment – in short, they seemed quite unable or unwilling to do so.

We might push the matter further. Working with the non-Gospel material does not just caution us as to the limitations of the historical Jesus project, as to what it can or cannot do. The process also offers a window onto the very doing of the exercise, onto the actual process of trying to remember Jesus and articulate who he is. These first-century questers were simultaneously trying to remember him, and thereby preserve the 'tradition', as well as make sense of Jesus as one in whom to put their faith. They demonstrate how

> There is no path to a secure portrait of Jesus independent of how he has been responded to . . . Part of the 'reality' we seek is that the history of Jesus did indeed begin the process that led to the definition of faith in the Christian sense.[19]

Such a pathway is one where 'history' and 'theology' combine,[20] and where trying to make sense of Jesus, trying to remember his significance, becomes a highly complicated task, particularly when trying to evaluate the implications of his humanity. As Sarah Coakley succinctly opines, Jesus 'is no less personally mysterious in his earthly life than in his risen existence';[21] as such, one can well imagine that the NT writers would respond and attest to this mysterious character in a variety of ways, each of which could be said to shed light on the 'historical' figure of Jesus. It is likely even attested by the Gospels themselves – certain characters, Nicodemus,

---

[19] Rowan Williams, 'Looking for Jesus and Finding Christ', in *Biblical Concepts and Our World*, ed. D. Z. Phillips and Mano van der Ruhr (Basingstoke: Palgrave Macmillan, 2004) 141–52 (151), quoted in Sarah Coakley, 'The Identity of the Risen Jesus: Finding Jesus Christ in the Poor', in *Seeking the Identity of Jesus: A Pilgrimage*, ed. Beverly Roberts Gaventa and Richard B. Hays (Grand Rapids: Eerdmans, 2008) 301–19 (307).

[20] Cf. Francis Watson, 'Veritas Christi: How to Get from the Jesus of History to the Christ of Faith without Losing One's Way', in *Seeking the Identity of Jesus: A Pilgrimage*, ed. Beverly Roberts Gaventa and Richard B. Hays (Grand Rapids: Eerdmans, 2008) 96–114: 'The concrete traits of the historical Jesus belong within account of the "historic, biblical Christ" and should not be allowed to take on an independent life of their own' (114).

[21] Coakley, 'Identity' 308.

for example, are also portrayed as struggling to grapple with exactly who this mysterious human figure of Jesus claims to be.[22]

Conclusion – the canonical Jesus

By considering the canonical Jesus, we open up a diversity of ways of remembering him. It can be remembrance by what he did and taught, by what he said and by what happened to him. But the non-Gospel texts also show that Jesus could be remembered by doing the kind of things that Jesus did (healing the sick, applying his teaching to new contexts, prioritizing the poor), by seeking to model/mimic his character (especially in times of suffering) or by recalling particular incidents of his life (especially the events leading up to his death). We might do so by having the same mindset as him (Phil. 2.5), by offering testimony to him (Acts 1.8), by clothing ourselves with him (Rom. 13.14) or by looking to him as faithful example (Heb. 12.1–2) and witness (Rev. 1.5). The canonical Jesus is the historical Jesus remembered, followed and obeyed.

---

[22] See David M. Allen, 'Secret Disciples: Nicodemus and Joseph of Arimathea', in *Jesus Amongst Friends and Enemies: A Historical and Literary Introduction to Jesus in the Gospels*, ed. Chris Keith and Larry W. Hurtado (Grand Rapids: Baker, 2011) 149–69.

Bibliography

Adams, Edward, *Parallel Lives of Jesus: A Guide to the Four Gospels* (Louisville: Westminster John Knox, 2011)

Adams, Edward, 'Paul, Jesus and Christ', in *The Blackwell Companion to Jesus*, ed. Delbert Royce Burkett, Blackwell Companions to Religion (Malden, MA: Wiley-Blackwell, 2011) 94–110

Adamson, James B., *The Epistle of James*, NICNT (Grand Rapids: Eerdmans, 1976)

Aitken, Ellen Bradshaw, 'Tradition in the Mouth of the Hero: Jesus as an Interpreter of Scripture', in *Performing the Gospel: Orality, Memory, and Mark*, ed. Richard A. Horsley, Jonathan A. Draper and John Miles Foley (Minneapolis: Fortress, 2006) 97–103

Allen, David M., 'Secret Disciples: Nicodemus and Joseph of Arimathea', in *Jesus Amongst Friends and Enemies: A Historical and Literary Introduction to Jesus in the Gospels*, ed. Chris Keith and Larry W. Hurtado (Grand Rapids: Baker, 2011) 149–69

Allen, David M., 'Why Bother Going Outside? The Use of the Old Testament in Heb 13.10–16' (forthcoming)

Allison, Dale C., Jr., *Constructing Jesus: Memory, Imagination, and History* (London: SPCK, 2010)

Allison, Dale C., Jr., *The Historical Christ and the Theological Jesus* (Grand Rapids: Eerdmans, 2009)

Allison, Dale C., Jr., 'The Historical Jesus and the Church', in *Seeking the Identity of Jesus: A Pilgrimage*, ed. Beverly Roberts Gaventa and Richard B. Hays (Grand Rapids: Eerdmans, 2008) 79–95

Allison, Dale C., Jr., 'The Pauline Epistles and the Synoptic Gospels: The Pattern of the Parallels', *NTS* 28 (1982) 1–32

Attridge, Harold W., *The Epistle to the Hebrews*, Hermeneia (Philadelphia: Fortress, 1989)

Attridge, Harold W., 'Jesus in the General Epistles', in *The Blackwell Companion to Jesus*, ed. Delbert Royce Burkett, Blackwell Companions to Religion (Malden, MA: Wiley-Blackwell, 2011) 111–18

Aune, David E., 'Jesus Tradition and the Pauline Letters', in *Jesus in Memory: Traditions in Oral and Scribal Perspectives*, ed. Werner H. Kelber and Samuel Byrskog (Waco: Baylor University Press, 2009) 63–86

Aune, David E., 'Stories of Jesus in the Apocalypse of John', in *Contours of Christology in the New Testament*, ed. Richard N. Longenecker, McMaster New Testament Studies (Grand Rapids: Eerdmans, 2005) 292–319

Backhaus, Knut, 'How to Entertain Angels: Ethics in the Epistle to the Hebrews', in *Hebrews: Contemporary Methods, New Insights*, ed. Gabriella Gelardini, *BibInt* 75 (Leiden: Brill, 2005) 149–75

Bales, William, 'The Descent of Christ in Ephesians 4:9', *CBQ* 72 (2010) 84–100

Barbarick, Clifford A., 'Milk to Grow On: The Example of Christ in 1 Peter', in *Getting 'Saved': The Whole Story of Salvation in the New Testament*, ed. Charles H. Talbert, Jason A. Whitlark and Andrew E. Arterbury (Grand Rapids: Eerdmans, 2011) 216–39

Barnett, Paul, *The Birth of Christianity: The First Twenty Years*, After Jesus 1 (Grand Rapids; Cambridge: Eerdmans, 2005)

Barnett, Paul, *Finding the Historical Christ*, After Jesus 3 (Grand Rapids: Eerdmans, 2009)

Barnett, Paul, *Paul: Missionary of Jesus*, After Jesus 2 (Grand Rapids: Eerdmans, 2008)

Barrett, Charles K., *A Critical and Exegetical Commentary on the Acts of the Apostles*, 2 vols, ICC (Edinburgh: T&T Clark, 1994)

Barrett, Charles K., '*Imitatio Christi* in Acts', in *Jesus of Nazareth: Lord and Christ: Essays on the Historical Jesus and New Testament Christology*, ed. Joel B. Green and Max Turner (Grand Rapids: Eerdmans, 1994) 251–62

Barrett, Charles K., 'Sayings of Jesus in the Acts of the Apostles', in *À cause de l'Évangile: Études sur les Synoptiques et les Actes offertes au Père Jacques Dupont, o.s.b., à l'occasion de son soixante-dixième anniversaire*, Lectio Divina 123 (Paris: Éditions du Cerf, 1985) 681–708

Bartholomä, Philipp F., 'Did Jesus Save the People out of Egypt? A Re-examination of a Textual Problem in Jude 5', *NovT* 50 (2008) 143–58

Barton, Stephen C., 'Memory and Remembrance in Paul', in *Memory in the Bible and Antiquity: The Fifth Durham-Tübingen Research Symposium (Durham, September 2004)*, ed. Stephen C. Barton, Loren T. Stuckenbruck and Benjamin G. Wold, WUNT 212 (Tübingen: Mohr Siebeck, 2007) 321–39

Bauckham, Richard J., *The Climax of Prophecy: Studies on the Book of Revelation* (Edinburgh: T&T Clark, 1993)

Bibliography

Bauckham, Richard J., 'The Divinity of Jesus Christ in the Epistle to the Hebrews', in *The Epistle to the Hebrews and Christian Theology*, ed. Richard Bauckham, Daniel R. Driver, Trevor A. Hart and Nathan MacDonald (Grand Rapids: Eerdmans, 2009) 15–36

Bauckham, Richard J., 'The Family of Jesus', in *Jesus Amongst Friends and Enemies: A Historical and Literary Introduction to Jesus in the Gospels*, ed. Chris Keith and Larry W. Hurtado (Grand Rapids: Baker, 2011) 103–25

Bauckham, Richard J., 'James and Jesus', in *The Brother of Jesus: James the Just and His Mission*, ed. Bruce Chilton and Jacob Neusner (Louisville: Westminster John Knox, 2001) 100–37

Bauckham, Richard J., *Jesus and the Eyewitnesses: The Gospels as Eyewitness Testimony* (Grand Rapids: Eerdmans, 2006)

Bauckham, Richard J., *Jude and the Relatives of Jesus in the Early Church* (Edinburgh: T&T Clark, 1990)

Bauckham, Richard J., 'Seeking the Identity of Jesus', *JSNT* 32 (2010) 337–46

Beilby, James K., Eddy, Paul R., Price, Robert M., Crossan, John Dominic, Johnson, Luke Timothy, Dunn, James D. G. and Bock, Darrell L., *The Historical Jesus: Five Views* (Downers Grove: InterVarsity, 2009)

Best, Ernest, '1 Peter and the Gospel Tradition', *NTS* 16.2 (1970) 95–113

Bevere, Allan R., 'The Cheirograph in Colossians 2:4 and the Ephesian Connection', in *Jesus and Paul: Global Perspectives in Honor of James D.G. Dunn for his 70th Birthday*, ed. B. J. Oropeza, C. K. Robertson and Douglas C. Mohrmann, Library of New Testament Studies 414 (London: T&T Clark, 2009) 199–206

Bird, Michael F., 'The Purpose and Preservation of the Jesus Tradition: Moderate Evidence for a Conserving Force in its Transmission', *BBR* 15 (2005) 161–85

Bird, Michael F. and Sprinkle, Preston M. (eds), *The Faith of Jesus Christ: Exegetical, Biblical, and Theological Studies* (Peabody: Hendrickson, 2009)

Blomberg, Craig L., *From Pentecost to Patmos: An Introduction to Acts through Revelation* (Nashville: Broadman & Holman, 2006)

Blount, Brian K., *Revelation: A Commentary*, NTL (Louisville: Westminster John Knox, 2009)

Bock, Darrell L., 'Blasphemy and the Jewish Examination of Jesus', in *Key Events in the Life of the Historical Jesus: A Collaborative Exploration*

182
</footer>

of Context and Coherence, ed. Darrell L. Bock and Robert L. Webb (Grand Rapids: Eerdmans, 2010) 589–667

Bock, Darrell L., *Studying the Historical Jesus: A Guide to Sources and Methods* (Grand Rapids: Baker Academic, 2002)

Borg, Marcus J. and Wright, N. T., *The Meaning of Jesus: Two Visions* (London: SPCK, 1999)

Boring, M. Eugene, *1 Peter*, ANTC (Nashville: Abingdon Press, 1999)

Boring, M. Eugene, 'Narrative Christology in the Apocalypse', *CBQ* 54 (1992) 702–23

Boxall, Ian, 'Jesus in the Apocalypse', in *The Blackwell Companion to Jesus*, ed. Delbert Royce Burkett, Blackwell Companions to Religion (Malden, MA: Wiley-Blackwell, 2011) 119–26

Braaten, Carl E., *Who Is Jesus? Disputed Questions and Answers* (Grand Rapids: Eerdmans, 2011)

Brown, Raymond Edward, *The Epistles of John*, AB 30 (Garden City, NY: Doubleday, 1982)

Bruce, F. F., *The Acts of the Apostles: The Greek Text with Introduction and Commentary*, 3rd rev. and enl. edn (Grand Rapids: Eerdmans, 1990)

Buckwalter, Douglas, *The Character and Purpose of Luke's Christology*, SNTSMS 89 (Cambridge: Cambridge University Press, 1996)

Bultmann, Rudolf, *Theology of the New Testament* 2 vols (London: SCM Press, 1952)

Burridge, Richard A., *Four Gospels, One Jesus? A Symbolic Reading* (London: SPCK, 1994)

Burridge, Richard A., *Imitating Jesus: An Inclusive Approach to New Testament Ethics* (Grand Rapids: Eerdmans, 2007)

Byron, John, 'Living in the Shadow of Cain: Echoes of a Developing Tradition in James 5: 1–6', *NovT* 48 (2006) 261–74

Byrskog, Samuel, *Story as History – History as Story: The Gospel Tradition in the Context of Ancient Oral History*, WUNT 123 (Tübingen: Mohr Siebeck, 2000)

Campbell, Douglas A., 'The Story of Jesus in Romans and Galatians', in *Narrative Dynamics in Paul: A Critical Assessment*, ed. Bruce W. Longenecker (Louisville: Westminster John Knox, 2002) 97–124

Claussen, Carsten, 'Early Christianity and the Synagogue: A Parting of the Ways', in *Who Was Jesus? A Jewish-Christian Dialogue*, ed. Paul Copan and Craig A. Evans (Louisville: Westminster John Knox, 2001) 97–110

Coakley, Sarah, 'The Identity of the Risen Jesus: Finding Jesus Christ in the Poor', in *Seeking the Identity of Jesus: A Pilgrimage*, ed. Beverly

Roberts Gaventa and Richard B. Hays (Grand Rapids: Eerdmans, 2008) 301–19

Couser, Greg A., '"The Testimony about the Lord", "Borne by the Lord", or Both? An Insight into Paul and Jesus in the Pastoral Epistles (2 Tim. 1:8)', *TynBul* 55 (2004) 295–316

Dalton, William J., *Christ's Proclamation to the Spirits: A Study of 1 Peter 3:18—4:6*, AnBib 23 (Rome: Pontifical Biblical Institute, 1965)

Davids, Peter H., 'James and Jesus', in *The Jesus Tradition outside the Gospels*, ed. David Wenham, Gospel Perspectives 5 (Sheffield: JSOT Press, 1985) 63–84

De Boer, Martinus C., 'Jesus the Baptizer: 1 John 5:5–8 and the Gospel of John', *JBL* 107 (1988) 87–106

Dunn, James D. G., *Beginning from Jerusalem*, Christianity in the Making 2 (Grand Rapids: Eerdmans, 2009)

Dunn, James D. G., *Jesus, Paul, and the Gospels* (Grand Rapids: Eerdmans, 2011)

Dunn, James D. G., *Jesus Remembered*, Christianity in the Making 1 (Cambridge: Eerdmans, 2003)

Dunn, James D. G., 'Jesus Tradition in Paul', in *Studying the Historical Jesus: Evaluations of the State of Current Research*, ed. Bruce Chilton and Craig A. Evans, New Testament Tools and Studies 19 (Leiden: E. J. Brill, 1994) 155–78

Dunn, James D. G., *A New Perspective on Jesus: What the Quest for the Historical Jesus Missed* (Grand Rapids: Baker Academic, 2005)

Dunn, James D. G., *The Theology of Paul the Apostle* (Grand Rapids: Eerdmans, 1998)

Eddy, Paul Rhodes and Boyd, Gregory A., *The Jesus Legend: A Case for the Historical Reliability of the Synoptic Tradition* (Grand Rapids: Baker Academic, 2007)

Ehrman, Bart D., *Did Jesus Exist? The Historical Argument for Jesus of Nazareth* (New York: HarperOne, 2012)

Eisenbaum, Pamela, 'Locating Hebrews within the Literary Landscape of Christian Origins', in *Hebrews: Contemporary Methods, New Insights*, ed. Gabriella Gelardini, *BibInt* 75 (Leiden: Brill, 2005) 213–37

Evans, Craig A., 'Exorcisms and the Kingdom: Inaugurating the Kingdom of God and Defeating the Kingdom of Satan', in *Key Events in the Life of the Historical Jesus: A Collaborative Exploration of Context and Coherence*, ed. Darrell L. Bock and Robert L. Webb (Grand Rapids: Eerdmans, 2010) 151–79

Evans, Craig A., 'Seeking the Identity of Jesus: A Pilgrimage', *Modern Theology* 27.1 (2011) 212–14

Fee, Gordon D., *The First Epistle to the Corinthians*, NICNT (Grand Rapids: Eerdmans, 1987)

Fee, Gordon D., *Pauline Christology: An Exegetical-Theological Study* (Peabody: Hendrickson, 2007)

Filson, Floyd V., *Yesterday: A Study of Hebrews in the Light of Chapter 13*, SBT 2/4 (London: SCM Press, 1967)

Fowl, Stephen E., *The Story of Christ in the Ethics of Paul: An Analysis of the Function of the Hymnic Material in the Pauline Corpus*, JSNTSup 36 (Sheffield: JSOT Press, 1990)

France, R. T., 'Exegesis in Practice: Two Samples', in *New Testament Interpretation*, ed. I. Howard Marshall (Carlisle: Paternoster, 1997) 252–81

France, R. T., 'Jesus the Baptist?', in *Jesus of Nazareth: Lord and Christ: Essays on the Historical Jesus and New Testament Christology*, ed. Joel B. Green and Max Turner (Grand Rapids: Eerdmans, 1994) 94–111

Fredriksen, Paula, *From Jesus to Christ: The Origins of the New Testament Images of Christ*, 2nd edn (New Haven: Yale Nota Bene, 2000)

Fredriksen, Paula, *Jesus of Nazareth, King of the Jews: A Jewish Life and the Emergence of Christianity* (New York: Knopf, 1999)

Funk, Robert W. and Hoover, Roy W., *The Five Gospels: The Search for the Authentic Words of Jesus* (New York: Macmillan, 1993)

Furnish, Victor Paul, *Jesus according to Paul*, Understanding Jesus Today (Cambridge: Cambridge University Press, 1993)

Furnish, Victor Paul, 'The Jesus–Paul Debate: From Baur to Bultmann', in *Paul and Jesus*, ed. A. J. M. Wedderburn, JSNTSup 37 (Sheffield: Sheffield Academic Press, 1989) 17–50

Garrow, A. J. P., *Revelation*, New Testament Readings (London: Routledge, 1997)

Gaventa, Beverly Roberts, 'Interpreting the Death of Jesus Apocalyptically: Reconsidering Romans 8:32', in *Jesus and Paul Reconnected: Fresh Pathways into an Old Debate*, ed. Todd D. Still (Grand Rapids: Eerdmans, 2007) 125–45

Gaventa, Beverly Roberts, 'Learning and Relearning the Identity of Jesus from Luke-Acts', in *Seeking the Identity of Jesus: A Pilgrimage*, ed. Beverly Roberts Gaventa and Richard B. Hays (Grand Rapids: Eerdmans, 2008) 148–65

Gaventa, Beverly Roberts and Hays, Richard B., *Seeking the Identity of Jesus: A Pilgrimage* (Grand Rapids: Eerdmans, 2008)

Gerhardsson, Birger, *Memory and Manuscript: Oral Tradition and Written Transmission in Rabbinic Judaism and Early Christianity*, ASNU 22 (Uppsala: Gleerup, 1961)

Gerhardsson, Birger, *The Origins of the Gospel Traditions* (Philadelphia: Fortress, 1979)

Gray, Patrick, 'Brotherly Love and the High Priest Christology of Hebrews', *JBL* 122 (2003) 335–51

Green, Gene L., 'Second Peter's Use of Jude: Imitatio and the Sociology of Early Christianity', in *Reading Second Peter with New Eyes: Methodological Reassessments of the Letter of Second Peter*, ed. Robert L. Webb and Duane Frederick Watson, Library of New Testament Studies 382 (London: T&T Clark, 2010) 1–25

Grieb, A. Katherine, 'Outside the Camp: *Imitatio Christi* and Social Ethics in Hebrews 13:10–14', in *Staying One, Remaining Open: Educating Leaders for a 21st-Century Church*, ed. Richard J. Jones and J. Barney Hawkins (New York: Morehouse, 2010) 109–23

Grieb, A. Katherine, '"Time Would Fail Me to Tell . . .": The Identity of Jesus Christ in Hebrews', in *Seeking the Identity of Jesus: A Pilgrimage*, ed. Beverly Roberts Gaventa and Richard B. Hays (Grand Rapids: Eerdmans, 2008) 200–14

Griffith, Terry, *Keep Yourselves from Idols: A New Look at 1 John*, JSNTSup 233 (Sheffield: Sheffield Academic Press, 2002)

Gundry, Robert H., 'Further "Verba" on Verba Christi in First Peter', *Bib* 55.2 (1974) 211–32

Habermas, Gary R., *The Historical Jesus: Ancient Evidence for the Life of Christ* (Joplin: College Press, 1996)

Hagner, Donald A., 'The Son of God as Unique High Priest: The Christology of the Letter to the Hebrews', in *Contours of Christology in the New Testament*, ed. Richard N. Longenecker, McMaster New Testament Studies (Grand Rapids: Eerdmans, 2005) 246–67

Hartin, Patrick J., 'James and the Jesus Tradition', in *The Catholic Epistles and Apostolic Traditions*, ed. Karl-Wilhelm Niebuhr and Robert W. Wall (Waco: Baylor University Press, 2009) 55–70

Hays, Richard B., 'The Story of God's Son: The Identity of Jesus in the Letters of Paul', in *Seeking the Identity of Jesus: A Pilgrimage*, ed. Beverly Roberts Gaventa and Richard B. Hays (Grand Rapids: Eerdmans, 2008) 180–99

Hemer, Colin J., 'The Speeches of Acts: pt 1: The Ephesian Elders at Miletus', *TynBul* 40 (1989) 76–85

Hengel, Martin, *Acts and the History of Earliest Christianity* (London: SCM Press, 1979)

Hengel, Martin, 'Eye-Witness Memory and the Writing of the Gospels', in *The Written Gospel*, ed. Markus N. A. Bockmuehl and Donald Alfred Hagner (Cambridge: Cambridge University Press, 2005) 70–96

Hengel, Martin, *The Four Gospels and the One Gospel of Jesus Christ: An Investigation of the Collection and Origin of the Canonical Gospels* (London: SCM Press, 2000)

Hoffmann, R. Joseph, 'Epilogue: The Canonical-Historical Jesus', in *Sources of the Jesus Tradition: Separating History from Myth*, ed. R. Joseph Hoffmann (New York: Prometheus, 2010) 257–65

Hoffmann, R. Joseph, 'On Not Finding the Historical Jesus', in *Sources of the Jesus Tradition: Separating History from Myth*, ed. R. Joseph Hoffmann (New York: Prometheus, 2010) 171–84

Hollander, Harm W., 'The Words of Jesus: From Oral Traditions to Written Record in Paul and Q', *NovT* 42 (2000) 340–57

Holtz, Traugott, 'Paul and the Oral Gospel Tradition', in *Jesus and the Oral Gospel Tradition*, ed. Henry Wansbrough, JSNTSup 64 (Sheffield: Sheffield Academic Press, 1991) 380–93

Horrell, David G., *1 Peter*, NTG (London: T&T Clark, 2008)

Horrell, David G., '"The Lord Commanded . . . But I Have Not Used . . .": Exegetical and Hermeneutical Reflections on 1 Cor 9: 14–15', *NTS* 43 (1997) 587–603

Horrell, David G., *Solidarity and Difference: A Contemporary Reading of Paul's Ethics* (London: T&T Clark, 2005)

Horrell, David G., 'Who Are "the Dead" and When Was the Gospel Preached to Them? The Interpretation of 1 Pet 4.6', *NTS* 49 (2003) 70–89

Hurtado, L. W., 'Jesus' Death as Paradigmatic in the New Testament', *SJT* 57 (2004) 413–33

Isaacs, Marie E., 'Hebrews 13: 9–16 Revisited', *NTS* 43 (1997) 268–84

Johnson, Luke Timothy, *The Acts of the Apostles*, SP 5 (Collegeville: Liturgical Press, 1992)

Johnson, Luke Timothy, *Hebrews: A Commentary*, NTL (Louisville: Westminster John Knox, 2006)

Johnson, Luke Timothy, *Living Jesus: Learning the Heart of the Gospel* (San Francisco: HarperSanFrancisco, 1999)

Bibliography

Johnson, Luke Timothy, 'The Use of Leviticus 19 in the Letter of James', *JBL* 101 (1982) 391–401

Johnson, Luke Timothy and Wachob, Wesley, 'The Sayings of Jesus in the Letter of James', in *Brother of Jesus, Friend of God: Studies in the Letter of James*, ed. Luke Timothy Johnson (Grand Rapids: Eerdmans, 2004) 136–54

Keith, Chris and Hurtado, Larry W., *Jesus among Friends and Enemies: A Historical and Literary Introduction to Jesus in the Gospels* (Grand Rapids: Baker Academic, 2011)

Kelber, Werner H., 'Conclusion: The Work of Birger Gerhardsson in Perspective', in *Jesus in Memory: Traditions in Oral and Scribal Perspectives*, ed. Werner H. Kelber and Samuel Byrskog (Waco: Baylor University Press, 2009) 173–206

Kilgallen, John J., 'Acts 20:35 and Thucydides 2.97.4', *JBL* 112 (1993) 312–14

Kim, Seyoon, 'The Jesus Tradition in 1 Thess 4.13—5.11', *NTS* 48 (2002) 225–42

Kim, Seyoon, *Paul and the New Perspective: Second Thoughts on the Origin of Paul's Gospel* (Grand Rapids: Eerdmans, 2002)

Koester, Helmut, *Ancient Christian Gospels: Their History and Development* (London: SCM Press, 1990)

Labahn, Michael, 'The Non-Synoptic Jesus: An Introduction to John, Paul, Thomas, and Other Outsiders of the Jesus Quest', in *Handbook for the Study of the Historical Jesus*, ed. Tom Holmén and Stanley E. Porter (Leiden: Brill, 2011) 1933–96

Lane, William L., *Hebrews 1—8; Hebrews 9—13*, 2 vols, WBC 47A–47B (Dallas: Word, 1991)

Laws, Sophie, 'Hebrews, Letter to the', in *Jesus: The Complete Guide*, ed. Leslie Houlden (London: Continuum, 2005) 328–31

Le Donne, Anthony, *Historical Jesus: What Can We Know and How Can We Know It?* (Grand Rapids: Eerdmans, 2011)

Le Donne, Anthony, *The Historiographical Jesus: Memory, Typology, and the Son of David* (Waco: Baylor University Press, 2009)

Lincoln, Andrew T., *Ephesians*, WBC 42 (Waco: Word Books, 1990)

Lincoln, Andrew T. and Wedderburn, A. J. M., *The Theology of the Later Pauline Letters*, New Testament Theology (Cambridge: Cambridge University Press, 1993)

Longenecker, Bruce W., 'Good News to the Poor: Jesus, Paul and Jerusalem', in *Jesus and Paul Reconnected: Fresh Pathways into an Old Debate*, ed. Todd D. Still (Grand Rapids: Eerdmans, 2007) 37–65

Longenecker, Richard N., *Contours of Christology in the New Testament*, McMaster New Testament Studies (Grand Rapids: Eerdmans, 2005)

Lowe, Bruce A., 'James 2:1 in the Pistis Christou Debate: Irrelevant or Indispensable?', in *The Faith of Jesus Christ: Exegetical, Biblical, and Theological Studies*, ed. Michael F. Bird and Preston M. Sprinkle (Peabody: Hendrickson, 2009) 239–57

Lüdemann, Gerd, 'Paul as a Witness to the Historical Jesus', in *Sources of the Jesus Tradition: Separating History from Myth*, ed. Joseph Hoffmann (New York: Prometheus, 2010) 196–212

Luther, Martin, *Luther's Works: The Catholic Epistles*, trans. Martin H. Bertram (St Louis: Concordia, 1967)

McCormack, Bruce L., '"With Loud Cries and Tears": The Humanity of the Son in the Epistle to the Hebrews', in *The Epistle to the Hebrews and Christian Theology*, ed. Richard Bauckham, Daniel R. Driver, Trevor A. Hart and Nathan MacDonald (Grand Rapids: Eerdmans, 2009) 37–68

Mackie, Scott D., *Eschatology and Exhortation in Hebrews*, WUNT 2.223 (Tübingen: Mohr Siebeck, 2007)

McKnight, Edgar V., *Jesus Christ in History and Scripture: A Poetic and Sectarian Perspective* (Macon: Mercer University Press, 1999)

McKnight, Scot, 'Jesus of Nazareth', in *The Face of New Testament Studies: A Survey of Recent Research*, ed. Scot McKnight and Grant R. Osborne (Grand Rapids: Baker Academic, 2004) 149–76

McKnight, Scot, *The Letter of James*, NICNT (Grand Rapids: Eerdmans, 2011)

Marshall, I. Howard, *The Acts of the Apostles*, NTG (Sheffield: JSOT Press, 1992)

Marshall, I. Howard, 'The Last Supper', in *Key Events in the Life of the Historical Jesus: A Collaborative Exploration of Context and Coherence*, ed. Darrell L. Bock and Robert L. Webb (Grand Rapids: Eerdmans, 2010) 481–588

Martin, Ralph P., *James*, WBC 48 (Waco: Word Books, 1988)

Matera, Frank J., *New Testament Christology* (Louisville: Westminster John Knox, 1999)

Melbourne, Bertram L., 'An Examination of the Historical-Jesus Motif in the Epistle to the Hebrews', *AUSS* 26 (1988) 281–97

Michaels, J. Ramsey, 'Catholic Christologies in the Catholic Epistles', in *Contours of Christology in the New Testament*, ed. Richard N.

Longenecker, McMaster New Testament Studies (Grand Rapids: Eerdmans, 2005) 268–91

Moffitt, David M., *Atonement and the Logic of Resurrection in the Epistle to the Hebrews*, NovTSup 141 (Leiden: Brill, 2011)

Moo, Douglas J., *The Letters to the Colossians and to Philemon*, The Pillar New Testament Commentary (Grand Rapids: Eerdmans, 2008)

Moyise, Steve, *The Later New Testament Writers and Scripture* (London: SPCK, 2012)

Neyrey, Jerome H., *2 Peter, Jude: A New Translation, with Introduction and Commentary*, AB 37C (London: Doubleday, 1993)

O'Brien, P. T., *The Letter to the Ephesians*, Pillar New Testament Commentary (Grand Rapids: Eerdmans, 1999)

Olbricht, Thomas H., 'Hebrews as Amplification', in *Rhetoric and the New Testament: Essays from the 1992 Heidelberg Conference*, ed. Stanley E. Porter and Thomas H. Olbricht, JSNTSup 90 (Sheffield: JSOT Press, 1993) 375–87

Painter, John, *1, 2, and 3 John*, SP 18 (Collegeville: Liturgical Press, 2002)

Painter, John, *Just James: The Brother of Jesus in History and Tradition*, Studies on Personalities of the New Testament (Minneapolis: Fortress, 1999)

Perkins, Pheme, 'Christ in Jude and 2 Peter', in *Who Do You Say That I Am? Essays on Christology*, ed. Jack Dean Kingsbury, Mark Allan Powell and David R. Bauer (Louisville: Westminster John Knox, 1999) 155–65

Pervo, Richard I., *Acts: A Commentary*, Hermeneia (Minneapolis: Fortress, 2009)

Pervo, Richard I., *Dating Acts: Between the Evangelists and the Apologists* (Santa Rosa: Polebridge, 2006)

Peterson, David, *Hebrews and Perfection*, SNTSMS 47 (Cambridge: Cambridge University Press, 1982)

Porter, Stanley E., 'Images of Christ in Paul's Letters', in *Images of Christ: Ancient and Modern*, ed. Stanley E. Porter, David Tombs and M. A. Hayes, Roehampton Institute London Papers 2 (Sheffield: Sheffield Academic Press, 1997) 95–112

Powell, Mark Allan, *Jesus as a Figure in History: How Modern Historians View the Man from Galilee* (Louisville: Westminster John Knox, 1998)

Powell, Mark Allan and Bauer, David R. (ed.), *Who Do You Say That I Am? Essays on Christology* (Louisville: Westminster John Knox, 1999)

Reese, Ruth Anne, *2 Peter and Jude*, The Two Horizons New Testament Commentary (Grand Rapids: Eerdmans, 2007)

Reumann, John, 'Christology of James', in *Who Do You Say That I Am? Essays on Christology*, ed. Mark Allan Powell and David R. Bauer (Louisville: Westminster John Knox, 1999) 128–39

Richard, Earl, 'The Functional Christology of 1 Peter', in *Perspectives on First Peter*, ed. Charles H. Talbert, NABPR Special Studies Series 9 (Macon: Mercer University Press, 1986) 121–39

Richardson, Christopher, 'The Passion: Reconsidering Hebrews 5.7–8', in *A Cloud of Witnesses: The Theology of Hebrews in Its Ancient Contexts*, ed. Richard Bauckham, Trevor Hart, Nathan MacDonald and Daniel Driver, Library of New Testament Studies 387 (London: T&T Clark, 2008) 51–67

Roetzel, Calvin J., *Paul: The Man and the Myth*, Studies on Personalities of the New Testament (Edinburgh: T&T Clark, 1999)

Rowston, Douglas J., 'The Most Neglected Book in the New Testament, *NTS* 21 (1975) 554–63

Sanders, E. P., *The Historical Figure of Jesus* (London: Penguin, 1993)

Schröter, Jens, 'Jesus and the Canon: The Early Jesus Traditions in the Context of the Origins of the New Testament Canon', in *Performing the Gospel: Orality, Memory, and Mark*, ed. Richard A. Horsley, Jonathan A. Draper and John Miles Foley (Minneapolis: Fortress, 2006) 104–22

Schweizer, Eduard, 'The Testimony to Jesus in the Early Christian Community', *HBT* 7 (1985) 77–98

Selwyn, Edward Gordon, *The First Epistle of St. Peter: The Greek Text* (London: Macmillan, 1946)

Small, Brian C., 'The Use of Rhetorical Topoi in the Characterization of Jesus in the Book of Hebrews', *PRSt* 37 (2010) 53–69

Smalley, Stephen S., *The Revelation to John: A Commentary on the Greek Text of the Apocalypse* (London: SPCK; Downers Grove: InterVarsity, 2005)

Smith, D. Moody, 'The Historical Figure of Jesus in 1 John', in *The Word Leaps the Gap: Essays on Scripture and Theology in Honor of Richard B. Hays*, ed. J. Ross Wagner, Christopher Kavin Rowe and A. Katherine Grieb (Grand Rapids: Eerdmans 2008) 310–24

Stanton, Graham, *Jesus of Nazareth in New Testament Preaching*, SNTSMS 27 (London: Cambridge University Press, 1974)

Stewart, Robert B. (ed.), *The Resurrection of Jesus: John Dominic Crossan and N. T. Wright in Dialogue* (Minneapolis: Augsburg Fortress, 2005)

Still, Todd D., 'Christos as "Pistos": The Faith(fulness) of Jesus in the Epistle to the Hebrews', *CBQ* 69 (2007) 746–55

Still, Todd D. (ed.), *Jesus and Paul Reconnected: Fresh Pathways into an Old Debate* (Grand Rapids: Eerdmans, 2007)

Strange, W. A., 'The Jesus-Tradition in Acts', *NTS* 46 (2000) 59–74

Strelan, Rick, *Strange Acts: Studies in the Cultural World of the Acts of the Apostles* (Berlin: Walter de Gruyter, 2004)

Talbert, Charles H., 'The Christology of the Apocalypse', in *Who Do You Say That I Am? Essays on Christology*, ed. Jack Dean Kingsbury, Mark Allan Powell and David R. Bauer (Louisville: Westminster John Knox, 1999) 166–84

Tannehill, Robert C., *The Narrative Unity of Luke-Acts: A Literary Interpretation* 2 vols, FF (Philadelphia: Fortress, 1986)

Theissen, Gerd, *The New Testament: A Literary History* (Minneapolis: Fortress, 2012)

Thiselton, Anthony C., *The First Epistle to the Corinthians: A Commentary on the Greek Text*, NIGTC (Grand Rapids: Eerdmans, 2000)

Thompson, Marianne Meye, *Colossians and Philemon*, The Two Horizons New Testament Commentary (Grand Rapids: Eerdmans, 2005)

Thompson, Marianne Meye, 'Jesus and His God', in *The Cambridge Companion to Jesus*, ed. Markus N. A. Bockmuehl, Cambridge Companions to Religion (Cambridge: Cambridge University Press, 2001) 41–55

Thompson, Marianne Meye, 'Jesus and the Victory of God Meets the Gospel of John', in *Jesus, Paul and the People of God*, ed. Nicholas Perrin and Richard B. Hays (London: SPCK, 2011) 21–40

Thompson, Michael B., *Clothed with Christ: The Example and Teaching of Jesus in Romans 12.1—15.13*, JSNTSup 59 (Sheffield: JSOT Press, 1991)

Trumbower, Jeffrey A., 'The Historical Jesus and the Speech of Gamaliel (Acts 5.35–9), *NTS* 39 (1993) 500–17

Tuckett, C. M., *Christology and the New Testament: Jesus and His Earliest Followers* (Louisville: Westminster John Knox, 2001)

Tuckett, Christopher, 'Sources and Methods', in *The Cambridge Companion to Jesus*, ed. Markus N. A. Bockmuehl (Cambridge: Cambridge University Press, 2001), 121–37

Twelftree, Graham H., 'Jesus the Baptist', *JSHJ* 7 (2009) 103–25

Wachob, Wesley Hiram, *The Voice of Jesus in the Social Rhetoric of James*, SNTSMS 106 (Cambridge: Cambridge University Press, 2000)

Wallis, Ian G., *The Faith of Jesus Christ in Early Christian Traditions*, SNTSMS 84 (Cambridge: Cambridge University Press, 1995)

Walter, Nikolaus, 'Paul and the Early Christian Jesus-Tradition', in *Paul and Jesus*, ed. A. J. M. Wedderburn, JSNTSup 37 (Sheffield: Sheffield Academic Press, 1989) 51–80

Warrington, Keith, *Discovering Jesus in the New Testament* (Peabody: Hendrickson, 2009)

Watson, Francis, '"I Received from the Lord . . .": Paul, Jesus and the Last Supper', in *Jesus and Paul Reconnected: Fresh Pathways into an Old Debate*, ed. Todd D. Still (Grand Rapids: Eerdmans, 2007) 103–24

Watson, Francis, 'Veritas Christi: How to Get from the Jesus of History to the Christ of Faith without Losing One's Way', in *Seeking the Identity of Jesus: A Pilgrimage*, ed. Beverly Roberts Gaventa and Richard B. Hays (Grand Rapids: Eerdmans, 2008) 96–114

Webb, Robert L., 'The Historical Enterprise and Historical Jesus Research', in *Key Events in the Life of the Historical Jesus: A Collaborative Exploration of Context and Coherence*, ed. Darrell L. Bock and Robert L. Webb (Grand Rapids: Eerdmans, 2010) 9–93

Webb, Robert L., 'The Roman Examination and Crucifixion of Jesus', in *Key Events in the Life of the Historical Jesus: A Collaborative Exploration of Context and Coherence*, ed. Darrell L. Bock and Robert L. Webb (Grand Rapids: Eerdmans, 2010) 669–773

Webb, Robert L., 'The Use of "Story" in the Letter of Jude: Rhetorical Strategies of Jude's Narrative Episodes', *JSNT* 31 (2008) 53–87

Wedderburn, Alexander J. M., 'Paul and Jesus: The Problem of Continuity', in *Paul and Jesus*, ed. A. J. M. Wedderburn, JSNTSup 37 (Sheffield: Sheffield Academic Press, 1989) 99–115

Wedderburn, Alexander J. M., 'Paul and the Story of Jesus', in *Paul and Jesus*, ed. A. J. M. Wedderburn, JSNTSup 37 (Sheffield: Sheffield Academic Press, 1989) 161–89

Wenham, David, 'Being "Found" on the Last Day: New Light on 2 Peter 3.10 and 2 Corinthians 5.3', *NTS* 33 (1987) 477–9

Wenham, David, *Paul and Jesus: The True Story* (Grand Rapids: Eerdmans, 2002)

Wenham, David, 'The Story of Jesus Known to Paul', in *Jesus of Nazareth: Lord and Christ: Essays on the Historical Jesus and New Testament Christology*, ed. Joel B. Green and Max Turner (Grand Rapids: Eerdmans, 1994) 297–311

Williams, Rowan, 'Looking for Jesus and Finding Christ', in *Biblical Concepts and Our World*, ed. D. Z. Phillips and Mano van der Ruhr (Basingstoke: Palgrave Macmillan, 2004) 141–52

Williamson, Ronald, *Philo and the Epistle to the Hebrews* (Leiden: Brill, 1970)

Wright, N. T., *Jesus and the Victory of God*, Christian Origins and the Question of God 2 (London: SPCK, 1996)

Wright, N. T., 'The Letter to the Romans', in *NIB* 393–770

Index of biblical references

OLD TESTAMENT

Genesis
1.1 150

Exodus
6.6 140

Leviticus
16.27 106
19 123, 129
19.11–18 122
19.12 123
19.13 123
19.15 123
19.16 123
19.17 123
19.18 122–3,
  125

Deuteronomy
7.8 140
21.22–23 38,
  139
25.4 88

Psalms
8 101
40.6–8 100
69.9 72
90.4 147
110 98
110.1 98

Isaiah
35.3 105
53 137–8, 140
53.4 137
53.5 137
53.6 137
53.7 137
53.9 137
53.12 137
64.4 65

Daniel
7 160
7.9 160
7.13 160
10.5–6 160

Joel
2 32

Amos
9 32

NEW TESTAMENT

Matthew
3.11 43
4.1–11 124
4.4 124
4.7 124
4.10 124
5.3 122–3
5.7 124
5.10 139
5.11–12 121,
  139
5.12 162
5.16 139
5.18 146
5.19 122
5.21 122
5.22 153
5.32 57–9
5.33–37 121
5.43–44 66
7.1–2 66
7.1–5 66
7.7 121
7.15 162
8.1–12 55
10.5–6 55, 118
10.10 57
10.32 162
11.15 162
11.29 73
15.24 55, 84
17.2 145, 161
19.1–9 57
19.28 118
19.28–29 118
21.39 107
22.1–14 163
22.39 122–3
23.1–8 126
23.8 126
23.12 124
24.30 162
24.30–31 63
24.35 146
24.36 64
24.42–44 63,
  119, 162
24.43 147, 162
24.44 147
25.35–36 124
26.18 162
26.26–28 61
26.52 162
27.3–10 31
27.9–10 31
27.27–31 138
27.37 82
28.16–20 26
28.19 55
28.19–20 130

Mark
1.1 66
1.10–11 89
6.3–4 11
7 32, 75
7.1–8 80
7.1–23 66
7.15 32, 48,
  66–7, 84
7.15–23 80
7.18 66–7
7.19 32, 66
7.24–30 34
8.27–32 39–40
9.2 145
9.2–8 134, 145
10.9 58
10.9–11 57
10.9–12 59
10.11–12 58
10.38–39 42
10.45 87,
  139–40

11.15–18 138
12.17 66
12.28–34 65
12.29–31 65
12.31 122
12.35–36 98
12.35–37 98
13.26–27 63
14.22–25 61
14.34–36 102
14.35–36 156
14.36 66
14.58 30
14.62 98
14.66–72 134
15.2 88
15.2–22 106
15.16–20 138
15.21 106
15.26 82
15.27 53
15.32 53
15.40 134
16.8 29

Luke
1.16 84
1.32–33 22
3.16 27
3.21–22 26
4.1 27
4.1–13 26, 124
4.2 26
4.13 104
4.14 27
4.15 26
4.43 26
6.20 122–3
6.20–21 32
6.22 139

6.23 121
6.27–28 66
6.27–35 66
6.27–42 123
6.28 139
6.29–30 66
6.31 121
6.32–34 139
6.36–38 66
6.40 128
6.47 128
7.40 26
8.10 26
9.2 26
9.32 145
9.58 72
10.7 57, 89
10.27 122–3
11.13 28
11.28 161–2
11.50 162
12.8 162
12.36–37 162
13.22–30 34
14.11 124
14.21 84
16.17 146
16.18 57–9
19.10 104
19.39 26
20.15 107
20.21 26
21.24 162
21.33 146
21.34–36 63
22.13–20 27
22.19–20 61
22.28–30 162
22.41–44 102
22.43–44 102

23.18 31
23.34 137
24.4–6 27
24.13–32 26
24.27 41
24.34 55
24.36–53 26
24.44 41
24.49 26, 28
24.50–51 26
24.51 29

John
1.1 150
1.32–33 154
3.22 42
3.26 153
4.1–2 153
4.2 42–3
7.3–5 11
13.34 152–3, 155
19.16–18 106
19.17 106
19.30 154, 158
19.32–33 105
19.34 153
20.25 81
21.25 4, 35

Acts
1.1 21–2, 26, 44
1.1–2 21
1.1–8 43
1.1–9 25, 174
1.1–11 25, 27
1.2 26–7, 30
1.3 26
1.3–5 26

1.3–9 26
1.4 26–8
1.4–5 22, 26–8, 44
1.5 28, 42
1.6 27, 40
1.8 24, 27, 42, 179
1.9 28
1.10–11 27
1.11 25
1.13–14 30
1.14 23, 30
1.15 133
1.15–26 23
1.16 31
1.16–19 31
1.17 30–1
1.18 31
1.19 31
1.21 29
1.21–23 24
1.22 27, 30, 43
2 32
2.3 28
2.22 23–4, 30, 32, 34, 36, 38–9
2.22–23 172
2.22–24 43, 167
2.22–36 22
2.23 23, 31, 38–9
2.24 39
2.25–36 34
2.29 25
2.32 23–4
2.33 39, 44
2.33–36 23

2.36 23, 26, 34, 39
2.38 41
2.43 36
2.44–45 32
3.2–8 119
3.6 24–5
3.12–26 39
3.13 31, 34, 39
3.14 31, 39, 151
3.14–15 34
3.15 23, 31, 39
3.16 40
3.17 31, 41
3.18 39
3.19 40
3.20 40
3.20–21 29, 41
3.22–23 41
3.23–26 41
4.10 24
4.27 31, 39
4.32–35 32
5 20
5.30 31, 38, 139
5.31 41
5.32 24
5.34–39 40
5.36 20
5.36–39 43
5.42 41, 84
6.8 36
6.14 30
6.38 34
7.37 41
7.52 151
7.55–56 25
7.58 46

8.12 36
8.32–35 41
8.36 41
9.22 41
10.7 34
10.36–41 172
10.37 27
10.37–43 23
10.38 30, 33
10.38–39 34
10.39 30, 33–4, 38, 139
10.40–41 24
10.43 41
11.16 28, 35
11.26 132
12.17 11
13.1 23
13.22–23 30
13.23 41
13.24 27
13.27 31
13.27–29 34
13.28 31
13.29 31, 38, 139
15 20
15.6–29 32
15.13–21 11
15.16–17 83
16.7 44
16.10–16 22
17.8 41
18.9–10 44
18.12–16 25
18.24–25 33
18.25 27
19.3–4 27
20.5—21.18 22
20.35 22, 34–5

22.8 24–5
22.14 39, 151
22.18 25
24.5 24
26.9 25
26.28 132
27.1—28.16 22
27.35 36
28.23 41
28.30–31 27
28.31 22, 44

Romans
1.3 52
1.3–4 53, 71
1.4 90
3.22 73
3.25 53
3.26 73
4.24–25 55
4.25 52, 174
5.10 52
5.19 73
6.4 53
6.6 53
8.15 66
8.32 52
8.34 55
10.9 52
12—13 65
12—15 65–6, 76
12.14 66
12.17 66
12.21 66
13.7 66
13.8–10 65
13.14 72, 76, 179
14 75

14.1—15.13 65
14.10 66
14.14 66
14.17 74
15.1–3 72
15.2–3 73
15.3 72
15.8 52
15.12 52
15.26 60
16.1–2 60

1 Corinthians
1.14–18 42
2.2 53, 172
2.6 105
2.6–8 53
2.8 52–3, 105
2.9 65
4.11–12 72
4.12–13 66
4.14–16 59
4.16–17 72
4.17 72
4.20 74
5.7 53
5.9 68
6.9–10 74
7.10 57–8, 167
7.10–11 58
7.10–12 48, 63, 70
7.11 58
7.12 58
7.15 59
7.25 59
8—10 48
8.6 71

9.1 46, 57
9.5 52
9.9 88
9.14 57–60, 63, 70, 89, 149, 167, 176
9.14–15 48
9.15 59–60
10.1–9 143
10.3–4 62
10.16 48, 62
10.17 62
11.1 52, 72
11.2 69
11.2–11 67
11.23 52–3, 60, 62
11.23–25 71, 169
11.23–26 47, 48, 60, 62, 64
11.25 61
11.26 61
14.37 57
15.1 61
15.1–8 69
15.3 8, 61
15.3–8 46, 61
15.3–9 54, 64
15.4 53
15.5 54
15.6 54
15.7 11, 54
15.11 69
15.20 79
15.45 75
15.50 74
16 67
16.22 64, 71

2 Corinthians
2.3–4 68
4.7–12 72, 175
5.16 46, 48
6.4–5 72
8.9 73
10.1 52, 72–3
11.1—12.10 56
11.3–4 56
11.4 56
12.3–7 72
12.7 72

Galatians
1.11–12 46
1.12 60
1.15 45
1.18 55
1.18–19 45, 67
1.19 11, 23, 52
2.1–10 20
2.7–8 133
2.9 11, 54
2.11 74
2.11–14 67
2.11–16 48
2.12 11
2.16 73
2.19 53
2.20 73
3.1 8, 69, 172
3.13 139
3.22 73
3.28 71–2
4.4 51–2
5.14 65
5.21 68, 74
6.2 65
6.17 72

Ephesians
1.20 84
1.20–21 83
1.20–22 86
1.20–23 83
1.22 83
2.5–6 83, 86, 90
2.13–22 83, 90
2.14 83
2.15 83
2.19 83
2.20 83
2.21 83
4.9 85–6, 140
4.10 83
4.14–24 84
4.15 83
4.20 84, 90
4.20–21 84
4.21 84–5, 90
4.22–24 85
4.22–32 85
4.29 84
5.23 83
5.25 83–4

Philippians
2.5 179
2.5–7 52
2.5–8 73
2.5–11 71, 73, 169
2.6 71
2.8 73
2.9–11 71
3.4–6 74
3.5 47
3.6 45
3.8–10 52

3.9 73
3.10 72, 74, 136, 175
4.15–17 60

Colossians
1.1 78
1.3–4 78
1.13 80
1.14 80
1.15 78–9
1.15–18a 78–9
1.15–20 78
1.16 79
1.18 79, 81, 83
1.19 79–80
1.20 80–1
1.22 80–2
1.24 82
2.2 78
2.6 80
2.6–7 84, 90
2.7 80
2.9 79–80
2.10 78
2.11–12 80–1
2.13–14 80
2.13–15 81
2.14 81–2
2.15 80–1
2.20 81
2.21–22 80
3.1 78, 90
3.3 81
4.3 82
4.10 82
4.11 78
4.12 78

1 Thessalonians
1.6 72
2.14–15 52
2.14–16 53
4.15 63
4.15–17 62–3
5.2 63–4, 119,
   147
5.2–3 63
5.3 63

2 Thessalonians
1.7 86
1.9 86
1.10 86
2.1 86
2.8 86

1 Timothy
1.15 89
2.5 87
2.5–6 87, 89,
   173
2.6 87
3.16 89–90,
   173
5.18 88–9
6.2–3 88
6.3 88
6.12 88
6.13 88, 160,
   167

2 Timothy
1.8 89
1.10 87
2.8 87, 89,
   173
2.11–13 89,
   173

Titus
1.4 87
2.13 87
2.14 87, 139
3.6 87

Hebrews
1.1–2 97
1.1–4 97
1.2 97
1.3 97–8, 100
1.4 98
1.4–14 97, 99
1.5–6 99
1.6 99
1.7–12 99
1.13–14 92, 99
2.2 8, 99
2.3 95, 104
2.3–4 94, 119,
   168, 172
2.5–18 97
2.6–8 101
2.6–9 97
2.10–11 101
2.12–13 100
2.12–14 101,
   172
2.14 103–4
2.14–18 93,
   150
2.15 101
2.16 101
2.17 96, 101,
   109
2.17–18 104
2.18 104
3.1 96, 99
3.1–6 99
3.2 108

3.6 108
3.7—4.11 109
3.14 109
4.11 93
4.14 97, 99
4.14–16 93,
   100
4.14—5.10 150
4.15 101, 103–5,
   136–7, 167
4.16 109
5.1–10 93, 100
5.5–6 92
5.5–10 101
5.7 102, 108
5.7–8 102, 104
5.8 103, 107
5.9 96, 103
6.4–6 92
6.20 97
7—10 100
7.1–28 92, 100
7.1—10.18 100
7.14 103, 104
7.22 100
7.24 100
7.25 100
7.26 105
7.27 100
8.1–13 100
9.1–10 100
9.11—10.18
   100
9.23–24 94
9.24 94
9.28 99–100,
   104
10.5–9 100,
   109
10.9 100

10.19–22 93
10.20 96
10.23 109
10.26–31 92
10.32 109
10.32–34 94,
   105, 110
10.33 108
10.34 108
11.1—12.2
   109
11.19 108, 110
11.26 110, 143
12.1 94, 175
12.1–2 179
12.1–3 110
12.2 53, 93,
   105, 107, 109
12.2–3 93, 96
12.2–4 105
12.3 94, 105,
   109–10
12.3–4 105
12.4 105
12.7 109
12.12 105
12.12–13 94
12.24 99
13.2 108
13.3 108
13.7 94, 108
13.8 96, 108
13.10 106
13.11–14 106
13.12 105–6
13.12–13 96,
   106
13.13 96,
   106–7, 175
13.13–14 94

13.17 108
13.20 108
13.24 94, 98

James
1.1 113–15,
   118, 126–7
1.2–4 121, 124
1.5 121, 127
1.9–11 127
2 117
2.1 115–19,
   121, 123,
   126, 175
2.1–9 112, 127
2.1–11 122
2.1–13 117
2.5 122
2.7 118
2.8 122–3
2.9 117
2.10 127
2.10–11 122
2.13 124, 127
2.14–16 112,
   124
2.14–26 117
2.19 117
2.23 117, 127
3.1 126
3.1–12 112
3.18 124
4.2–3 121
4.4 126–7
4.7 124
4.10 124
4.11 123
4.15 119
4.17 124
5.1–5 127

5.4 123
5.6 125, 151
5.7–8 126
5.8 119
5.9 123
5.11 127
5.12 121, 123
5.12b 122
5.13–16 112
5.14–16 119
5.16 119
5.20 123

1 Peter
1.1 133
1.2 137
1.3 135
1.6 135
1.8 134
1.18 140
1.19 135, 137
1.20 135–6
2.4 136
2.5 136
2.7 137
2.11–17 138
2.12 139
2.19–20 139
2.21 135–8,
   175
2.21–22 138
2.21–25 138
2.22 136–7
2.22–23 135–6
2.22–24 138
2.22–25 137,
   167, 175
2.23 137
2.24 38, 137,
   139–40

2.24a 137
2.24b 137
2.25 135, 137
3.9 139
3.14 139
3.18 136
3.18–20 85,
   137
3.19–20 140–1
3.20–21 140
3.22 141
4.1 134, 137
4.1–2 135
4.6 85, 141
4.12 135
4.12–14 136
4.13–14 139
4.16 132, 136
5.1 133–4,
   137
5.1b 134
5.4 135
5.12 133

2 Peter
1.1 144
1.2 144
1.11 144
1.16 145
1.16–18 144–5
1.17 145
1.17–18 145
3 144
3.1 143
3.2 144, 146
3.3–10 144
3.4 144
3.5–6 146
3.8 146–7
3.8–9 147

3.8–10 144,
   146
3.9 146–7
3.10 146–7
3.10a 146
3.12 146
3.13 144
3.16 9
3.18 144

1 John
1.1 150, 153
1.1–3 150,
   167, 172
1.3 151–2, 173
1.5 151
1.7 151
2.1 151–2
2.2 151
2.3–6 152
2.6 151
2.7 152
2.13–14 151
2.18 151
2.22 151, 154
2.28 151
3.8 151
3.15 153
3.16 151
3.23 151–2
4.2 151
4.14 151
5.1 151
5.6 90, 153
5.6–8 153
5.9 154

2 John
3 154
5 153, 155

7 154–5
9 154

3 John
7 149

Jude
1 142
4 142
5 142–3
17 142
21 142
25 142

Revelation
1.1 158
1.3 162

1.3b 162
1.5 158–9, 167, 172, 175, 179
1.5–6 159, 163
1.7 162
1.10 158
1.12 160
1.12–20 160, 162
1.13–16 161–2
1.14 160
1.17–20 156
2.2 158
2.7 162
2.13 159

3.2 162
3.3 162
3.5 162
3.14 159, 172, 175
3.20 162
3.21 160, 162
5.5 158
5.9 158
5.9–10 158
5.12 158
6.10 160
7.17 160
11.2 162
11.8 158
12 157
12.1–5 158

13.10 162
13.11 162
14.12 160
16 159
16.13 162
16.15 162
16.17 158
18.20 158
18.24 162
19.7 162
19.9 162
19.11–16 156
19.16 160
19.20 162
21.14 156, 158
22.13 160
22.16 157–8

Index of names and subjects

1 Clement 16

Abraham, figure of 117
Adams, Edward 13, 56, 73, 90
Adamson, James B. 122
agrapha 6, 124
Allen, David M. 106, 179
Allison, Dale C., Jr. 2, 9, 14, 52–3, 62, 65–6, 82, 102, 123, 137, 167, 172–3
Acts of the Apostles 5, 20–44, 50, 90, 166–7, 172, 174–6; dating of 21; and earthly Jesus 25–30; and history 20, 26, 28–9, 37–8; portrait of Jesus 20–44; relationship to Gospel of Luke 21–2, 26–7, 32, 43, 50; sermonic passages 37–41; structure of 23–4; textual traditions 20; use of Scripture 32–4, 40–1; *see also* Luke, Gospel of
Aitken, Ellen Bradshaw 100
Ascension (of Jesus) 22–3, 25–6, 28–30, 44, 100, 151
Aune, David E. 51, 155, 157, 159
Attridge, Harold W. 93, 102, 107, 145, 152–3

Backhaus, Knut 108
Bales, William 86
Barabbas 31
Barbarick, Clifford A. 135, 147
Barnett, Paul 2, 14, 20–1, 46, 55
Barrett, Charles K. 28, 32, 36

Bartholmä, Philipp F. 143
Barton, Stephen C. 48
Bauckham, Richard 4, 7, 9, 11, 68, 98, 113, 116, 119, 121, 123, 127, 130, 142–3, 163, 167
Bauer, David R. 14
Beatitudes 32, 123–4, 139, 161
Beilby, James K. 1
Best, Ernest 139
Bevere, Alan R. 81
Bird, Michael F. 64, 73, 173, 175
Blomberg, Craig L. 35
Blount, Brian K. 157
Bock, Darrell L. 1, 6, 98
Borg, Marcus 3
Boring, M. Eugene 134, 136, 162–3
Boxall, Ian 155, 164
Boyd, Gregory A. 55
Braaten, Carl 5, 13
Brown, Raymond Edward 153
Bruce, F. F. 28
Buckwalter, Douglas 36
Bultmann, Rudolf 47
Burridge, Richard A. 13, 74
Byron, John 125
Byrskog, Samuel 17, 38

Cain and Abel 125
Campbell, Douglas A. 71, 73
canon, concept of 16, 87, 165, 170–1
canonical Jesus 4, 8, 15–19, 34, 165–79

Christ of faith 1–3, 8, 14, 23, 55, 75, 96, 166, 177; *see also* historical Jesus
Christology 13, 50, 73, 78, 97, 115, 144
Claussen, Carsten 25
Coakley, Sarah 178
Colossians 78–82, 156, 168; Christ hymn 78–80; portrait of Jesus 78–82
Corinth 8, 52, 56–61, 64, 67, 72; first epistle 45, 47–8, 57, 60, 68, 149, 169; second epistle 45
Council of Jerusalem 20, 32, 176
Couser, Greg A. 88, 89
Crossan, John Dominic 1, 3
crucifixion 8, 52–4, 73, 80–2, 90, 104–5, 107, 126, 137–9, 153, 157–9

Dalton, William J. 141
Davids, Peter H. 54, 114, 121, 124, 176
De Boer, Martinus C. 153
Deutero–Pauline corpus 4, 45, 77–91, 148, 172
Didache 11, 16
divorce, teaching on 57–9
dominical logia 5, 22, 28, 34–5, 57–64, 70–1, 78, 88–9, 93, 120, 124, 139–40, 149, 162–3, 169
Dunn, James D. G. 1, 7, 9, 10, 26, 29, 46, 49–50, 70, 75–6, 128, 169–70

Eddy, Paul R., 1, 55
Ehrman, Bart D. 6, 31, 58, 101
Eisenbaum, Pamela 92
Elijah 117, 119, 145

Ephesians 83–6, 90, 140, 168; portrait of Jesus 83–6
Eucharist 47–8, 60–2
Evans, Craig A. 125, 175

Fee, Gordon D. 50, 61, 86
Filson, Floyd V. 96–7
Fowl, Stephen E. 80, 89–90
France, R. T. 43, 141
Fredriksen, Paula 9, 47, 50, 54, 166
Funk, Robert F. 3
Furnish, Victor Paul 45, 51, 69, 77, 79, 82–3

Galatians, epistle to 8, 45, 67–9
Gamaliel 20, 40
Garrow, A, J. P. 156
Gaventa, Beverley Roberts 4, 7, 17–18, 34, 37, 41, 52
Gentiles, inclusion of 32–4, 55, 74, 83–4, 118
Gerhardsson, Birger 54, 57, 80, 173
Gray, Patrick 101
Green, Gene L. 128, 142
Grieb, A. Katherine 18, 99, 107
Griffith, Terry 154
Gundry, Robert H. 139

Habermas, Gary R. 52
Hagner, Donald A. 101
Hartin, Patrick J. 118, 129–30
Hays, Richard B. 4, 7, 17–18, 49, 54, 63, 68–9, 71, 73
Hebrews, epistle to 8, 10, 13, 18, 88, 92–111, 113, 132, 135, 167–9, 171–2, 175; and angels 99; centrality of Jesus 92–7; death of Jesus 102–10,

113; heavenly high priest
97–100; human Jesus 100–10;
limitations of 93–5; portrait
of Jesus 110–11

Hemer, Colin J. 35

Hengel, Martin 8, 49–50, 69

Herod 31

historical Jesus 1–3, 8–10, 12, 14,
20–1, 46, 127–30, 155–6, 159,
165–7, 170, 175–8; continuity
with Christ of faith 2–3, 55,
75, 82, 96; quest/project 1–3,
14, 46, 76, 120, 125, 164, 169,
177–8; sources for 2–11, 45–6,
56, 87

history 8–11, 170–1; and
apocalyptic genre 156–9; and
canon 16, 170–1; and divine
action 94; and narrative
17–18, 31, 95–6, 137–9; and
theology 1–3, 8–11, 28–9,
83–4, 95, 178–9

Hoffmann, Joseph R. 170, 174

Hollander, Harm W. 67

Holtz, Traugott 57, 63, 65

Hoover, Roy W. 3

Horrell, David G. 59, 73–4, 139,
141

Hurtado, L. W. 88, 110, 163, 168

incarnation 28, 71, 79–80, 86,
89, 97, 123, 135, 143, 154–5,
167

Isaac, figure of 108, 110

Isaacs, Marie E. 106

James, epistle of 10–12, 18, 70,
112–32, 139, 142, 162, 167–9,
171–2, 174–5; authorship of
113–14; Christology of 112–15;

James the Just 113–14, 130;
mentions of Jesus 113–19;
portrait of Jesus 125–31;
use of Jesus tradition 120–5

James, figure of 10, 54, 67,
113–14, 142

James the Just 11, 23, 113–14,
125, 130, 142

Jesus of faith 13–15, 166, 177–8

Jesus Justus 78

Jesus of Nazareth 1–3, 13–14,
23–5, 38–9, 41, 44–5, 49, 51–7,
72–3, 76, 79, 101–2, 120, 125,
148–9, 155, 158, 165–7, 169,
172, 175; apocalyptic prophet
63–4, 126, 146–7; appearance of
161; Ascension of 25, 28–30,
44, 71, 90, 140–1; baptism
of 26–8, 30, 47, 52, 89, 153–4;
baptismal ministry 41–3, 153;
birth of 30, 51–2, 89, 158;
crucifixion of 38, 52–4, 73,
80–2, 90, 104–5, 107, 126,
137–9, 153, 157–9; death of
18, 31, 38–9, 44, 47, 52–4, 62,
73–5, 80–2, 84, 86, 95–6,
102–8, 113, 126, 133–4, 136–7,
147, 151, 153–4, 158–9, 167,
173–4; descent to Hades 86,
140–1; disciples of 28–9, 42,
46, 54–5, 130, 133, 142, 152,
156, 158; earthly ministry 30,
32–4, 57–64, 93, 97, 104,
113–14, 119, 126, 130, 155–6,
159, 182; Eucharist 47–8,
60–2; exaltation of 39, 78–9,
83, 90, 108, 118; exemplar
figure 36, 72–4, 82, 85, 88, 96,
108–9, 116–17, 123, 128–30,
132, 135–7, 143–4, 151, 168,

175, 177; faithfulness of 73–4, 109–10, 116–17, 123, 127, 159–60, 175; family of 30, 52, 113, 130, 142; Gentiles, ministry to 32–4, 55, 74; Gethsemane 72, 102, 156, 162; Golgotha 103, 105–6; healing others 24, 30, 33, 40–1, 43, 119, 179; high priest 92, 95–100, 102–3, 106, 109–11; identity of 3, 7–9, 14, 16–19, 22, 25, 29, 44, 56, 69, 70–2, 76, 97–105, 112, 135, 145, 152, 163, 165–70, 177; kingdom of God 26–7, 36, 40, 68, 74; lineage of 52, 87, 89, 103–4, 158; Messiah 15, 22–3, 39, 41, 43, 52–3, 115–18, 142, 151; name of 13, 40, 56–7, 137, 143, 151, 155; poor, treatment of 32, 74, 117, 122–3, 125, 129, 131, 175, 179; restoration of Israel 118; resurrection of 8, 16–17, 25–7, 29, 38–9, 44, 47, 49, 54–5, 75–6, 79–80, 84, 86, 89–90, 108–10, 113, 118, 126, 135, 147, 158; revolutionary figure 40, 138, 158; second coming 25, 63–4, 71, 86, 100, 119, 126, 135, 144, 146–8; sinlessness of 95, 103, 105, 135–7, 167; social reformer 122–4, 126–7; Son of God 15, 50, 66, 99, 103, 107, 135, 151, 154; Son of Man 101–2, 118, 147, 157, 160–2, 164; story of 37–41, 70–4, 80–2, 84–5, 89–90, 95–7, 167; teacher 26–7, 43, 47, 57–8, 64, 66, 125–9, 155; teaching of 57–66,

104, 120–7, 139–40, 154–5, 167, 174; Temple cleansing 30, 47, 110, 138; temptation of 26, 101, 104, 111, 124–5, 135; titles of 39–41, 98–9, 142, 151, 160; Transfiguration 134, 145–6, 161; trial of 88, 159–60; wisdom teaching 125–7, 168; worship of 5, 13, 16, 51–2, 99, 111, 115, 163, 173, 177

Jesus Seminar 3, 62

Jesus tradition 5–10, 12, 16, 21–3, 33–4, 37–8, 46–70, 75–6, 80, 84–5, 87–90, 93–5, 98–9, 101, 104–5, 110, 114, 118–32, 134–5, 140–1, 144–8, 152, 155, 159, 162–3, 166–70, 172–6; flexibility of 57–8, 64, 123–4, 163, 173

Jesusology 13–14, 41, 76, 78, 109, 143, 151–2, 156, 158, 168, 171; plurality of images 168–71

Job 117

John, epistles of 5, 169; 1 John 149–54, 168, 172; 2 John 154–5; 3 John 149, 154, 168

John, Gospel of 3, 102, 106, 152–4

John the Baptist 27–8, 30, 42–3, 52, 154

Johnson, Luke Timothy 1, 2, 17, 20, 51, 71, 85, 92, 94, 101, 103, 117, 120–3, 170

Josephus 5, 11, 20

Judas the Galilean 20, 40

Judas Iscariot 31, 62

Jude, epistle of 128, 132, 141–3

Jude, figure of 142

Keith, Chris 168
Kelber, Werner H. 62
Kilgallen, John J. 35
Kim, Seyoon 63–5, 74
Koester, Helmut 87, 121, 139

Labahn, Michael 6
Lane, William L. 105–6
Laws, Sophie 93, 102, 106
Le Donne, Anthony 9–10
Lincoln, Andrew T. 80–1, 83–5
Longenecker, Bruce W. 74
Longenecker, Richard N. 14
Lowe, Bruce A. 116–17
Lüdemann, Gerd 48, 55, 58
Luke, Gospel of 13, 21–2, 28, 30–3, 41, 50, 61, 97, 102, 108, 174; *see also* Acts of the Apostles

McCormack, Bruce L. 101
Mackie, Scott D. 104
McKnight, Edgar 5
McKnight, Scott 2, 11, 15, 116, 118, 126, 129
Manen/Menachem 23
Mark, Gospel of 10, 13, 29, 33, 59, 61, 66, 95, 102, 140, 174
Marshall, I. Howard 21, 61
Martin, Ralph P. 123
Marx, Karl 15
Matera, Frank J. 14, 22, 113, 135, 148
Matthew, Gospel of 29, 31, 61, 121–2, 139
Melbourne, Bertram L. 109
Melchizedek 92, 99–100, 104
memory 7, 9–10, 15, 17, 94, 158, 161, 163, 169, 171, 177
Michaels, J. Ramsey 136

mission teaching 32–6, 55, 58–60, 67
Moffitt, David M. 94, 109
Moo, Douglas J. 79, 81
Moses 29, 41, 92, 99, 110, 145
Moyise, Steve 32

narrative approaches 17–18, 37–41, 50, 70–2, 95–7, 136–9
Neyrey, Jerome H. 143, 146–7
non–Gospel material 2–19, 165–79; minimal use of Jesus tradition 4–5, 68, 70, 87, 89–90, 93–4, 119, 134–5, 144, 155, 165–8, 171, 175–9; portrait of Jesus 165–75; as sources 2–14; value of 6–11

O'Brien, P. T. 85
Olbricht, Thomas H. 93

Painter, John 11, 130, 151
Passion narrative 69, 95, 102, 133–4, 136–8, 172–3
Pastoral Epistles 87–90
Paul 4–6, 8, 13–14, 18, 25, 34–6, 41, 45–76, 112–13, 128, 132–7, 139, 144, 147, 166, 167–8, 172, 174–6; Damascus road 20, 24–5, 46, 56, 60, 67; on death of Jesus 52–4, 60, 62, 69, 73–5, 113, 137, 139, 174; and Deutero–Paulines 77–8; imitation of Jesus 72–4, 76, 136, 168, 174, 176; knowledge of Jesus 45–7, 51–6, 67–8; missionary preaching 8, 49–50, 68–9, 84–5; persecutor 24–5; portrayal of Jesus 45–76; silence on Jesus 47–50, 56–7,

59–60, 67–70, 93, 134–5, 166; story of Jesus 59, 69–75; on teaching of Jesus 57–66; use of Jesus tradition 57–66; use of Scripture 47, 59, 67, 71

Perkins, Pheme 144, 148

Pervo, Richard I. 21, 26, 35

Peter, epistles of 5, 6, 132–48, 166, 172

Peter, figure of 35, 38–9, 41, 54–5, 57, 67, 112, 133–4, 143, 145, 174

Peter, first epistle 13, 18, 88, 132–41, 143, 151, 160, 162, 167–9, 174–5; authorship 133–5; on death of Jesus 136–40; on exemplary function 143–4, 147–8; on Jesus tradition 137–40

Peter, second epistle 16, 128, 132, 142–8; authorship 143; on Parousia 144, 146–8; relationship to 1 Peter 143–4; on Transfiguration 145–6

Peterson, David 103

Philip 34, 41, 174

Philippians, epistle to 45, 67–8, 74, 169

Philo of Alexandria 94

Pontius Pilate 31, 88, 160

Porter, Stanley E. 55

Powell, Mark Allen 14, 17

Price, Robert M. 1

Q source 12, 54, 57, 64

Rahab 117

Reese, Ruth Anne 144–5

remembered Jesus 14, 23, 33, 37–41, 76, 86, 95–6, 104, 111,

125–9, 138, 154, 163, 169–70, 174, 176–8

resurrection 8, 11, 16–17, 25–7, 29, 38–9, 44, 49, 54–5, 75–6, 79–80, 84, 90, 108–9, 113, 118, 126, 147, 158; resurrection appearances 25–7, 54–5, 90

Reumann, John 113, 118

Revelation, book of 13, 18, 149, 155–64, 168, 171–2, 174–5; earthly Jesus 157–61; genre of 156–7; heavenly Lord 149, 155–7, 160; portrait of Jesus 163–4; Synoptic tradition 162–3

Richard, Earl 148

Richardson, Christopher 103

Romans, epistle to 4, 45, 65–7, 72

Rome 24, 36, 44, 94–5, 98; Jesus' response to 138, 173; responsibility for Jesus' death 23, 31, 39, 52–3, 81, 95, 105, 138, 158

Rowston, Douglas J. 141

Sanders, E. P. 63, 118

Schröter, Jens, 48–9

Schweizer, Eduard 8

Scripture, use of 32–4, 40–1, 47, 59, 67, 71, 89, 100, 111, 122–3, 137–9; Jesus' use of 100, 129, 139–41

Selwyn, Edward Gordon 134

Sermon on Plain/Mount 66, 120–4, 139, 161, 171

Simon of Cyrene 106

Small, Brian C. 96

Smalley, Stephen S. 159

Smith, D. Moody 1, 150–2

Sprinkle, Preston M. 73
Stanton, Graham 39–41
Stephen, figure of 25, 36, 41, 46, 174
Stewart, Robert B. 3
Still, Todd 51, 93, 109
Strange, W. A. 9, 21, 32–4, 37, 176
Strelan, Rick 28–9
Synoptic Gospels 2–5, 9–12, 17, 29–30, 32, 41–3, 101–2, 106, 120–5, 138, 141, 144, 146, 171; as historical Jesus sources 2–5, 9–12, 171

Talbert, Charles H. 161
Tannehill, Robert C. 28
Tertullus 25
Theissen, Gerd 53, 66
Theudas 20, 40
Thessalonians 64, 68; first epistle 45, 64; Jesus of 62–4; second epistle 86, 168
Thiselton, Anthony C. 58
Thomas, Gospel of 3, 17, 54, 65
Thompson, Marianne Meye 3, 79, 111
Thompson, Michael B. 76
Trumbower, Jeffrey A. 40

Tuckett, C. M. 14, 56, 94, 113
Twelftree, Graham H. 42
Twelve, the 11, 36, 54–5, 68, 156, 158; *see also* Jesus of Nazareth, disciples of
twelve tribes 115, 118

Wachob, Wesley Hiram 116, 118, 120–2
Wallis, Ian G. 117
Walter, Nikolaus 51, 65, 68
Warrington, Keith 4, 22, 92, 143
Watson, Francis 9, 49, 56, 60, 178
Webb, Robert L. 6, 53, 141
Wedderburn, Alexander J. M. 69, 71, 74–5, 80–1
Wenham, David 51–2, 65, 147
Williams, Rowan 178
Williamson, Ronald 94
wisdom teaching 57, 114, 125–7, 160; *see also* Jesus of Nazareth, teacher
witness, theme of 23–5, 36, 44, 89, 133–4, 145, 159–60, 164, 167, 172, 174–5, 179; eyewitness 4, 7, 47, 94, 133–4, 145, 166–7
Wright, N. T. 3, 7, 64, 72, 126